JOURNEYS

A Reading and Literature Program

Revised Edition with Writing Supplement

TEACHER'S MANUAL

with Tests

Cascade

JOURNEYS

A Reading and Literature Program

Teacher's Manual
with Tests

Cascade

WITH ANSWER KEY TO TEST BOOKLET

Curriculum and Writing

Richard J. Smith

Professor of Curriculum and Instruction,
University of Wisconsin.
Formerly, Director of Reading Development,
Public Schools of Madison, Wisconsin.
Formerly, Reading Coordinator, Public Schools
of Ripon, Wisconsin.

HBJ HARCOURT BRACE JOVANOVICH, PUBLISHERS

Orlando San Diego Chicago Dallas

We do not include a teacher's manual automatically with each shipment of a classroom set of textbooks. We prefer to send a teacher's manual only when it is part of a purchase order or when it is requested by the teacher or administrator concerned or by one of our representatives. A teacher's manual can be easily mislaid when it arrives as part of a shipment delivered to a school stockroom, and, since it contains answer materials, we would like to be sure it is sent *directly* to the person who will use it, or to someone concerned with the use or selection of textbooks.

If your class assignment changes and you are no longer using or examining this Teacher's Manual, you may wish to pass it on to a teacher who may have use for it.

Acknowledgments

For permission to reprint copyrighted material, grateful acknowledgement is made to the following sources:

Dorothy Boles and Triangle Communications Inc.: From "The Contest" by Paul Darcy Boles in *Seventeen*® Magazine. Copyright © 1975 by Triangle Communications Inc. All rights reserved.

The Caxton Printers, Ltd., Caldwell, ID: From "Say It With Flowers" in *Yokohama, California* by Toshio Mori.

CBS Radio, a division of CBS Inc.: From "A Shipment of Mute Fate" by Les Crutchfield. Copyright © 1953 by Columbia Broadcasting System, Inc. All rights reserved.

Chilton Book Company, Radnor, PA/Scholastic Books, New York, NY: From "Our Indian Heritage" (Retitled: "Gifts of the Indian") in *The Day They Hanged the Sioux* by C. Fayne Porter. © 1964 by C. Fayne Porter.

Manuela Williams Crosno: From "Otero's Visitor" in *New Mexico Quarterly*, Vol. 7, No. 4, November 1937. All rights reserved.

Doubleday & Company, Inc.: From "The Meadow Mouse" in *The Collected Poems of Theodore Roethke.* Copyright © 1963 by Beatrice Roethke as Administratrix of the Estate of Theodore Roethke.

Norma Millay (Ellis): From "Portrait of a Neighbor" by Edna St. Vincent Millay in *Collected Poems.* Copyright 1922, 1950 by Edna St. Vincent Millay. Published by Harper & Row, Publishers, Inc.

Blanche C. Gregory, Inc. and Lilian Jackson Braun: From "The Sin of Madame Phloi" by Lilian Jackson Braun. Copyright © 1962 by Davis Publications.

Harper & Row, Publishers, Inc.: From "Pete at the Zoo" in *The World of Gwendolyn Brooks.* Copyright © 1960 by Gwendolyn Brooks. From "For My Grandmother" in *On These I Stand* by Countee Cullen. Copyright 1925 by Harper & Row, Publishers, Inc.; renewed 1953 by Ida M. Cullen. From "Where the Sidewalk Ends" in *Where the Sidewalk Ends: The Poems and Drawings of Shel Silverstein.* Copyright © 1974 by Snake Eye Music, Inc.

Lawrence Hill & Co., Westport, CT: From "Last Cover" in *The Best Nature Stories of Paul Annixter.* Copyright © 1974 by Jane and Paul Annixter.

CONTENTS

WOODNOTES

PROFILES

PERSPECTIVES

WINTER THUNDER

VISTAS

MOSAIC

THE HOBBIT

ABOUT THE MANUAL

A scope and sequence chart begins each unit. This chart provides an overview of the unit and lists the skills taught in the unit. Lesson plans for each selection follow the scope and sequence chart. A lesson plan usually contains the following parts:

1. **Summary**

   A short summary of the selection.

2. **Before Reading**

   Suggestions for preparing and motivating the students to read the selection. These suggestions help students set a purpose for reading.

3. **Glossary Words**

   A list of the words from the selection contained in the glossary. It contains the page number, column (a or b), and paragraph in which the word first appears. The paragraph number refers to the first complete paragraph in the column. Line numbers indicate that the word is in the paragraph fragment at the top of the column. Starred words receive special attention in the Teaching the Glossary Words section.

4. **Teaching the Glossary Words**

   Suggestions for teaching the words in the glossary list.

5. **Check Test**

   Five true-or-false questions that determine whether or not the students have read the selection.

6. **After Reading**

   A question to stimulate discussion after the students have finished reading the selection.

7. **Close Up**

   Answers to Close Up Questions. Answers appear with the questions from the textbook.

8. **Literature Skill**

   Answers to the literature skill questions. Answers appear with the questions from the textbook.

9. **Additional Activities**

Activities that help students respond to the selections.

10. **Teaching the Reading Skill**

Suggestions to use before assigning the reading exercise.

11. **Answers to the Reading Skill Exercise**

Answers appear with the questions from the textbook.

12. **Teaching Word Attack**

Suggestions to use before assigning the word attack exercise.

13. **Answers to Word Attack**

Answers appear with the questions from the textbook.

14. **Word Attack Check Test**

A short check test to determine whether or not students have mastered the word attack skill.

15. **Answers to Word Attack Check Test**

16. **About the Author**

Biographical information with other books by the author.

17. **Teaching Writing** (page 219)

Suggestions for teaching writing activities with the selections and suggestions for teaching the writing supplement. Answers to activities and exercises are included here.

Each unit ends with answers to the end-of-unit quizzes from the textbook and a special reading skill review test.

OBJECTIVES

Literature Skills

TYPES OF LITERATURE DEFINED

Teaching Objective: Students will develop an understanding of various types of literature.

1. Students will develop an understanding of a personal narrative.
2. Students will develop an understanding of a short story.
3. Students will develop an understanding of a lyric poem.
4. Students will develop an understanding of an essay.
5. Students will develop an understanding of a play.

PLOT AND CHARACTER

Teaching Objective: Students will identify the elements of plot and characterization and recognize how they function in literature.

1. Students will define plot and identify the plot of a short story.
2. Students will identify the elements that create suspense in a short story.
3. Students will develop an understanding of dilemma in a short story.
4. Students will develop an understanding of how a character is developed and identify these elements of characterization in a true story.
5. Students will develop an understanding of a conflict between two characters in a play.
6. Students will develop an understanding of a conflict between a character and nature in a short story.
7. Students will develop an understanding of an internal conflict in a short story.

POINT OF VIEW

Teaching Objective: Students will develop an understanding of point of view and identify the point of view from which a story is told.

1. Students will develop an understanding of first-person narration in nonfiction and identify the narrator.
2. Students will develop an understanding of first-person narration in fiction and identify the narrator.

3. Students will read a story told in the first person and recognize how the story would change if another character told it.
4. Students would develop an understanding of third-person narration in fiction when it is limited to one character.
5. Students will develop an understanding of third-person narration in fiction when it is omniscient.

SETTING

Teaching Objective: Students will develop an understanding of setting and recognize how it functions in literature.

1. Students will develop an understanding of how setting functions in a short story.
2. Students will visualize the setting of a short story.
3. Students will recognize time as an important element of setting in a play.
4. Students will develop an understanding of how the setting of a short story can affect its plot.
5. Students will develop an understanding of how the setting of a short story can affect characters.

MOOD

Teaching Objectives: Students will recognize mood in literature and recognize details that help to create it.

1. Students will identify the mood of quiet happiness in a short story and recognize the details that help to create it.
2. Students will identify the mood of terror in a short story and recognize how foreshadowing and the use of specific details helps to create it.
3. Students will identify humor in nonfiction and recognize the details that help to create it.

THEME

Teaching Objective: Students will interpret theme in literature, identify and develop strategies for finding theme, and state the theme of what they have read.

1. Students will identify what a character learns in a short story and note it as a key to theme.
2. Students will identify significant statements in a true story and note them as a key to theme.
3. Students will write statements expressing the theme of a selection.
4. Students will recognize symbols in literature and note them as a key to theme.

POETRY

Teaching Objective: Students will appreciate and enjoy poetry.

1. Students will recognize poetry.
2. Students will recognize free verse.
3. Students will interpret and enjoy poems containing figurative language and vivid imagery.
4. Students will interpret implied meaning.
5. Students will develop an understanding of limericks.
6. Students will appreciate and enjoy descriptive poems.
7. Students will identify and interpret metaphors.
8. Students will recognize mood in poetry.
9. Students will recognize tone in poetry.

LONG SELECTIONS

Teaching Objective: Students will recognize elements of literature in long selections and interpret a selection they have read over a series of days.

1. Students will develop an understanding of plot development in a novel.
2. Students will develop an understanding of motivation in a novel.
3. Students will develop an understanding of characterization in a novel.
4. Students will develop an understanding of conflict in a novel.
5. Students will develop an understanding of characterization in drama.
6. Students will develop an understanding of motivation in drama.
7. Students will develop an understanding of plot development in drama.

Reading Skills

SENTENCE MEANING

Teaching Objective: Students will recognize sentence parts and use them to gain meaning from sentences.

1. Students will use quotation marks to gain meaning from dialogue.
2. Students will use punctuation marks to gain meaning from sentences.
3. Students will use punctuation marks to read sentences in poetry.
4. Students will find core parts in sentences.
5. Students will read and interpret sentences with words left out.

RELATIONSHIPS

Teaching Objective: Students will develop an understanding of relationship patterns in literature.

1. Students will identify time order and be able to place events from a story in their proper time order.
2. Students will identify connectors that show cause and effect and develop an understanding of their function.
3. Students will identify cause and effect and see how it functions in a short story.
4. Students will identify comparison and contrast and see how it functions in sentences.
5. Students will identify contrast relationships and see how they function in a play.
6. Students will identify spatial order and be able to determine the spatial relationship of one object to another.
7. Students will identify simple and significant listing and demonstrate their ability to make lists.

JUDGMENTS

Teaching Objective: Students will read critically and will evaluate statements in literature.

1. Students will distinguish between primary and secondary sources.
2. Students will identify statements of fact and statements of opinion.
3. Students will identify mixed statements of fact and opinion.
4. Students will recognize stereotypes.
5. Students will identify loaded words.

INFERENCES

Teaching Objective: Students will find the meaning of material when it has not been directly stated.

1. Students will make inferences based on evidence in a short story.
2. Students will make valid inferences about characters in a short story.
3. Students will make inferences about a character's feelings in a play.
4. Students will make valid inferences about realistic and fantastic details in science fiction.
5. Students will make valid inferences about future actions and events in a short story.
6. Students will identify valid inferences.
7. Students will make valid inferences about past events in a short story.
8. Students will make valid inferences about an author's tone in nonfiction.

MAIN IDEA

Teaching Objective: Students will identify and interpret main ideas both when they are stated and when they are implied.

1. Students will find the topic sentence of a paragraph and recognize it as the main idea.
2. Students will distinguish between the topic and the main idea of a paragraph.
3. Students will identify details that support main ideas.
4. Students will find implied main ideas in paragraphs.
5. Students will recognize the outline form and outline the information in a selection.
6. Students will read an essay for main ideas.

FLEXIBILITY

Teaching Objective: Students will select the appropriate method and rate of reading.

1. Students will set a purpose for reading an article.
2. Students will scan for facts.
3. Students will develop an understanding of the techniques of skimming and then skim an article.
4. Students will recognize the outline form and outline the information in an article.
5. Students will read an article for main ideas.

READING A LONG SELECTION

Teaching Objective: Students will apply reading skills to read a selection over a series of days.

1. Students will make inferences in a long selection.
2. Students will develop an understanding of cause and effect in a long selection.
3. Students will develop an understanding of comparison and contrast in a long selection.
4. Students will make judgments while reading a long selection.

Word Attack Skills

DICTIONARY

Teaching Objective: Students will use a dictionary.

1. Students will develop an understanding of the function of a glossary and use the glossary to find the meaning of unfamiliar words.
2. Students will develop an understanding of the function of a pronunciation key and use the pronunciation key to pronounce words.

3. Students will recognize guide words and use them to locate words in a dictionary.
4. Students will identify principal parts of a verb and find these parts in a dictionary.
5. Students will use a dictionary to divide a word into syllables.

STRUCTURE

Teaching Objective: Students will identify prefixes, suffixes, and root words and use word structure to find the meaning of words and to build new words.

1. Students will identify contractions and understand their meaning.
2. Students will identify root words and use them to build new words.
3. Students will identify negative prefixes and see their function.
4. Students will identify and build compound words and use their structure to find their meaning.

CONTEXT

Teaching Objective: Students will use the context of a word to find its meaning.

1. Students will recognize that words have more than one meaning and then choose the meaning that fits the context.
2. Students will use context to choose the correct homophone.
3. Students will use context clues to find the meaning of an unfamiliar word.
4. Students will identify direct context clues and use them to find the meaning of an unfamiliar word.
5. Students will identify words used as nouns and verbs and see that their meaning within a sentence depends on how they are used.
6. Students will identify jargon and use context clues to identify its meaning.
7. Students will use context to find the meaning of words from Spanish.

MEANING

Teaching Objective: Students will find the meaning of unfamiliar words.

1. Students will find the synonym of a word.

FIGURATIVE LANGUAGE

Teaching Objective: Students will identify and interpret figurative language.

1. Students will identify and interpret figurative language.
2. Students will identify and interpret similes.
3. Students will identify and interpret figurative comparisons.

IMAGERY

Teaching Objective: Students will identify and interpret imagery.

1. Students will identify vivid adverbs and see how they create strong images.
2. Students will identify vivid compound words and see how they create strong images.

COMPOSITION SKILLS

Teaching Objective: Students will write complete sentences and narrative, descriptive, and expository paragraphs.

1. Students will combine three sentences by removing repeated words and using a coordinating conjunction.
2. Students will combine two sentences by using a signal word that shows the relationship between the two sentences.
3. Students will develop an understanding of narration and write narrative paragraphs.
4. Students will develop an understanding of description and write descriptive paragraphs.
5. Students will develop an understanding of exposition and write expository paragraphs.
6. Students will use the writing process to generate ideas and compose written works.

Teaching Guide to the Selections

WOODNOTES

SELECTION	TYPE	LITERATURE SKILL	READING SKILL	WORD ATTACK SKILL
Cat-About-Town by James Herriot pp. 3–17	non-fiction	Types of Literature. Understanding the personal narrative	Sentence Meaning. Using quotation marks	Dictionary. Using a glossary
Last Cover by Paul Annixter pp. 18–29	fiction	Types of Literature. Understanding the short story	Sentence Meaning. Using punctuation marks	Context. Choosing the meaning that fits the context
The Meadow Mouse by Theodore Roethke pp. 31–35	poetry	Types of Literature. Understanding the lyric poem	Sentence Meaning. Using punctuation to read sentences in poetry	Dictionary. Using a pronunciation key
Unforgettable Grizzly Bears by George Laycock pp. 36–43	non-fiction	Types of Literature. Understanding the essay	Sentence Meaning. Finding core parts	Dictionary. Using guide words
Pete at the Zoo by Gwendolyn Brooks *For My Grandmother* by Countee Cullen p. 45	poetry	Poetry. Finding implied meaning		
A Shipment of Mute Fate by Les Crutchfield pp. 46–63	drama	Types of Literature. Understanding the play	Sentence Meaning. Reading sentences with words left out	Structure. Understanding contractions

SELECTION	TYPE	LITERATURE SKILL	READING SKILL	WORD ATTACK SKILL
Review Quiz pp. 64–65				
Composition. Sentence Combining p. 66				
Before Going On p. 67			Flexibility. Reading for a purpose	
Further Reading *The Story of Tuffy* by Margaret Davidson pp. 68–71	non-fiction			

Cat-About-Town

JAMES HERRIOT
pp. 3–17

Summary   In this amusing true story, James Herriot operates on and saves the life of a stray cat. He and his wife then adopt the cat and name him Oscar. Shortly afterward, Oscar starts disappearing each night. The Herriots find that Oscar attends social gatherings; he is really a socialite, a "cat-about-town."

BEFORE READING

Ask students to turn to p. 3. Have one student read the title of the story and the author's name aloud. Tell them that James Herriot is a veterinarian who lives in England. This selection is a true story about a cat he helped and then adopted.

Ask students what is meant by the term "man-about-town." What could be meant by the term "cat-about-town"? Ask one student to read the headnote aloud. Then have them read the story to find out where Oscar does go each night. (Flexibility: Setting a Purpose)

Glossary Words

(Starred words appear in Teaching the Glossary Words section)

*abdomen (p. 3, b, 1)
*ancestry (p. 5, b, 5)
*despondent (p. 7, b, ℓ. 7)
*distraught (p. 7, a, 12)
*emaciate
    (emaciated, p. 4, a, 3)
*medley (p. 6, b, 2)

*pelvis (p. 3, a, 6)
*saunter
    (sauntered, p. 6, b, 1)
*suture
    (sutured, p. 5, a, 4)
*ventral (p. 3, b, 1)

TEACHING THE GLOSSARY WORDS

Write the glossary words on the chalkboard. Say each word aloud and have the students repeat it after you. (All of these words are taught in the Word Attack lesson on p. 17.) Tell students to look up these words as they read the story and copy in their notebooks the sentence in which each word appears. Explain that sometimes the glossary word appears in a slightly different form in the selection. For example, in this story, the verb *emaciate* is used in the past tense as an adjective. The entry word, though, is *emaciate*. (Word Attack: Dictionary, Context)

CHECK TEST

(F)   1. James Herriot finds Oscar and brings him to the surgery.

(F)	2.	Tristan doesn't think they should try to save Oscar.
(T)	3.	Helen spoon-feeds Oscar until he regains his strength.
(F)	4.	Sep Gibbons refuses to take Oscar back.
(F)	5.	Helen doesn't want to go to Wederly to see Oscar.

AFTER READING

Remind the students that Herriot's first instinct was to put the cat out of its misery. Then ask them why it is a good idea to examine all the possibilities before making a decision. (Judgments)

CLOSE UP (Comprehension Questions)

1. **Why is Jim shocked when he examines the cat?** (Relationships: Cause/Effect)
   The cat is emaciated and badly wounded—his intestines are spilling out of him.
2. **Jim wants to put the cat out of its misery. Why does he change his mind?**
   When Tristan strokes the cat, it purrs. Jim can't bring himself to destroy such a courageous and good-natured cat without first trying to save its life.
3. **After the operation, Jim says that he has a "feeling of sweeping undesirable things under the carpet." What does he expect to happen to the cat?**
   He expects the cat to develop peritonitis—high fever, vomiting, and a tense abdomen—because he and Tristan were unable to wash all the dirt and grit out of its intestines.
4. **Jim and Helen decide to keep the cat, and they work together to make him well.**
   (a) How does Helen help the cat?
   Helen provides a box for a bed and spoon-feeds him liquids and soft foods.
   (b) How does Oscar help himself?
   He moves as little as possible until he has healed.
5. **What secret aspect of Oscar's personality do Helen and Jim discover?**
   They discover that Oscar is a social animal, a natural mixer who takes off at night to attend town activities, such as card games, sales, and concerts.
6. **(a) Why do the Herriots decide to return Oscar to the Gibbons?** (Inferences)
   Oscar belonged to the Gibbons family. They obviously loved him since they kept trying to find him. (He had got lost only because they had moved.) Oscar was delighted to see them again.
   (b) Do you think they made the right decision? Why or why not? (Judgments)
   Answers will vary, but most students will agree that returning him was the right thing to do: the Gibbons family missed him and had given him a good home; besides, he really belonged to them.

THE PERSONAL NARRATIVE (Literature Skill Questions)

1. **James Herriot appears in the story as the character Jim. What pronoun does he use to refer to himself?**

Jim refers to himself with the first-person singular pronoun: *I.*

2. **(a) Who is Helen?**
Helen is Jim's wife.
(b) Who is Tristan?
Tristan is Jim's friend and veterinary assistant.

3. **Herriot has written several books about his experiences as a veterinarian in northern England. Based on this story from his book *All Things Wise and Wonderful,* how do you think Herriot feels about the animals he takes care of? Find details in the story to support your answer.** (Inferences)
Herriot feels concern for and takes delight in the animals that he cares for: He spends two painstaking hours stitching up the stray cat. He and Helen spend hours searching for Oscar the first two times he disappears. He has to fight back tears when Oscar leaves with the Gibbons.

ADDITIONAL ACTIVITIES

1. Make a list of things you like or do not like about cats.
2. Make a list of names you think would be good names for cats. For each name, describe the kind of cat you think the name would fit.

TEACHING SENTENCE MEANING (Reading Skill)

Read the explanatory material in the book aloud while the students read it silently. Then have them complete the exercise and check their answers. Help students correct any items they did incorrectly.

SENTENCE MEANING (Reading Skill Exercise)

Using Quotation Marks

▶ **Read the passage below. Jim (I) is speaking to Helen. Then answer the questions that follow the passage.**
"What's happened?" I asked.
"It's Oscar—he's gone!"
"Gone? What do you mean?"
"Oh, Jim, I think he's run away."
I stared at her. "He wouldn't do that. He often goes down to the garden at night. Are you sure he isn't there?"
"Absolutely. I've searched right into the yard. I've even had a walk round the town. And remember." Her chin quivered. "He . . . he ran away from somewhere before."
a. **Who says, "It's Oscar—he's gone"?**
Helen
b. **Who says, "Gone? What do you mean?"**
Jim
c. **Who says, "I think he's run away"?**
Helen

d. Who says, "He wouldn't do that"?
Jim
e. Who says that he ran away before?
Helen

TEACHING WORD ATTACK

Read the explanatory material in the book aloud while the students read it silently. Have them inspect the glossary to find firsthand the various information you are telling them about (e.g., *lugubrious,* accent marks, parts of speech). Give them five or ten minutes to leaf through the glossary, studying any entries that interest them. Then have them complete Exercises 1 and 2. For Exercise 1 you may want them to copy only one or two entries.

WORD ATTACK (Exercises)

Using a Glossary

1. **The following words are from "Cat-About-Town." Look up each word in the glossary. On a separate piece of paper, copy the complete glossary entry for each one.**
   a. **pelvis**　　　　　　　　　f. **ancestry**
   b. **abdomen**　　　　　　　g. **saunter**
   c. **ventral**　　　　　　　　h. **medley**
   d. **emaciated**　　　　　　i. **distraught**
   e. **suture**　　　　　　　　j. **despondent**
   Check students' answers against the glossary entries.

2. **From the list of words in Exercise 1, choose a word to complete each sentence below.**
   a. Oscar was quite <u>emaciated</u> and sickly; he had little flesh on his bones.
   b. Jim had to <u>suture</u> the muscle with catgut.
   c. Oscar's coat was a <u>medley</u> of bright, unusual colors.
   d. Tristan thought that Oscar must have a ginger Tom somewhere in his <u>ancestry</u>.
   e. Helen and Jim were very sad and missed Oscar deeply; even Sam seemed <u>despondent</u>.

WORD ATTACK CHECK TEST

▶ Check the glossary to find the part of speech for each of the following words:
   a. despondent　　　　　　d. abdomen
   b. saunter　　　　　　　　e. emaciate
   c. ancestry　　　　　　　　f. medley

ANSWERS TO WORD ATTACK CHECK TEST

▶ a. adjective　　　　　　　　b. verb

c. noun
d. noun

e. verb
f. noun

ABOUT THE AUTHOR

James Herriot has written several books about his experiences as a veterinarian. Among them are *All Creatures Great and Small*, *All Things Bright and Beautiful*, and *All Things Wise and Wonderful*. The British Broadcasting Corporation (BBC) recently produced a television series based on *All Creatures Great and Small*. In addition to being a writer, Mr. Herriot continues to practice veterinary medicine in the Yorkshire Dales of northern England, where he works hand in hand with the real "Tristan and Siegfried Farnon," the delightful characters from his books.

Last Cover

Paul Annixter
pp. 18–29

Summary Stan narrates this short story about his brother Colin and Colin's pet fox, Bandit. Colin has two loves, art and Bandit, and these loves pose two problems. His father objects to his becoming an artist, and Bandit runs off to the woods and becomes a chicken thief. At the end of the story, Colin convinces his father of the value of art by drawing a picture of where Bandit had hidden from the hunters.

BEFORE READING

Aldous Huxley once said, "There is no substitute for talent. Industry and all the virtues are of no avail." Ask students to define *talent*. For what types of things can a person have talent? For example, can a person have a talent for music? Can a person have a talent for conversation? Can a person have a talent for art? Ask students to discuss the meaning of the quotation.

Then tell students they are going to read a story about a conflict between a boy and his father. The boy's talent is for art, but the father's is for nature. Have them read the story to find out how the boy gains his father's support for his talent. (Flexibility: Setting a Purpose)

Glossary Words

*harry
  (harried, p. 24, b, 1)
*incredulous (p. 26, a, ℓ. 1)
 instinct (p. 24, b, 1)
*intricate (p. 25, b, 1)
 kit (p. 18, a, 5)

loll
  (lolling, p. 22, a, ℓ. 9)
pox (p. 20, b, 5)
*sanctuary (p. 25, a, 1)
*vixen (p. 21, a, 2)

TEACHING THE GLOSSARY WORDS

Write the glossary words on the chalkboard. Say each word aloud and have the students repeat it after you. Then have students look up the starred words in the glossary. Write the following sentences on the board and tell the students to decide which word best fits in each blank.

Bandit's eyes looked bright and _____ . You could tell he was worried about the hunters. (harried)

They saw the _____ dash into the woods and knew that Bandit had found a mate. (vixen)

Bandit took refuge, or _____ , in the stream where the boys used to swim. (sanctuary)

Father looked at the _____ pencil drawing, which revealed Bandit's head among the maze of twigs and branches. (intricate)

Mother was _____ . She found it hard to believe Bandit had been so clever. (incredulous)

Have the students look up the remaining words for homework. (Word Attack: Dictionary, Context)

CHECK TEST

(T)   1. From the first, Bandit makes tension in the family.
(F)   2. Colin is like Father, "the sort of stuff that can take it—tough and strong . . . ."
(T)   3. Father predicted from the first that Bandit would run away.
(F)   4. After he runs away, Bandit feeds entirely on wild game.
(T)   5. A "chance hunter" kills Bandit as Bandit creeps from his hiding place in the deep pool.

AFTER READING

Ask students if they think a wild animal can be completely tamed. Why or why not?

CLOSE UP (Comprehension Questions)

1. **Stan is tough and strong, while his brother Colin is delicate and often sick. What does Stan mean when he says that Mother fears that Colin may be pre-destined?** (Word Attack)
   She fears that he will die young—he is small, delicate, and often sick.

2. **Find two reasons for Father's objecting to Colin's art.** (Relationships: Cause/Effect)
   Father says that since Colin became interested in art, he's had "an invalid for help around the place." Also, Father's love is for the land and all that it pertains to it. He has no understanding of what seems to him "a passive 'white-livered' interpretation of nature through brush and pencil instead of rod and rifle."

3. **(a) How does the pet fox create tension in the family?**
   Everyone but Father goes "a bit silly over the little thing." Father doesn't like the idea of adopting a baby fox; he predicts that Bandit will leave when he's grown, forget the boys, and become an egg and chicken thief.
   (b) Why does Father decide to call the fox Bandit?
   Father calls the fox Bandit after he steals a chicken for the first time.

4. **After Bandit disappears, Colin finds the fox in the woods. (a) How does Bandit show that he still loves Colin?** (Relationships: Cause/Effect)
   Bandit allows Colin to put an arm around him.
   (b) What telltale sign shows that Bandit is also a wild hunter?
   A chicken feather "on his thin chops" shows this.

5. **How does Colin maintain his bond with Bandit?**
   He shows himself frequently to Bandit, so that the fox won't forget him.

6. **(a) Why does Colin's picture of Bandit show Father that they value the same things?** (Inferences)
   The picture shows how closely Colin has observed Bandit in his habitat. As a keen woodsman, Father can appreciate the verisimilitude of the picture. Also, it was a picture made especially for a "born hunter."
   (b) Why does this picture make Father respect Colin's talent? (Inferences)
   The picture conveys "as if by nature's art itself" the clever way in which Bandit camouflaged himself. It shows that Colin perceived the natural scene clearly and thoroughly—qualities Father admires.

7. **Why do you think this story is called "Last Cover"?** (Main Idea)
   "Last Cover" is the title because Colin's picture represents Bandit's last hiding place. Also, since his father now respects his art, this may be the last time Colin uses a box cover for his drawings; he will have professional supplies in art school.

THE SHORT STORY (Literature Skill Questions)

1. **(a) List the characters in "Last Cover."**
   The characters are Stan, Colin, Mother, and Father (and Bandit).
   (b) Which character do you think is the most important? Why?

Colin might be considered the most important because he's the one we are concerned about, the one who faces a crisis in development in the story. At the beginning of the story, he is shattered by Bandit's disappearance; by the end of the story, he has dealt with the situation. He has faced it *and* made it into something else: a painstaking work of art.

2. **The main conflict in this story is between Colin and Father. What two things does Father want Colin to give up?**
   Father wants Colin to give up his love for Bandit and his passion for art.

3. **At what point does this conflict reach its highest point of intensity?**
   This conflict is most intense when Colin gives his pencil drawing to Father.

4. **How is this conflict resolved?**
   Father studies the picture and finally picks out the picture's secret (Bandit's head "woven craftily into the maze of twigs and branches, as if by nature's art itself"). What Father always scorned about Colin was his "passive 'white-livered' interpretation of nature through brush and pencil instead of rod and rifle." This new drawing represents a "rod and rifle" interpretation of nature and shows Father that Colin has a hunter's eye. Father realizes that Colin drew the picture "especially for him." He no longer disapproves of Colin's interest in art: in fact, when the time comes for Colin to go to art school, Father is his "solid backer."

ADDITIONAL ACTIVITIES

1. Make a list of names you think would fit a pet fox.
2. Draw a sketch of Bandit as you think he looked.
3. Pick one part of the story that you think would make a good television scene. Explain why it would be effective on television.
4. Find three facts about foxes from an encyclopedia.

TEACHING SENTENCE MEANING (Reading Skill)

Tell the students to read the explanatory material in their books. When they are finished, ask them to tell you what they learned about punctuation marks. Have them read aloud the two paragraphs that are used to illustrate the importance of pauses in getting meaning. Then have them complete the reading skill exercise and check their answers.

SENTENCE MEANING (Reading Skill Exercise)

Using Punctuation Marks

▶ **Copy the following sentences on a separate piece of paper. Then find each sentence in the story and add the punctuation marks. (Remember: If you add a period, be sure to capitalize the letter following the period.)**
   a. "For six hours I had walked, reading signs, looking for a delicate print in the damp soil or even a hair that might have told of a red fox passing that way— but I had found nothing."
   b. "I'm not sure I can tell you what you want to know about my brother; but

everything about the pet fox is important, so I'll tell all that from the beginning."

c. "I'm just ordinary, like Father. I'm the sort of stuff that can take it—tough and strong—but Colin was always sort of special."

d. "Father wasn't as hard as he made out, I knew, but he had to hold a balance against all Mom's frothing. For him, the thing was the land and all that pertained to it."

e. "Wild things' memories were short, we knew; we'd have to find him soon or the old bond would be broken."

f. "Noon came, and Colin had not come in to eat. After dinner Father didn't go back to the field."

TEACHING WORD ATTACK

Have the students read the explanatory material in their books. Then have them complete the skill exercise and check their answers.

WORD ATTACK (Exercise)

Choosing the Meaning That Fits the Context

▶ **Read each sentence below. From the two meanings following each sentence, choose the meaning that fits the context.**

a. **"That fox learned to *pine* for table scraps and young chickens."**
   (2) to yearn for or desire

b. **"From the first, the tame fox had made *tension* in the family."**
   (1) strained relationships or uneasiness

c. **". . . Father and Laban Small had been *running* a vixen through the hills with their dogs."**
   (1) chasing or pursuing

d. **"It was Colin who felt out, like an Indian, the *stretch* of woods where Bandit had his den."**
   (2) an unbroken piece of land

e. **"On his thin *chops,* I saw a telltale chicken feather."**
   (2) jaw or cheek

ABOUT THE AUTHOR

"Paul Annixter" (1894–   ) is the pen name of Howard A. Sturtzel. He began writing stories at the age of nineteen when he was working on a timber claim in northern Minnesota. The claim never amounted to much financially, but he considered it a gold mine since it provided subject matter for his stories. Annixter wrote and published over 500 short stories prior to 1950. His books include *Swiftwater* and four collections of short stories: *Brought to Cover, The Hunting Horn, Devil of the Woods,* and *Pride of Lions.* In 1955, he began collaborating with his wife. Their books include *Horns of Plenty, The Phantom Stallion, Windigo,* and *Vikan the Mighty.*

The Meadow Mouse

THEODORE ROETHKE
pp. 31–35

Summary   The poet finds a baby mouse in the meadow. He brings it home and cares for it. In the morning the mouse is gone. The poet worries about its fate and the fate of all innocent creatures.

BEFORE READING

Have the students turn to pp. 30–31. Ask one student to read the title of the poem and the poet's name aloud. Then have them look at the photograph. Ask them how this photograph makes them feel. How does the photograph make them feel about the mouse? Ask them to list words that describe the mouse. Then have them read the poem to discover how the poet feels about the mouse. (Flexibility: Setting a Purpose)

Glossary Words

*absurd (p. 31, ℓ. 7)
 cartoon (p. 31, ℓ. 7)
*hapless (p. 32, ℓ. 29)
*minuscule (p. 31, ℓ. 11)
   (Also spelled miniscule)
*nuzzle
   (nuzzled, p. 32, ℓ. 22)

*paralytic (p. 32, ℓ. 28)
 quaker (p. 31, ℓ. 6)
*shrike (p. 32, ℓ. 25)
 trough (p. 31, ℓ. 12)
 twitch
   (twitching, p. 31, ℓ. 16)

TEACHING THE GLOSSARY WORDS

Write the glossary words on the chalkboard. Say each word aloud and have the students repeat it after you. Have the students look up the starred words in the glossary. Then have them decide which word fits in each sentence below.

Because he was such a _____ fellow, people called him Unlucky Louis. (hapless)

The tiny field mouse ran for safety as the _____ circled overhead. (shrike)

The cat climbed up on my shoulder and _____ (d) against my cheek. (nuzzled)

The _____ was unable to move from the wheelchair. (paralytic)

She looked _____ after she fell in the mud puddle. (absurd)

The mouse looked like a _____ puppy. (minuscule)

CHECK TEST

(F)   1. The speaker puts the mouse in a wire cage.
(F)   2. The mouse is so frightened it refuses to eat.
(F)   3. The mouse stays with the speaker for several years.
(T)   4. The speaker fears that the mouse will be killed.
(F)   5. The mouse reminds the poet of other strong predatory animals.

AFTER READING

Have students look up the words *pity*, *compassion*, *commiseration*, *sympathy*, and *empathy*. Ask them to determine which word best describes the poet's feeling toward all innocent and vulnerable creatures. (Word Attack: Context)

CLOSE UP (Comprehension Questions)

1. **Why does the poet describe the mouse as "a little quaker"?** (Word Attack: Context)
The mouse is trembling with fear.

2. **(a) How does the mouse change after it eats the three kinds of cheese?** (Relationships: Comparison/Contrast)
Instead of trembling, it lies quietly in a corner. It no longer struggles to escape.
(b) Why do you think the poet hopes that the mouse no longer trembles? (Inferences)
He hopes the mouse is comfortable. He doesn't want it to fear him.

3. **In the second part of the poem, the mouse has left the shoe-box house. What does the poet fear will happen to the mouse?**
He fears that it will become the prey of another animal.

4. **Reread lines 25–29. How do you think the poet feels about all fragile and helpless creatures?** (Sentence Meaning)
The poet fears for and is moved by "All things innocent, hapless, forsaken."

THE LYRIC POEM (Literature Skill Questions)

1. **(a) To what does the poet compare the mouse's feet?** (Relationships: Comparison/Contrast)
He compares them to "small leaves" and to a little lizard's feet.
(b) To what does he compare the mouse's wriggling movements? (Relationships: Comparison/Contrast)
He compares them to those of a "minuscule puppy."

2. **(a) How do these comparisons make you feel about the mouse?** (Inferences)
They make you feel that the mouse is a helpless, harmless creature.
(b) How do you think the poet feels about the mouse? Why? (Inferences)
He feels protective and compassionate. He compares the mouse to small,

delicate things. He uses the word "puppy," which implies warmth and love.

3. **In line 22, the poet calls the mouse "My thumb of a child that nuzzled in my palm." On the basis of this image, how do you think the poet feels about the mouse?** (Imagery)
The poet feels tender and protective toward the mouse.

4. **(a) What five creatures are mentioned in lines 23–25?** (Relationships: Listing)
The hawk, the owl, the shrike, the snake, and the tomcat are mentioned.
(b) How are these creatures different from the mouse? (Relationships: Comparison/Contrast)
They are all hunters, rather than the creatures being hunted.

5. **This poem is written in *free verse*. This means that there is no regular rhyme or rhythmic pattern. Do you think this makes the poem *more* or *less* effective? Why?** (Judgments)
Students' answers will vary, but the value of free verse can be pointed up: since a rhythm and rhyme scheme is not imposed in advance on every line, each line can create its own effects. For example, line 12 can be long and complex to suggest the variety of paraphernalia that the poet produced for his orphan; line 9 can be short and simple; line 29 can be repetitive and mournful.

TEACHING SENTENCE MEANING (Reading Skill)

Have the students read the explanatory material in their books. Then ask them the following questions: (1) What do commas, dashes, and semicolons tell you to do? (2) What do periods, question marks, and exclamation marks tell you to do? Then have the students complete the skill exercises and check their answers.

SENTENCE MEANING (Reading Skill Exercises)

Using Punctuation to Read Sentences in Poetry

1. **Read aloud the first eleven lines of this poem, pausing at each comma and stopping at the period.**
Evaluate individual students' responses.

2. **Look at lines 12–16. Which punctuation mark tells you to take a longer pause than you would for a comma?**
The semicolon tells you this.

3. **Read aloud lines 17–19. Remember to raise the pitch of your voice at the end of line 18.**
Evaluate individual students' responses.

4. **Look at the second part of this poem. (a) How many times should you pause?**
You should pause twelve times.
(b) How many times should you stop?
You should stop four times.

TEACHING WORD ATTACK

Have the students read the explanatory material and complete the skill exercises. Check their answers.

WORD ATTACK (Exercises)

Using a Pronunciation Key

1. **Look up each of the following words in the glossary. On a separate piece of paper, write the diacritical marks you find after each word.**
   a. quake (kwāk)
   b. absurd (ăb-sûrd′)
   c. cartoon (cär-to͞on′)
   d. minuscule (mĭn′ə-sky͞ool′)
   e. shrike (shrīk)
   f. trough (trôf)
   g. twitch (twĭch)
   h. nuzzle (nŭz′əl)
   i. nestle (nĕs′əl)
   j. paralytic (păr′ə-lĭt′ĭk)

2. **Say aloud each of the words in Exercise 1. Then answer the following questions.**
   a. **Does the *a* in *quake* sound like the *a* in *quart* or in *tape*?**
      tape
   b. **Does the *a* in *cartoon* sound like the *a* in *barge* or in *that*?**
      barge
   c. **Does the *i* in *shrike* sound like the *i* in *big* or in *line*?**
      line
   d. **Does the *c* in *cartoon* sound like the *c* in *court* or in *center*?**
      court
   e. **Which letter is silent in *nestle*?**
      t
   f. **Does the *u* in *nuzzle* sound like the *u* in *ugly* or in *use*?**
      ugly
   g. **Does the *gh* in *trough* sound like the *gh* in *tough* or in *ghost*?**
      tough
   h. **Does the *ou* in *trough* sound like the *ou* in *cough* or in *count*?**
      cough
   i. **Does the first *u* in *minuscule* sound like the *u* in *minus* or in *minute*?**
      minus
   j. **Does the second *u* in *minuscule* sound like the *u* in *rule* or in *mule*?**
      mule

WORD ATTACK CHECK TEST

► Refer to the glossary to find answers to the following questions.
   a. How many syllables does the word *paralytic* have?
   b. Are the *a*'s in the word *paralytic* pronounced alike or differently?
   c. Is the *y* in *paralytic* pronounced like the *i* in *it* or like the *i* in *like*?
   d. Is the *a* in *quaker* pronounced like the *a* in *carpet* or the *a* in *cake*?
   e. Which letter in the word *shrike* is silent?

ANSWERS TO WORD ATTACK CHECK TEST

▶ a. four (*par   a   lyt   ic*)   d. *cake*
  b. differently   e. the letter *e*
  c. *it*

ABOUT THE AUTHOR

Theodore Roethke (1908–1963) was many things—a world-famous American poet, a tennis coach, a professor of English, a man admired by his contemporaries and rivals. In 1941, he published his first book of poems, *Open House*. By 1953, he had won a Pulitzer Prize for *The Waking*. During his career, he wrote several children's poems and "greenhouse" poems, which appear in the collected work *I Am! Says the Lamb*. Roethke's last teaching position was at the University of Washington, where he was given the honorary title of "poet in residence" in 1962. When he died, John Ciardi, a fellow poet, published an elegy (a poem written in honor of the dead) to Roethke. It remains a fitting tribute to Roethke's talents.

Unforgettable Grizzly Bears

GEORGE LAYCOCK
pp. 36–43

Summary The narrator tells about three renegade bears: Old Two Toes, Bloody Paws, and Old Mose. He explains that most grizzly-bear attacks on humans do not have to happen. There are certain precautions people can take when they are in the bear's territory.

BEFORE READING

Ask students to imagine they are camping in the woods in Montana or Wyoming. What animals would they fear meeting? List these animals on the chalkboard. (If the students do not mention grizzly bears, add them to the list yourself.) Why would each of these animals be dangerous? Then have students turn to p. 36. Have them read the selection to find out why the author calls these grizzly bears "unforgettable." (Flexibility: Setting a Purpose)

Glossary Words

*maul
  (mauled, p. 40, b, 4)

*renegade (p. 36, a, 2)
*wrangler (p. 38, a, 4)

TEACHING THE GLOSSARY WORDS

Write the glossary words on the chalkboard. Say each word aloud and have the students repeat it after you. Then write the following sentences on the board.

The most famous renegade bear was Old Mose. This outlaw was shot and injured many times, but he wasn't killed until 1904.

The camper had been mauled by the bear. Despite his cuts and bruises, he pleaded for the bear's life.

The job of the wrangler was to take the string of pack ponies across the narrow mountain trail.

Have the students use context clues to figure out the meaning of the underlined words. Then have them check their answers in the glossary. (Word Attack: Context, Dictionary)

CHECK TEST

(F)   1. Old Mose, a renegade bear, was never shot or injured during his career.
(F)   2. Jake Ratcliff killed Old Mose and collected a $575 reward.
(F)   3. When hiking in grizzly-bear country, you should make as little noise as possible.
(T)   4. In general, a person cannot outrun a grizzly.
(F)   5. The author concludes that outlaw bears probably are born that way.

AFTER READING

The grizzly is an endangered species. Ask students what actions could be taken to prevent the species from becoming extinct. (You may want them to write to the National Wildlife Federation, 1412 16th Street, NW, Washington, D.C. 20036.)

CLOSE UP (Comprehension Questions)

1. **(a) How did Old Two Toes get its name?**
   Old Two Toes lost the tips of three toes in a bear trap.
   (b) Why did the ranchers offer a reward for Old Two Toes?
   Old Two Toes' raids were destroying cows, steers, calves, and colts.
2. **Why did Bloody Paws become a legend?** (Relationships: Cause/Effect)

Bloody Paws "was said to have dispatched more than 500 sheep, including fifty-two in a single night."

3. **(a) Why did Old Mose try to kill Jake Ratcliff?** (Relationships: Cause/Effect)
Jake had repeatedly fired his gun at Old Mose.
(b) What fatal mistake did Ratcliff make?
Jake had been pretending to be dead. When he moved his head to see if the bear was gone, Old Mose renewed his attack.

4. **Do you think Old Mose was really a man-killer? Why or why not?** (Judgments)
Students' answers will vary. Some will say he was, because he killed Jake Ratcliff. Others will say he wasn't—that he killed Ratcliff only because he had been provoked by the rifle shots. The bear was just defending himself.

THE ESSAY (Literature Skill Questions)

1. **The topic of this essay is grizzly bears. List five facts the essay gives you about grizzlies.** (Relationships: Listing)
Possible answers are : (1) Only 1,000 to 1,200 grizzlies are left south of Canada. (2) They are mostly in Idaho, Wyoming, and Montana. (3) Grizzlies are still secure in parts of Alaska and northern Canada. (4) The explorers Lewis and Clark first reported the existence of grizzly bears. (5) A fifteen-year-old bear can weigh half a ton.

2. **According to the author, why have grizzly bears and people never made good neighbors?** (Relationships: Cause/Effect)
People seldom want grizzlies coming close to them or their livestock. Grizzlies want nothing to do with people—people have been trying to kill them since Lewis and Clark first reported their existence.

3. **(a) Why would a grizzly attack a person?** (Relationships: Cause/Effect)
Grizzlies are most likely to attack a person who gets too close when they are feeding their young. They will also attack when they think they have been cornered or when they have been attacked.
(b) What should a person do if attacked by a grizzly?
Nobody can outrun a grizzly. A person should either climb a tree or stand or lie perfectly still (i.e., play dead).

4. **Reread the last two paragraphs of this essay. (a) What conclusion does the author reach about grizzlies?** (Main Idea)
The author observes that it is humans who are constantly encroaching on the bears' territory, and concludes that if we had more respect for the wilderness, more of these "magnificent wild creatures" might be left in the world. Also, he believes if people had held this attitude, there might have been fewer anti-human renegades.
(b) Do you agree with this conclusion? Why or why not? (Judgments)
Answers will vary. Some students may feel that it is natural to be afraid of and hostile to creatures that are capable of killing us. Others may feel that all creatures have a right to live, and that the extinction of a species impoverishes us all.

TEACHING SENTENCE MEANING (Reading Skill)

Read the explanatory material in the book aloud while the students read it silently. Then have them complete the skill exercises and check their answers.

SENTENCE MEANING (Reading Skill Exercises)

Finding Core Parts

1. **Find the two core parts in each sentence below. Write them on a separate piece of paper. (If the simple subject is a proper name, be sure to include the full name.)**
   a. **For the rest of his life, the hunter limped badly.**
   hunter   limped
   b. **The horses walked near the inside of the trail.**
   horses   walked
   c. **On the mountainside above them, Old Two Toes rose to his full height.**
   Old Two Toes   rose
   d. **The horse stumbled over the cliff to its death.**
   horse   stumbled

2. **Find the three core parts in each sentence below. Write them on a separate piece of paper.**
   a. **Then one day, far up in the mountains, a wrangler took a horse across a narrow trail.**
   wrangler   took   horse
   b. **Because of his position on the mountain, the bear had the advantage.**
   bear   had   advantage
   c. **Bloody Paws surprised Jake Madden in the middle of the trail.**
   Bloody Paws   surprised   Jack Madden
   d. **With lightning speed, Madden fired the gun at the grizzly at point-blank range.**
   Madden   fired   gun

3. **Usually the simple subject is a noun or a pronoun. [A noun is a word that names a person, place, thing, or idea. A pronoun is a word that takes the place of one or more nouns *(I, he, she, it, you, we, they)*.] In each of the following sentences, the subject is a noun. Replace each noun subject with an appropriate pronoun.**
   a. **The cowboy found tracks made by the bear.**
   He found tracks made by the bear.
   b. **Old Two Toes swatted a cow in the head.**
   He (or It) swatted a cow in the head.
   c. **The incident caused a fury in town.**
   It caused a fury in town.
   d. **The bullet only grazed the bear.**
   It only grazed the bear.
   e. **Lewis and Clark were the first people to report seeing grizzlies.**
   They were the first people to report seeing grizzlies.

TEACHING WORD ATTACK

Have the students read the explanatory material in their books and complete the skill exercises. Check their answers.

WORD ATTACK (Exercises)

Using Guide Words

1. **Find each of the following words in the glossary. On a separate piece of paper, write the guide words you find at the top of the glossary pages on which the words appear.**

   a. **scan**
   provocation/shrike

   b. **corral**
   bevel/cranky

   c. **grub**
   encounter/hatch

   d. **swat**
   sinister/tranquility

   e. **shamble**
   provocation/shrike

   f. **steer**
   sinister/tranquility

   g. **infuriate**
   hogan/invalid

   h. **cranky**
   bevel/cranky

   i. **mill**
   inventory/nominal

   j. **wrangler**
   transition/writhe

2. **Imagine the guide words at the top of the page are *major* and *malice*. Which of the following words would fall on this page?**
   a. maker
   d. malfunction

3. **Imagine the guide words at the top of the page are *sense* and *sequin*. Which of the following words would fall on this page?**
   b. sequel
   c. separate

ABOUT THE AUTHOR

George Laycock (1921–   ) is a field editor of *Audubon*. He contributes articles and short stories to *Audubon*, *Field and Stream*, and *Boys' Life*. He wrote the books *Animal Movers*, *Alaska: The Embattled Frontier*, and *Wingspread*. His book *Never Pet a Porcupine* won the Boys' Clubs of America Junior Book Award in 1966.

Pete at the Zoo

GWENDOLYN BROOKS

For My Grandmother

COUNTEE CULLEN
p. 45

Summaries   "Pete at the Zoo" is a remarkably sensitive portrayal of a child's fear of night. In "For My Grandmother," the poet tenderly remembers his grandmother's indomitable spirit.

BEFORE READING

Explain to students that sometimes the meaning of a poem is suggested rather than directly stated. Tell students to keep the following question in mind as they read these poems: Who is each poem really about? Then have them read each poem to find out what it suggests about each person. (Inferences; Flexibility: Setting a Purpose)

CLOSE UP (Comprehension Questions)

1. **At first, "Pete at the Zoo" seems to be about an elephant. What does the poet wonder about the elephant?**
   The poet wonders if the elephant feels lonely after the people leave the zoo.
2. **Reread the last two lines of this poem. (a) Whom do you think the poem is really about? Why?** (Inferences)
   It is about Pete. He wonders if the elephant fears being alone, as he does.
   (b) What does "hunch up . . ./Against the dark of night" mean? (Sentence Meaning)
   To hunch up means to bend or draw up into a hump. Often we hunch up or pull our bodies together when we are afraid. Pete must be afraid of being alone in the dark.
3. **(a) In the second poem, what has happened to the grandmother?**
   She has died.
   (b) What does the poet mean when he says "she would grow again"? (Figurative Language)
   She believed that she would live again—possibly through her children.

ABOUT THE AUTHORS

Gwendolyn Brooks (1917–   ) won the Pulitzer Prize in 1950 for *Annie Allen,* a collection of poems about a black girl growing up in Chicago. Countee Cullen (1903–1946) published his first collection of poems, *Color,* in 1925. He was the editor of *Caroling Dusk* (1927).

A Shipment of Mute Fate

LES CRUTCHFIELD
pp. 46–63

Summary The bushmaster is the deadliest snake in the world. Chris wants to transport one to New York aboard the liner *Chancay*. During the voyage, the bushmaster escapes from its cage, and Chris must recapture it before it kills.

BEFORE READING

Ask students to name places or objects that make people frightened. Write their responses on the chalkboard. (If the students do not mention snakes, add them to the list yourself.)

Then have students turn to p. 46. Ask one student to read the title of the play and the author's name aloud. Ask the students to look at the illustration. To what do they think the term "mute fate" refers? Why would a snake be called "mute fate"? Have students read the play to find out what happens when a dangerous snake escapes from its box aboard a ship. (Flexibility: Setting a Purpose)

Glossary Words

companionway (p. 53, a, 8)
gaudy (p. 49, b, 9)
incipient (p. 56, b, 5)
*lethal (p. 57, b, 2)
*ominous (p. 51, a, 8)
seethe
  (seethed, p. 56, b, 5)

*sinuous (p. 57, b, 2)
sodden (p. 53, b, 15)
throe (p. 56, b, 5)
transition (p. 48, b, 8)
veer
  (veered, p. 58, a, ℓ. 4)

TEACHING THE GLOSSARY WORDS

Write the glossary words on the chalkboard. Say each word aloud and have the students repeat it after you. Then write the following sentences on the board.

"As I moved, the snake slid out of the cupboard in a single <u>sinuous</u> slide—and drew back into a loose coil on the galley floor—never taking his eyes off me."

"The <u>lethal</u> coils tightened a little—then were still again."

"But in spite of the calm seas and pleasant weather, I was becoming possessed with an <u>ominous</u> anxiety."

"Again every light burned, and the whole ship <u>seethed</u> in the throes of <u>incipient</u> panic."

Have students look up the underlined words in the glossary. Then have them rewrite each sentence replacing each underlined word with a word or several words that mean the same as the underlined word.

Have them look up the remaining words for homework. (Word Attack: Glossary, Context)

CHECK TEST

(T)   1. At first, the Captain refuses to allow the bushmaster on board.

(T)   2. According to Chris, the bushmaster will go after any creature that walks.

(F)   3. Mrs. Willis takes pity on the snake and lets it out of its cage.

(F)   4. The Captain decides to tell the passengers and crew that the snake has escaped.

(F)   5. At the end of this play, *homo sapiens* win out against mute fate.

AFTER READING

The Captain elected not to tell the passengers that the snake had escaped. He wished to avoid a panic. Ask the students if they agree with his decision. Did he have a valid reason for withholding information? Should the passengers have been told they were in danger? Ask them to explain their answers. (Judgments)

CLOSE UP (Comprehension Questions)

1. **(a) How does Chris gain permission to bring the bushmaster on board?** (Relationships: Cause/Effect)
Chris goes over the Captain's head and cables the shipping company's main office in New York.
(b) Why does he want a live snake? (Relationships: Cause/Effect)
It will be "the *only* live bushmaster ever brought to the United States."
2. **Several characters believe that the snake has almost supernatural powers.**
(a) Why does Sanchez say, "No turn him loose in Venezuela. Because he know I the one who catch him—and he know where I live!"? (Relationships: Cause/Effect)
Sanchez fears that the snake has the power to seek him out and kill him (in revenge).
(b) According to the Captain, who broke the glass on the bushmaster's zoo cage?
The Captain says that the night watchman at the zoo was found dead one morning, and the people in charge never found out what happened—but

"the way they figured it—the glass was broken from the inside!" In other words, they believed, and the Captain believes, the snake broke the glass.

3. **(a) What freak accident allows the bushmaster to escape from the chest?**
An enormous wave hits the ship on the port bow, causing a desk in the Captain's cabin to slide into the chest and break both it and the box inside wide open.
(b) When Chris finds the snake in the cupboard, why does he feel that the snake has been waiting for him? (Inferences)
The snake stayed quiet when Bowman was in the galley. It begins to move only when Chris alone is there. Also, Chris has begun to believe the snake has supernatural power. He has begun to think it is his "mute fate."

4. **The bushmaster backs Chris into a corner and prepares to attack. How is Chris saved?** (Relationships: Cause/Effect)
Clara, the "mangy, brave, beautiful alley cat" that Mrs. Willis sneaked aboard, repeatedly provokes the snake to strike. When the snake eventually tires, Clara blinds it and then kills it with a bite to its neck. (She does this to protect her three new kittens.)

5. **(a) Why is "Mute Fate" an appropriate name for the bushmaster?** (Main Idea)
The bushmaster brings death. It kills soundlessly by coiling and squeezing.
(b) How does love triumph over mute fate? (Inferences)
Mrs. Willis' love for her cat Clara prompts her to disobey the new steward's rule and smuggle her aboard. Then, Clara's love for her kittens makes her brave and cunning and enables her to defeat the snake.

THE PLAY (Literature Skill Questions)

1. **The main character in this play is Chris. You learn about him in two important ways—from what he tells you directly and from what he says to other characters. (When Chris is speaking directly to you, the audience, the word *narrating* appears after his name.) (a) How does Chris feel as he looks at the *Chancay*?**
Chris feels a cold chill and a mysterious sense of dread.
(b) Why does he feel this way? (Inferences)
He knows that he is bringing an extremely dangerous snake aboard. He may have a premonition of the terror to come.

2. **Chris tells the Captain that he wants to bring a live bushmaster aboard. (a) What does the Captain tell Chris?**
The Captain refuses to allow the snake aboard because "something might happen," and on a liner the safety of the passengers comes first.
(b) How do you know that Chris doesn't plan to accept this decision? (Inferences)
Chris says that he didn't spend two months in "that stinking back country" to be stopped "on the edge of the wharf." He is determined not to let "a pigheaded ship captain" stop him at the last minute.

3. **A flashback is a look into the past. It tells you about something that happened earlier in the story. (a) Find the flashback in this play.**

The flashback starts on p. 49, *a* and ends on p. 50, *a*.

(b) What purpose does the flashback serve?

It heightens the sense of impending danger. It shows what a dangerous enemy a bushmaster can be.

4. **When you read a play, you imagine the words as you think the actors would say them. On page 53, how do you think the actor playing Mr. Bowman would say, "Huh? . . . Great Jehosaphat! We're taking it on the port bow! Hang on!"?** (Inferences)

The actor would say "Huh?" softly, calmly, and almost absent-mindedly, and then "Great Jehosaphat!", etc., very excitedly, his voice increasing in both pitch and volume.

5. **(a) Find three directions for sound effects. (b) What does each of these directions help you to visualize?**

There are many directions for sound effects. Here are three examples: (1) "(Sound: Wooden box set on wooden wharf, boat whistles, etc. . . . Sound: Steps on gangplank; fade.)" These directions allow us to visualize the busy goings on of life at the wharf.
(2) "(Sound: Wave crashes across the foredeck . . . seems to shake the whole ship . . . and subsides.)" This sound helps us imagine the size and impact of the wave.
(3) "(Sound: The thuds change to the frantic scraping of a heavy snake.)" Since each thud means a coiled strike, the scrape means that the battle has heated up. Sound effects here help us to visualize the extraordinary combat between the skinny cat and the eight-foot snake.

ADDITIONAL ACTIVITIES

▶ Select one or two speeches from this play, rehearse them, and speak them as you think a professional actor would speak them.

TEACHING SENTENCE MEANING (Reading Skill)

Read the explanatory material in the book aloud while the students read it silently. Write the following sentences on the chalkboard.

Going away for the holidays?

Been to the movie yet?

Watched television last night.

Dropped a stitch.

See you later.

Breakfast at eight.

Have students fill in the missing parts of each sentence. Then have them complete the skill exercises and check their answers.

SENTENCE MEANING (Reading Skill Exercises)

Reading Sentences with Words Left Out

1. Add the word or words necessary to make a complete sentence from each of the following items.
   a. "This very bad country."
      This is a very bad country.
   b. "Got a cable from the head office this morning."
      I got a cable from the head office this morning.
   c. "Missed again—by a fraction of an inch."
      It missed again—by a fraction of an inch.
   d. "The scrawny cat that Mother Willis sneaked aboard in La Guaira."
      It is the scrawny cat that Mother Willis sneaked aboard in La Guaira.
   e. "Sorry to go over your head, Captain Wood—but I had to."
      I'm sorry to go over your head, Captain Wood—but I had to.

2. Add the words necessary to make a compound sentence from the following item. [A compound sentence is made up of two complete sentences joined together by a conjunction *(and, or, but)*.]
      "Most happy to have had you aboard on the trip down two months ago, Christopher, and I'm very glad you're coming along with us on the run back to New York."
   I am (*or* I'm) most happy to have had you aboard on the trip down two months ago . . .

TEACHING WORD ATTACK

Have the students read the explanatory material in the book and complete the skill exercise. Then check their answers.

WORD ATTACK (Exercise)

Understanding Contractions

▶ On a separate piece of paper, write the two words that have been combined to form each of the following contractions.
   a. "*Who's* Mr. Bowman?"
      Who is
   b. "I *don't* believe a word of it."
      do not
   c. "Mr. Bowman said I had to leave her ashore—and I just *couldn't!*"
      could not
   d. "*I'd* gone too far to stop."
      I had
   e. "*How's* the best-looking stewardess on the seven seas?"
      How is
   f. "*You've* carried worse things!"
      You have
   g. "There *isn't* anything worse—and any skipper *afloat'll* bear me out."

is not, afloat will

h. *"You're* getting two hundred dollars for it."
You are

i. "Here—*what's* the matter?"
what is

j. *"It'd* never move—just lie there and look at you as long as you were in sight."
It would

WORD ATTACK CHECK TEST

▶ Write a contraction for each of the word groups below:

a. I shall
b. he had
c. it is
d. how have
e. I would

f. do not
g. will not
h. could not
i. they will
j. I have

ANSWERS TO WORD ATTACK CHECK TEST

▶ a. I'll
b. he'd
c. it's
d. how've
e. I'd

f. don't
g. won't
h. couldn't
i. they'll
j. I've

REVIEW QUIZ

ON THE SELECTIONS

p. 64

1. In "Cat-About-Town," how does Sam, the Herriots' dog, feel about Oscar? Find one detail that supports your answer. (Inferences)
Sam, the dog, adores Oscar. They become fast friends. When Oscar returns to the Gibbons family, Sam sniffs disconsolately in the areas where Oscar's bed used to lie and collapses on the rug with a long lugubrious sigh.

2. How does Oscar show that he remembers Helen?
Oscar takes one look at Helen and leaps onto her lap.

3. **In "Last Cover," why are the boys afraid that Bandit will forget them?** (Relationships: Cause/Effect)

They realize that "wild things' memories (are) short." If they don't find him soon, the bond between them and the fox will be broken.

4. **How does Colin prove to his father that he also considers nature important?** (Relationships: Cause/Effect)

Colin's painstaking re-creation of nature's "mazy" complexity in his picture of Bandit shows Father than he has been a careful observer of nature.

5. **In "The Meadow Mouse," what does the poet fear may happen to the mouse?** (Sentence Meaning)

The poet fears that the mouse may be caught by a predator.

6. **How is the mouse like "The turtle gasping in the dusty rumble of the highway"?** (Relationships: Comparison/Contrast)

The mouse, like the turtle, is vulnerable and unprotected in a dangerous environment.

7. **In "Unforgettable Grizzly Bears," why is Old Two Toes easy to track?** (Relationships: Cause/Effect)

Old Two Toes's paw print is unmistakable: he lost the tips of three toes in a trap.

8. **According to this essay, why don't grizzlies and human beings make good neighbors?** (Relationships: Cause/Effect)

Humans always try to kill grizzlies. Sometimes for no reason. Grizzlies are always a threat to farmers and ranchers, since they kill livestock.

9. **In "A Shipment of Mute Fate," Mrs. Willis is kind to a cat and brings it on board. How does her kindness later prevent disaster?** (Relationships: Cause/Effect)

The cat kills the deadly bushmaster.

10. **Why doesn't the Captain want to tell the passengers that the snake has escaped?** (Relationships: Cause/Effect)

He doesn't want to start a panic.

ON SENTENCE MEANING

p. 65

1. **Copy the following item on a separate piece of paper. Then put quotation marks around the exact words of the speaker.**

    "I'm afraid so, Helen," I said. "We've done our best for him but I honestly don't think he has much chance."

2. **Copy the following item on a separate piece of paper. Then add a semicolon, two commas, and a period in the appropriate places.**

    "We'd taken the young fox into the kitchen; all of us, except Father, gone a bit silly over the little thing."

3. **Which three punctuation marks tell you to stop?**

    The period, the question mark, and the explanation mark tell you to stop.

4. **Find the three core parts in the following sentence.**

    Around 1902, the cowboys rode the trails of western Montana.

    cowboys   rode   trails

5. Make a complete sentence from the following item.
   "Better start looking for a place to camp."
   Accept any answers that supply a subject. Here is an example:
   "You had better start looking for a place to camp."

ON TYPES OF LITERATURE

p. 65

▶ **Decide whether the following statements are true or false.**
   a. A personal narrative is a fictional story.
   false
   b. A short story is only about real-life people and events.
   false
   c. A lyric poem expresses an emotional response to a person, place, object, or idea.
   true
   d. An essay usually provides factual information and tells about events that really occurred.
   true
   e. A play is a story that is meant to be performed.
   true

COMPOSITION (Exercise)

Sentence Combining

p. 66

▶ **Combine each group of three sentences into one sentence. Remember to use the first sentence as your base. Then remove the repeated words in the second and third sentences. Finally, use the comma and connecting word that appear in parentheses.**
   a. Helen fed the cat milk.
   Helen fed the cat strained broth. (,)
   Helen fed the cat baby food. (, and)
   Helen fed the cat milk, strained broth, and baby food.
   b. I caught the mouse by the tail.
   I brought him inside. (,)
   I cradled him in my hand. (, and)
   I caught the mouse by the tail, brought him inside, and cradled him in my hand.
   c. Chris feared the bushmaster.
   Sanchez feared the bushmaster. (,)
   Captain Wood feared the bushmaster. (, and)
   Chris, Sanchez, and Captain Wood feared the bushmaster.
   d. It was the biggest grizzly in the area.
   It was the meanest grizzly in the area. (,)
   It was the most powerful grizzly in the area. (, and)

It was the biggest, meanest, and most powerful grizzly in the area.

BEFORE GOING ON

p. 67

The Story of Tuffy, the Dolphin Who Was Trained to Save Lives

MARGARET DAVIDSON
pp. 68–71

Summary   This essay tells how dolphins assist aquanauts in their experiments. It focuses on Tuffy and the tasks he performs, and it shows how he was trained to save lives.

Glossary Words

*aquanaut (p. 69, a, 1)   scan (p. 71, a, 4)
*astronaut (p. 69, a, 1)   sonar (p. 71, a, 4)

TEACHING THE GLOSSARY WORDS

Write the glossary words on the chalkboard. Say each word aloud and have the students repeat it after you. Then write the following words on the board.

aquarium   aquamarine
aquaplane

Tell them these words and the word *aquanaut* are based on the word part *aqua–*, which means "water." Have them define the three words. Ask them what they think an aquanaut does. Have them check their answers in the glossary.

Then tell them that *astro–* is a word part that means "pertaining to outer space." Ask them what an astronaut does. Then have them list other words based on this word part (e.g., astrology, astronomer, astronomy).

Have them look up the remaining two words for homework and write sentences using them. (Word Attack: Structure, Context)

TEACHING FLEXIBILITY (Reading Skill)

Have the students read the explanatory material in their books and study the five purpose-setting questions in the skill exercise. Then have them read the selection and answer the questions.

FLEXIBILITY (Reading Skill Exercises)

Reading for a Purpose

1. **Keep the following questions in mind as you read "The Story of Tuffy, the Dolphin Who Was Trained to Save Lives." After you finish reading, write the answers to the questions on a separate piece of paper.**

   a. **What three specific tasks did the aquanauts perform underwater?**
   They measured the underwater currents, they took pictures of the ocean floor, they put metal tags on the tails of some fish, and they studied underwater plants. (Accept any three.)

   b. **What were Tuffy's two jobs?**
   He carried things (tools, mail, medicines) to the aquanauts and he saved lives.

   c. **Why did the aquanauts pretend to be lost?**
   They did this to test Tuffy.

   d. **Why did Tuffy swim first to Sealab, and then to the lost aquanaut?**
   He did this to get the lifeline rope.

   e. **Why did Tuffy "bop" the aquanaut over his head?**
   The aquanaut did not reward him as usual with chopped fish.

2. **Reread the article using the following procedure.**

   a. **Reread paragraphs 1 and 2. Write a sentence summarizing them.**
   Example: A 300-pound dolphin named Tuffy assisted aquanauts on a
   project called Sealab II.
   (Students' answers will vary.)

   b. **Reread paragraphs 3–6. Write one or two sentences summarizing them.**
   (Students' answers will vary.) **Then answer the following questions.**
   (1) What was "home" for the aquanauts?
   Sealab (a "big metal capsule . . . which rested on the bottom of the ocean") was their "home."
   (2) What tasks did the aquanauts have?
   They measured underwater currents, photographed the ocean floor, put metal tags on the tails of some fish, and studied underwater plants.
   (3) What tasks did Tuffy have?
   He carried mail and tools and occasionally medicines from the surface to the aquanauts below.
   (4) What was Tuffy's most important task?
   He also had been trained to save lives.

   c. **Reread paragraphs 7–10. Write one or two sentences summarizing them.**
   Students' answers will vary.

   d. **Reread paragraphs 11–13. Write one or two sentences summarizing them.**
   Students' answers will vary.

e. **Reread paragraphs 14–17. Write one or two sentences summarizing them.**

Students' answers will vary.

f. **Write a paragraph summarizing the entire article.**

Students' answers will vary.

ABOUT THE AUTHOR

Margaret Davidson (1936–   ) wrote the books *Louis Braille: The Boy Who Invented Reading for the Blind; Dolphins;* and *Frederick Douglass Fights for Freedom.* Her book *Helen Keller's Teacher* won the Junior Book Award of Boys' Clubs of America. Her interests include art, reading, museums, and peace work.

READING SKILLS UNIT TEST (Woodnotes)

1. **Put quotation marks around the exact words of the speakers in the sentences below.**

   a. **Did you go up in the foothills? Mom asked.**

      "Did you go up in the foothills?" Mom asked.

   b. **That was only pranking when he was little, Colin said desperately.**

      "That was only pranking when he was little," Colin said desperately.

   c. **Father shook his head. Late winter's a high time for foxes.**

      Father shook his head. "Late winter's a high time for foxes."

   d. **What sleepers are they? I asked.**

      "What sleepers are they?" I asked.

   e. **Mom was into him then, quick. Not a single frame of Colin's has ever gone to waste. The boy has real talent, Sumter, and it's time you realized it.**

      Mom was into him then, quick. "Not a single frame of Colin's has ever gone to waste. The boy has real talent, Sumter, and it's time you realized it."

2. **Punctuate the sentences below with the punctuation marks indicated in parentheses after each one.**

   a. **" 'Sorry to bother you Jim but could you come down for a minute' " (, , ?)**

      " 'Sorry to bother you, Jim, but could you come down for a minute?' "

   b. **"A teen-age girl was standing by the table her hand resting on a stained roll of blanket" (, .)**

      "A teen-age girl was standing by the table, her hand resting on a stained roll of blanket."

   c. **"Tristan head bowed continued his stroking" (, , .)**

      "Tristan, head bowed, continued his stroking."

   d. **"Then from under the shapeless heap of blanket we heard it again the deep purring which increased in volume till it boomed in our ears like a distant motorcycle" (; .)**

"Then from under the shapeless heap of blanket we heard it again; the deep purring which increased in volume till it boomed in our ears like a distant motorcycle."

e. **"He didn't say anything but continued to look at me steadily"** (, .)

"He didn't say anything, but continued to look at me steadily."

3. **Identify the three core parts in each sentence below.**

a. **"Again and again they ran tests."**

they   ran   tests

b. **"Tuffy would scan the water with his sonar."**

Tuffy   would scan   water

c. **"Each man carried a small plastic bag of chopped fish."**

man   carried   bag

d. **"I remember the way my mother looked up as I came into the kitchen."**

I   remember   way

4. **What is one good way to read for a specific purpose?**

Look for answers to specific questions.

PROFILES

SELECTION	TYPE	LITERATURE SKILL	READING SKILL	WORD ATTACK SKILL
You Can't Take It With You by Eva-Lis Wuorio pp. 75–81	fiction	Plot and Character. Defining plot	Relationships. Understanding time order	Meaning. Understanding synonyms
The Promised Visit by Grey Cohoe pp. 82–93	fiction	Plot and Character. Understanding suspense	Relationships. Understanding cause and effect	Dictionary. Finding verb forms in a dictionary
Say It with Flowers by Toshio Mori pp. 95–103	fiction	Plot and Character. Understanding dilemma	Relationships. Understanding cause and effect	Context. Understanding homophones
Final Curve by Langston Hughes *Faces* by Ted Jones p. 105	poetry	Poetry. Understanding figurative language		
A Running Brook of Horror by Daniel Mannix pp. 106–121	non-fiction	Plot and Character. Understanding characteriza-tion	Relationships. Understanding comparison and contrast	Context. Using context to find the meaning of unfamiliar words
The Dying Detective Michael and Mollie Hardwick (Adapted from a short story by Arthur Conan Doyle) pp. 122–139	drama	Plot and Character. Understanding conflict—person against person	Relationships. Understanding contrast relationships	Context. Finding the meaning that fits the context

SELECTION	TYPE	LITERATURE SKILL	READING SKILL	WORD ATTACK SKILL
The Adventure of the Dying Detective by Isaac Asimov *Arthur* by Ogden Nash *The Old Lady from Dover* by Carolyn Wells p. 141	poetry	Poetry. Understanding the limerick.		
Big Red by Jim Kjelgaard pp. 143–153	fiction	Plot and Character. Understanding conflict— person against nature	Relationships. Understanding spatial order	Structure. Finding root words
The Wall by Noël Murchie pp. 154–169	fiction	Plot and Character. Understanding internal conflict	Relationships. Understanding spatial order	Context. Understanding jargon
Review Quiz pp. 170–171				
Composition. Sentence Combining p. 172				
Before Going On p. 173 Further Reading *Skateboarding* by Karen Folger Jacobs pp. 175–183	essay		Flexibility. Scanning for facts	

You Can't Take It With You

EVA-LIS WUORIO
pp. 75–81

Summary   Uncle Basil is a miser. The family argue that he shouldn't be so parsimonious since—after all, "He can't take it with him."
Uncle Basil proves the family wrong: He lines his coffin with envelopes stuffed with his money and has it cremated along with him.

BEFORE READING

Write the title of the story on the chalkboard. Ask students what people mean when they say, "You can't take it with you." Be sure students understand that the pronoun *it* refers to money. Then tell students they are going to read a humorous story about a man who didn't want his family to inherit his money and so schemed to take it with him when he died. Have them read the story to find out if he is successful. (Sentence Meaning; Flexibility: Setting a Purpose)

Glossary Words

*behest (p. 78, b, 2)
*churl (p. 75, a, 2)
*cremation (p. 77, a, 4)
*curmudgeon (p. 76, a, 1)
*dour (p. 76, b, 3)
*drivel (p. 77, a, 3)

*foible (p. 76, b, 1)
*nominal (p. 77, b, 6)
*parsimonious (p. 75, b, 1)
*unanimous (p. 75, a, 2)
*unorthodox (p. 76, b, 1)
*usurer (p. 75, a, 2)
*vintage (p. 77, b, ℓ. 1)

TEACHING THE GLOSSARY WORDS

Write the glossary words on the chalkboard. Say each word aloud and have the students repeat it after you. (Since your students may find these words difficult to pronounce, you may want to have the students repeat each word two or three times.) Then have students use their glossary to complete the puzzle on the following page. (Word Attack; Dictionary)

Across

1. a disagreeable person
2. request
3. a person who lends money at an extremely high rate
4. gloomy; ill-humored
5. minimal; much less than
6. a miser or extremely stingy person
7. unconventional; not traditional

Down

1. burning of a corpse
3. complete agreement
8. silly talk
9. small fault
10. stingy

CHECK TEST

(F)　1. The family agree that Uncle Basil is a miser.
(T)　2. Basil isn't as deaf as the family believes he is.
(F)　3. Basil made his millions as an exclusive caterer.
(F)　4. Basil bought a fully lined coffin for himself.
(F)　5. At the end of the story, the family refuse to let Basil be cremated.

AFTER READING

Ask students when they first suspected Basil's plan. Why was Basil able to "take it with him" in spite of his family's wishes? (Relationships: Cause/Effect)

CLOSE UP (Comprehension Questions)

1. **Uncle Basil's family complain about his stinginess and greed. (a) Why do Aunt Clotilda, Percival, and Letitia need money?**
Aunt Clotilda wants a new string of pearls because the one she has is getting old. Percival needs money because he has smashed his Aston Martin. Letitia wants a new fur even though it is summer.
(b) How is Basil's greed different from his family's greed? (Relationships: Comparison/Contrast)
Basil wants to keep *his own* money; the family want someone else's money (Basil's). Basil wants to live comfortably on his own money. The family want to use his money for things they do not need.

2. **Uncle Basil likes Verner more than he likes the other members of his family. How is Verner different from the other family members?** (Relationships: Comparison/Contrast)
Verner is not demanding, calculating, and self-centered like the rest of the family. Ironically, he also is "somewhat slow-witted."

3. **Basil would not have gotten away with his plan if his family had cared more about him and less about his money. What do they say when Verner suggests they buy Basil a better coffin?**
They reject the idea: they think, "After all, it (will) only be burned, so what (does) it matter?"

4. **Throughout the story, Basil's family tell him, "You can't take it with you." How does Basil prove that they are wrong?** (Relationships: Cause/Effect)
Basil manages to take it with him by lining his coffin with his fortune, then having himself (and the coffin) cremated.

PLOT (Literature Skill Questions)

1. **The opening situation presents a conflict. (a) What do the family want from Uncle Basil?**
The family want Uncle Basil's money.

(b) What does Uncle Basil want?

He wants to keep his money. In fact, he wants to take it with him when he dies.

2. **The conflict comes to a head at the funeral. Why is the funeral the climax, or high point?**

   The funeral is the point in the story when you find out who wins—the family or Uncle Basil.

3. **What is the resolution of this story?**

   The resolution occurs when you find out how Uncle Basil managed to take his money with him.

TEACHING RELATIONSHIPS (Reading Skill)

Read the explanatory material in the book aloud while the students read it silently. Then have them complete the skill exercises and check their answers.

RELATIONSHIPS (Reading Skill Exercises)

Understanding Time Order

1. **Read each of the following sentences. Then find the signal word that indicates time order in each sentence.**

   a. **"That happened a good decade before the morning his housekeeper, taking him his tea, found him peacefully asleep forever."**
   before

   b. **"The cremation was to take place immediately after the death, and they would find the coffin ready in the garden shed."**
   after

   c. **"The family returned to the little house as the housekeeper was leaving."**
   as

   d. **"Another foible of Uncle Basil's was that, while he still was in excellent health, he had Verner drive him out to an old-fashioned carpenter shop, where he had himself measured for a coffin."**
   while

2. **Make a time line for the following events. Just draw a horizontal line across a page. Starting at the left-hand side of the line, place the events on the line in correct time order. (The event that happened first should be at the left-hand side of the line.)**

   a. **Verner finished lining the coffin with thick envelopes.**
   b. **Uncle Basil found gold in the Transvaal.**
   c. **The lawyer read the contents of Uncle Basil's envelope.**
   d. **Uncle Basil had a coffin built for himself.**
   e. **Uncle Basil died.**
   f. **Uncle Basil hired Verner.**

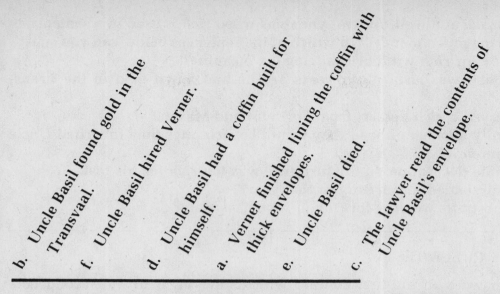

b. Uncle Basil found gold in the Transvaal.

f. Uncle Basil hired Verner.

d. Uncle Basil had a coffin built for himself.

a. Verner finished lining the coffin with thick envelopes.

e. Uncle Basil died.

c. The lawyer read the contents of Uncle Basil's envelope.

3. **Why is it important that Uncle Basil's coffin was built before he died?**
This meant Basil was able to have Verner slowly and carefully line the coffin with envelopes containing Basil's money, without making his family suspicious.

TEACHING WORD ATTACK

Read the explanatory information in the textbooks aloud while the students read it silently. Then have the students complete the exercises and check their answers.

WORD ATTACK (Exercises)

Understanding Synonyms

1. **Which of the following words are synonyms for *miser*? You may use a dictionary to help you.**
   a. scrimp
   b. benefactor
   c. cheapskate
   d. spendthrift
   e. squanderer
   f. pinchfist
   g. hoarder
   h. economist
   i. money-grubber
   j. relative
   Items *a, c, f, g,* and *i* are synonyms for *miser.*

2. **Which of the following words are synonyms for *stingy*? You may use a dictionary to help you.**
   a. parsimonious
   b. unpleasant
   c. miserly
   d. penny-pinching
   e. generous
   Items *a, c,* and *d* are symonyms for *stingy.*

3. **Why can a miser be described as a *Scrooge*? You may use a dictionary to help you answer.**
   Scrooge, a character in Charles Dickens' *A Christmas Carol*, was a miser.

4. The words *rich* and *wealthy* are synonyms when *rich* is used in a sentence to mean "having much money." In which of the sentences below can you substitute *wealthy* for *rich* without changing the meaning?

    a. Uncle Basil was *rich;* many years ago he had found gold in the Transvaal.

    b. They served a *rich* dessert from Fortnum and Mason.

    c. The family members hoped they would be *rich* after they inherited Uncle Basil's money.

    d. The ornate decoration on the furniture was too *rich* for his taste.

    e. The land yielded a *rich* harvest that year.

You can substitute *wealthy* for *rich* in sentences a and c.

WORD ATTACK CHECK TEST

▶ Match each word in the first column with its synonym in the second column.

a. stingy	(1) squanderer
b. spendthrift	(2) hateful
c. benefactor	(3) wealthy
d. loathsome	(4) miserly
e. rich	(5) helper

ANSWERS TO WORD ATTACK CHECK TEST

▶ a. (4)   d. (2)

  b. (1)   e. (3)

  c. (5)

ABOUT THE AUTHOR

Eva-Lis Wuorio is a Canadian citizen who was born in Finland. She has spent the last several years in Finland writing her books. These include *Code: Polonaise,* a novel about wartime Poland based on Polish government documents and her interviews with refugees during and following World War II; *To Fight in Silence,* a World War II novel about the Danish underground; and *Escape If You Can,* a collection of thirteen haunting short stories.

The Promised Visit

GREY COHOE
pp. 82–93

Summary   While driving on a lonely road during a storm, a young man stops to give a ride to a hitchhiker named Susan Billy. She tells him where to drop her off and mentions that she might visit him some night. Later, he goes looking for her only to find that Susan Billy died ten years before. He believes the Susan Billy he met was a ghost when he finds the sweater he lent her hanging on one of the logs of the hogan where she is buried.

BEFORE READING

Have students turn to p. 82. Ask one student to read the title of the story and the author's name aloud. Then have the students study the illustration. On the basis of this illustration, ask them what kind of story they think this will be. Why? (Students should see that the story will be mysterious or "spooky.") Then have them look at the title. Ask them what type of visit they would dread. Have students read the story to find out the secret behind the "promised" visit. (Flexibility: Setting a Purpose)

Glossary Words

hogan (p. 88, b, 3)   sagebrush (p. 89, a, ℓ. 1)
myth (p. 84, a, 3)   superstition (p. 84, b, 1)

TEACHING THE GLOSSARY WORDS

Write the glossary words on the chalkboard. Say each word aloud and have the students repeat it after you. As they read, have them copy in their notebooks the sentences in which they find these words, and write the meaning under each sentence. (Word Attack: Glossary; Context)

CHECK TEST

(T)   1. The person telling this story is driving back from a scholarship interview.
(T)   2. Crosses mark the places where people died along the highway.
(F)   3. At first, the boy refuses to pick up the hitchhiker.
(F)   4. The boy drives the hitchhiker to her house and meets her family.
(T)   5. At the end of the story, the boy finds out that Susan Billy died ten years ago.

AFTER READING

Have a student read the last paragraph of the story aloud. Ask the students to discuss how the boy now feels about Susan Billy's "promised" visit and why he feels this way. How would they feel if they were in his place? (Inferences)

CLOSE UP (Comprehension Questions)

1. **Why do the dark clouds make the young man tremble as he drives through the storm?** (Relationships: Cause/Effect)
   Many people have died mysteriously on the road he is driving, especially in thunderstorms. There are fearsome myths about angry clouds in Navajo lore. In fact, the young man's mother once mentioned a monster that lived in the thunderclouds. His grandmother had told him about a ghost who had caused her son's death on the highway during a storm.

2. **After the storm passes, he feels as though he has awakened from a nightmare. (a) What does he see that suddenly frightens him again?**
   He sees an object standing about fifty yards ahead. (He has always feared dark objects at night.) It turns out to be a girl hitchhiking.
   (b) Why is this sight unusual? (Relationships: Comparison/Contrast)
   It is unusual for someone to be standing on the highway at so late an hour in such miserable weather.

3. **(a) Why does the man try to keep Susan talking at the road to her house?** (Relationships: Cause/Effect)
   Susan is the prettiest girl he has ever seen. He would like to know her better, and he doesn't want their acquantance to end.
   (b) How does he feel when she says she may visit him some night?
   He is proud and delighted by her interest.

4. **(a) What does the young man find out about Susan a few days later?**
   He learns that she died ten years ago.
   (b) What does his sweater prove?
   The appearance of his sweater at her burial hogan proves that he lent it to her ghost.

5. **At the end of the story, does the young man still want a visit from Susan Billy? Why or why not?** (Inferences)
   He seems to still want Susan Billy to visit him, because he loves her. But he is somewhat afraid of what will happen when she visits.

SUSPENSE (Literature Skill Questions)

1. **Early in the story, the young man thinks about all the people who have died along the road. What do his thoughts on death lead you to suspect may happen?** (Inferences)
   They lead you to suspect that either he will meet the ghost of a person who has died along the road or that he himself will die.

2. **(a) What two tales about storms haunt the driver?**
He is haunted by a story his mother told him. This story is about a monster that lives in the thunderclouds. Also, he is haunted by a story his grandmother told him. This story is about her son, who saw a ghost on the highway and drove through the rain-soaked image.
(b) Why do you think the author includes these tales? (Inferences)
The author mentions these tales in order to foreshadow a supernatural happening.

3. **Susan Billy tells the man very little about herself. Does this add suspense to the story? Why or why not?** (Judgments)
Susan's laconic and evasive statements add further suspense to the story. We want to know who she is, where she lives, and why she is on the road at such an unlikely time. We also want to know why she is withholding information.

4. **At the end of the story, the man finds out who Susan Billy really is. Do you still wonder what will happen to him? Why or why not?**
We still wonder what will happen to him—after all, he is certain that he will meet Susan again. We wonder what that meeting will be like. Will he take the chance that she will not kill him, or will he try to escape from her—and death? If he does try, will he succeed or fail?

ADDITIONAL ACTIVITIES

1. **Composition.** Write a letter to the author of this story, telling him why you did or did not enjoy reading it.
2. If you were going to write a ghost story, what place and time would you use for your setting? Explain your answer.

TEACHING RELATIONSHIPS (Reading Skill)

Read the explanatory material in the book aloud while the students read it silently. Then have them complete the skill exercises and check their answers.

RELATIONSHIPS (Reading Skill Exercises)

Understanding Cause and Effect

1. **Identify the word or words that signal a cause-and-effect relationship in each item below.**
   a. **He applied in the spring so he could go to school after graduation.**
      so
   b. **Since he didn't want to believe in superstitions, he thought of something else.**
      Since
   c. **As a result of the rain, the roads were slippery.**
      As a result
   d. **He gave her his sweater because he didn't want her to catch pneumonia.**
      because

e. He knew she liked him, for her eyes told him as much.
for

2. Copy each sentence below on a separate piece of paper. Draw one line under the part of the sentence that shows the cause, and two lines under the part that shows the effect.
    a. What he heard in her voice was love; therefore, he knew she would find him again.
    b. His mind raced ahead to his next meeting with her; accordingly, he lost all track of time.
    c. It was his maroon sweater; thus, he had no choice but to believe in ghosts.
    d. The girl was dead; consequently, he knew his love was hopeless.
    e. Because she loved him, the ghost did not lead him to his death.

TEACHING WORD ATTACK

Read the explanatory material in the book aloud while the students read it silently. Then have them complete the skill exercise and check their answers.

WORD ATTACK (Exercise)

Finding Verb Forms in a Dictionary

► Read each of the following sentences. Then write each of the *italicized* verbs in the form indicated in parentheses. You may use a dictionary to help you find the correct spelling.
    a. She was *hitchhike* (present participle).
       hitchhiking
    b. He *meet* (past) her for the first time that night.
       met
    c. He had *see* (past participle) her up ahead of him.
       seen
    d. He had *prepare* (past participle) for the rainy night.
       prepared
    e. He is *control* (present participle) the car in spite of the storm.
       controlling
    f. After a while, the clouds *slide* (past) away.
       slid
    g. People *tell* (past) of that storm for years.
       told
    h. Many people had *die* (past participle) along that road.
       died

WORD ATTACK CHECK TEST

► Write each of the *italicized* verbs in the following sentences in the form indicated in parentheses.

a. The myth *give* him something to think about. (past)
b. He knew he would be *see* her again on some stormy night. (present participle)
c. He had *think* about her every day since he had *leave* her on the road that dark, stormy night. (part participle)
d. He was *surprise* by her father's words. (past)
e. He is *wonder* what he will do when he meets her again. (present participle)

ANSWERS TO WORD ATTACK CHECK TEST

► a. gave
   b. seeing
   c. thought; left

   d. surprised
   e. wondering

ABOUT THE AUTHOR

Grey Cohoe (1944–   ), a Navajo artist, studied writing and graphic arts at the Institute of American Indian Arts in Santa Fe. Since then, his poems, short stories, and prints have earned him awards and acclaim. His short story "Grandfather Tells the Cat Story" appears in the book *Ethnic American Short Stories*.

Say It with Flowers

TOSHIO MORI
pp. 95–103

Summary   Teruo, the new clerk at a florist shop, keeps throwing out the old flowers, and insists on selling only fresh ones to the customers. This practice costs the boss money and eventually gets Teruo into trouble.

BEFORE READING

Write the following statement on the chalkboard: Honesty is the best policy. Ask students what this statement means. Are there any times when honesty could get a person into trouble? Have students cite examples. Is what is moral or right always the most practical course? Why or why not? Then tell the students they are going to read a story about a boy who must choose between doing what he considers moral and what is practical. Have them read the story to find out which he chooses. (Flexibility: Setting a Purpose)

Glossary Words

*disarm
  (disarmed, p. 95, b, 5)
*ensue
  (ensuing, p. 96, b, 10)
*glutton (p. 96, a, 1)

*harmonize (p. 95, a, 1)
*indignantly (p. 100, a, 11)
*inevitable (p. 97, b, 3)
*temperament (p. 95, a, 1)

TEACHING THE GLOSSARY WORDS

Write the glossary words on the chalkboard. Say each word aloud and have the students repeat it after you. Then write the following sentences on the chalkboard. Have students use the glossary to find out which word best fits in each blank.

"He was curious almost to a fault, and was a_____for work." (glutton)

"In the _____ weeks we watched Teruo develop into a slick salesclerk but for one thing." (ensuing)

"He was a quiet fellow with very little words for anybody, but his smile _____ a person." (disarmed)

"There was something about this young man's appearance which I could not altogether _____ with a job as a clerk in a flower shop." (harmonize)

"I had seen clerks come and go, and although they were of various sorts of _____ (s) and conducts, all of them had the technique of waiting on the customers . . . ." (temperaments)

" 'What!' the boss cried _____." (indignantly)

"Then one early morning the _____ happened." (inevitable)

(Word Attack: Dictionary; Context)

CHECK TEST

(F)   1. Teruo has worked in the flower shop for about five years.
(F)   2. Tommy tells Teruo to sell the fresh flowers in the back room first.
(F)   3. Mr. Sasaki fires Teruo as soon as he sees him sell the fresh flowers.
(T)   4. Teruo persuades the woman not to buy the orchid because it will not keep.
(F)   5. At the end of the story, Teruo pleads with Mr. Sasaki to let him keep his job.

AFTER READING

Ask students if they think Mr. Sasaki was correct in firing Teruo. Why or why not? (Judgments)

CLOSE UP (Comprehension Questions)

1. **Teruo works hard and is eager to learn the florist business. Explain the following sentence: "He was curious almost to a fault, and was a glutton for work."** (Sentence Meaning)
   Teruo is not content to just do his job; he wants to do a good job. He asks an excessive amount of questions and is eager for more work and responsibility.

2. **What does Teruo find out when he asks how to tell the age of the flowers?**
   He find out that the flowers he has been selling are not fresh.

3. **Tommy tells Teruo he must sell the old flowers. (a) What does Tommy think Teruo's "business" should be?**
   Tommy tells Teruo that his "business" is to live.
   (b) Who is more practical—Tommy or Teruo? Why? (Relationships: Comparison/Contrast)
   Tommy is more practical. He places survival ahead of moral questions.

4. **(a) Are the flowers Mr. Sasaki sells really old? Why or why not?**
   The flowers are four to five days old. They are not old for a florist shop, although they would be old for a wholesale market.
   (b) How does he show kindness to Teruo? (Inferences)
   Mr. Sasaki knows Teruo needs the job. He does not fire him when he sees Teruo sell the fresh flowers, but gives him another chance.

5. **Mr. Sasaki says that Teruo doesn't have any business sense. (a) What does the term "business sense" mean?** (Word Attack)
   "Business sense" means understanding what needs to be done in order to make money and keep a business going.
   (b) Do you agree with his judgment of Teruo? Why or why not? (Judgments)
   Students' answers will vary. Some will say that Mr. Sasaki's judgment is correct. A good business person would not give away flowers. He would be more interested in making a profit than in making his customers happy. Others will say that Teruo's practices were good for business. People knew they could trust him and so would frequent his shop.

6. **You may have seen the phrase "Say it with flowers" in an advertisement for a florist. (a) What does this phrase usually mean?** (Sentence Meaning)
   It usually means to show your affection for someone (express your feelings) through giving flowers.
   (b) What does Teruo try to "say with flowers"? (Inferences)
   Teruo tries to say that he cares for his customers and will not cheat them.

DILEMMA (Literature Skill Questions)

1. **Teruo's situation is a dilemma. He will lose his job unless he lies to the cus-**

tomers. **What will he lose if he does lie to the customers?** (Relationships: Cause/ Effect)

He will lose his self-respect.

2. **(a) How does Teruo feel the first time he lies to someone about the flowers?**

He feels guilty. He says, "I'm lousy. The people'll get to know my word pretty soon."

(b) How does he feel when Mr. Sasaki finds him selling fresh flowers?

Teruo feels sick. He doesn't know whether to explain to Mr. Sasaki or to keep quiet.

3. **What forces Mr. Sasaki to fire Teruo?** (Relationships: Cause/Effect)

Teruo sells the fresh flowers instead of the old ones. He charges people less for the flowers than they are worth. And he gives away a dozen fresh roses.

(b) Do you think Teruo wanted Mr. Sasaki to fire him? Why or why not? (Inferences)

Teruo seems to have wanted Mr. Sasaki to fire him. When he came to work that morning, he seemed unusually high-spirited, as though he had made a decision and was no longer troubled. He did not hide any of his actions from Mr. Sasaki. Indeed, he seemed to flaunt them. In fact, he went on a "mad spree" after Mr. Sasaki's warning at lunchtime.

4. **(a) How does Teruo feel when he is fired?**

Teruo is delighted. (He is extremely grateful and cheerful.)

(b) How does he act?

He deposits his week's wages in the cash register (presumably to cover the cost of the flowers he gave away), waves to Mr. Sasaki, and exits whistling, with shoulders straight and head held high.

TEACHING RELATIONSHIPS (Reading Skill)

Have the students read the explanatory material in their books and complete the skill exercise. Check their answers. If you think the students may have difficulty doing the exercise correctly, do the items with them one at a time, making sure they have the correct answer for each one before they do the next.

RELATIONSHIPS (Reading Skill Exercise)

Understanding Cause and Effect

▶ **Copy each of the following sentences on a separate piece of paper. Then draw one line under the part of the sentence that is the cause. Draw two lines under the part of the sentence that is the effect.**

  a. The delivery boy did not say anything about Teruo because he wanted to be on the safe side.

  b. Since Tommy was the head clerk, he trained Teruo.

  c. Mr. Sasaki was satisfied with Teruo, so he moved ahead his yearly business trip.

d. Because <u>the delivery boy had worked in a nursery</u>, <u>he knew how to tell the age of flowers.</u>

e. <u>Teruo knew the flowers were old</u>, for <u>they were brought in five days ago.</u>

f. <u>Teruo found it hard to say that the flowers were fresh</u>, since <u>he knew it wasn't true.</u>

g. <u>Tommy sold the old flowers</u> so that <u>he could keep his job.</u>

h. <u>Tommy didn't get angry at Teruo</u>, since <u>he felt Teruo was just a "green kid."</u>

i. <u>Mr. Sasaki knew Teruo needed the job</u>; consequently, <u>he gave Teruo a second chance.</u>

j. <u>Teruo persuaded the customer buy Columbia roses</u>, since <u>they were the freshest of the lot.</u>

TEACHING WORD ATTACK

Read the first sentence in the explanatory material aloud. Then ask different students to pronounce the words in each group. Have other students tell what the words in each word group mean. Finally, have the students complete the word attack exercise and check their answers.

WORD ATTACK (Exercise)

Understanding Homophones

▶ **Choose the correct homophone to complete each sentence below. You may use a dictionary to help you.**

a. "... but at the _____ (time, thyme) I kept my mouth shut."
time

b. "Mr. Sasaki undoubtedly remembered last year's rush when Tommy, Mr. Sasaki, and I had to do everything and had our hands tied behind _____ (hour, our) backs from having _____ (so, sew) many things to _____ (do, dew) at _____ (one, won) time."
our, so, do, one

c. "When Teruo reported _____ (four, for) work the following morning, Mr. Sasaki left him _____ (in, inn) Tommy's hands."
for, in

d. "We got to _____ (no, know) one another pretty well after that."
know

e. "We soon learned that he _____ (new, knew) nothing about the florist business."
knew

f. "Every morning for several _____ (days, daze) Tommy repeated the prices of the _____ (flours, flowers) for him."
days, flowers

g. "All I do is follow your instructions and _____ (sell, cell) the ones you tell me to . . . ."
sell

h. "I guess in this _____ (whether, weather) they'll hold a day or two."
   weather

i. "When the customers ask _____ (whether, weather) the flowers are fresh, say yes firmly."
   whether

j. ". . . I _____ (no, know) you _____ (knead, need) a job, but you've got to be a good clerk _____ (here, hear) or _____ (your, you're) going out."
   know, need, here, you're

WORD ATTACK CHECK TEST

▶ Choose the correct homophone to complete each sentence below.

a. The _____ (flour, flower) matched her beauty.

b. The petals of the _____ (rose, rows) were wet with _____ (do, dew).

c. The _____ (Morning, Mourning) Glory Flower Shop _____ (sells, cells) only fresh flowers.

d. Teruo got to _____ (no, know) the world of business pretty fast.

e. You _____ (knead, need) to have business sense.

ANSWERS TO WORD ATTACK CHECK TEST

▶ a. flower
b. rose, dew
c. Morning, sells

d. know
e. need

ABOUT THE AUTHOR

Toshio Mori (1910–   ) writes short stories about second generation Japanese-Americans. He draws upon his experiences in doing so. His stories have been published in *Common Ground*, *Writer's Forum*, and *Clipper*. "Say It With Flowers" appeared in the book *The Best American Short Stories of 1943*. His novels include *Woman from Hiroshima* and *Yokohama, California*.

Faces

TED JOANS

Final Curve

LANGSTON HUGHES
p. 105

Summaries "Faces" is a celebration of people who are proud and free. "Final Curve" raises the question: How does it feel to come face-to-face with yourself?

BEFORE READING

Ask students to look at the photograph on p. 104. What is the girl doing? How do they think she feels? How does this photograph make them feel? Why? Then ask students what the expression "to face yourself" means. (For example, How can you "face yourself" after what you have done?) Have students read these two poems to find out how the poets feel about "facing oneself." (Figurative Language)

CLOSE UP (Comprehension Question)

▶ **Do you think it takes courage to come to terms with yourself, to face who you are? Why or why not?** (Judgments)
Students' answers will vary. Some will say that it does take courage to face your limitations and accept yourself for what you really are.

ABOUT THE AUTHORS

Ted Joans (1928–   ) was born in Cairo, Illinois. In addition to being a poet, he is also a painter and a jazz musician. Many of his poems have been anthologized. His books of poetry include *Beat, All of Ted Joans, The Hipsters, Black Bow-Wow*, and *Afrodisia*.

Langston Hughes (1902–1967), a world-famous American writer, won the Witter Bynner Prize for undergraduate poetry while attending Lincoln University. A prolific writer, his poem "The Negro Speaks of Rivers" had been translated into twelve languages by the time he was nineteen. He published his first book of poems, *The Weary Blues,* in 1926, and followed up its success with the publication of several novels, short stories, and essays—all works concerned with depicting black American life. He edited several anthologies, including *The Poetry of the Negro* (with Arna Bontemps) and *The Best Short Stories by Negro Writers,* and also published an autobiography, *The Big Sea*. In addition, Hughes was a lyricist, librettist, and newspaper columnist—the famous Harlem character, Jesse B. Simple, was born in his columns.

A Running Brook of Horror

DANIEL MANNIX
pp. 106–121

Summary   In this suspenseful true story, Jule and Daniel Mannix interview Grace Wiley, an expert snake handler, and learn about her remarkable technique. They want to take a picture of Grace with the king cobra. Grace removes her glasses to pose for the picture and subsequently misjudges the king cobra's striking distance. It grabs hold of her finger and she quickly dies from the bite.

BEFORE READING

Have students turn to p. 106. Have one student read the title of the selection, the author's name, and the headnote aloud. Tell the students that the title is John Ruskin's description of a snake. Ask them why a snake could be described as a "running brook of horror." Then tell them they are going to read a true story of a woman who worked fearlessly with snakes. Have them read the story to find out in what ways Grace Wiley is remarkable. (Figurative Language; Flexibility: Setting a Purpose)

Glossary Words

*amputate
   (amputated, p. 117, b, 2)
   (amputation, p. 116, a, 3)
*conception (p. 118, b, 2)
*dexterity (p. 108, a, ℓ. 4)
*feint
   (feinting, p. 108, b, 3)
*frustrate
   (frustrated, p. 112, a, 2)

*hypodermic (p. 112, a, ℓ. 7)
*indulgently (p. 108, b, 1)
*intrinsically (p. 109, b, 1)
*provocation (p. 112, b, 3)
*psychological (p. 109, b, 1)
*slough
   (sloughing, p. 113, a, 2)
*tourniquet (p. 116, a, 2)
*uncanny (p. 109, a, ℓ. 7)

TEACHING THE GLOSSARY WORDS

Write the glossary words on the chalkboard. Say each word aloud and have the students repeat it after you. Then have the students find each word in the following puzzle. Tell them the words may read from left to right, from right to left, from top to bottom, from bottom to top, or diagonally. After they find each word, have them look it up in the glossary and write a sentence using it. (Word Attack: Dictionary, Context)

```
I N D U L G E N T L Y A H
N G C O N C E P T I O N Y
T E F Y B C F K G E G E P
R O R I T O A Q U A M T O
I N U G E I N N A D E A D
N O S R O M R S N R O T E
S E T H N P S E N Y M U R
I S R F E I N T T A P M
C H A O N P Q R S X R M I
A G T A N H O U Y I E A C
L U E D D E N S E P R D O
L O P R O V O C A T I O N
Y L C I A O L P H C Y S P
P S Y C H O L O G I C A L
```

CHECK TEST

(T) 1. In captivity, rattlers often grow sluggish.
(F) 2. Grace is afraid of the new batch of cobras.
(T) 3. Grace handles rattlesnakes differently than she does cobras.
(F) 4. A cobra stabs instead of biting.
(F) 5. The cobra that bites Grace has a W on its hood.

AFTER READING

Ask students if they agree with the author that Grace Wiley was a remarkable woman. Why or why not? (Judgments)

CLOSE UP (Comprehension Questions)

1. **Grace Wiley based her technique on her knowledge of the physical and psychological differences in snakes. (a) Why could she allow a cobra to strike her open palm?** (Relationships: Cause/Effect)
A cobra has to bite in order to inject its poison. Grace knew that it couldn't get a grip on her flat palm.
(b) Why would she *not* allow a rattlesnake to strike her palm? (Relationships: Cause/Effect)
A rattlesnake doesn't have to bite to inject its poison; it stabs with its fangs.

2. **When handling the cobra, Grace depended on her practiced eye to determine a safe position for her hand. (a) Why did she remove her glasses when Daniel Mannix photographed her?** (Relationships: Cause/Effect)
Grace thought she would look better in the photo without her glasses.
(b) Why was this a tragic mistake? (Inferences)
Grace needed keen vision to judge the cobra's striking distance. She needed to see the cobra's movements to know when to deflect its bite with her palm. Without her glasses she misjudged the distance and was bitten on the finger.

3. **(a) Why did Grace call the new Indian cobra from Siam "my snake"?**
The new Indian cobra had a "G" pattern on the back of its head, which Grace identified with her name.
(b) After reading the story's ending, what else do you think this name means? (Inferences)
It is "her snake" because it causes her death.

CHARACTER (Literature Skill Questions)

1. **List two things that made Grace one of the most remarkable people the author had ever met.** (Relationships: Listing)
Here are some examples. She knew more about handling snakes than anyone else. Her collection of reptiles was extraordinary, one of the world's finest. Originally, she had been afraid of even garter snakes. Even after she was fatally bitten, she was calm and thoughtful. (She carefully put the cobra back in its cage, told Jule not to worry, and showed concern about the fate of her frogs and snakes.)

2. **Reread the fourth paragraph in the story. Find the sentence that tells you what Grace Wiley looked like.** (Imagery)
"She was a surprisingly little lady, scarcely over five feet, and probably weighed less than a hundred pounds."

3. **How did Grace Wiley feel about the hamadryads?**

Grace felt reverence toward them. She called the male of her couple "the king of kings" (i.e., of king cobras).

4. **(a) How did Mrs. Tanner feel about Grace?**
Mrs. Tanner thought Grace was a beautiful and talented person, but she could not understand why she wanted to "mess around with those awful snakes."
(b) How did the directors of the Museum of Natural History at the Minneapolis Public Library feel about her? (Relationships: Comparison/Contrast)
The directors felt that her style of handling snakes was reckless. They felt it endangered not only her own life but also the lives of others.

5. **On the basis of Grace Wiley's actions, do you think the directors' judgment of Grace was right? Why or why not?** (Judgments)
Students' answers will vary. Some will say that her actions got results. She was an acknowledged expert. She was successful at handling snakes and had a good reputation—Dr. Mann, the director of the National Zoological Park in Washington, D.C., said, "Grace is probably the only non-Oriental who knows the real secrets of this curious business [snake charming]." Others will feel that by vainly removing her glasses, Grace shows that the directors' judgment was right.

TEACHING RELATIONSHIPS (Reading Skill)

Have the students read the explanatory material in their books, and complete the skill exercise. Check their answers.

RELATIONSHIPS (Reading Skill Exercise)

Understanding Comparison and Contrast

▶ **Answer the question following each item below.**
a. **"Man-eating tigers are said to kill 600 natives a year, but cobras kill 25,000 people a year in India alone."**
How are tigers different from cobras?
They kill fewer people in a year's time.
b. **"The snake swayed like a reed in the wind, feinting for the strike."**
How is the snake like a reed in the wind?
They both sway.
c. **"As rapidly as an expert boxer drumming on a punching bag, the snake struck three times against Grace's palm, always, for some incredible reason, with his mouth shut."**
How is the snake like an expert boxer?
It strikes as fast as a boxer punches.
d. **"The cobra hesitated a split second, his reared body quivering like a plucked banjo string."**
How is the snake's body like a plucked banjo string?
They both quiver.
e. **"Although the cobra is intrinsically a far more dangerous snake than the**

rattlesnake, Grace would never have attempted to handle a diamondback rattler in the manner she handled this cobra."
How is the cobra different from the rattlesnake?
The cobra is more dangerous. It also is easier to handle.

TEACHING WORD ATTACK

Read the explanatory material in the book aloud while the students read it silently. Then talk through each item in Exercise 1, one at a time. Ask the students to define the *italicized* words and identify the context clues that helped them formulate each definition. Then have them do Exercise 2 and check their answers.

WORD ATTACK (Exercises)

Using Context to Find the Meaning of Unfamiliar Words

1. Write the meaning of each *italicized* word. Use context to help you figure out the meaning. Then look up each word in a dictionary to check your answers.
   a. "Grace lives in a little house full of poisonous snakes *imported* from all over the world."
   brought into the country
   b. "The cobra hesitated a split second, his reared body *quivering* like a plucked banjo string."
   trembling
   c. "Because of the *deceptively* coiled S, no one can tell exactly how far a rattler can strike."
   misleading
   d. "Grace knew snakes perfectly and could tell by tiny, *subtle* indications what the reptile would probably do next."
   slight; hard to detect
   e. "When a king cobra *rears* up, he stands higher than the head of a kneeling man."
   rises
   f. "Grace slid her open hand over his head and stroked his hood. The snake hissed again and struggled violently under her touch. Grace continued to *caress* him."
   touch; stroke
   g. "Because of his method of rearing, a cobra cannot strike directly upward (a rattler can strike up as easily as in any other direction), and Grace could actually touch the top of the snake's head. The snake became puzzled and frustrated. He felt that he was fighting an *invulnerable* opponent who, after all, didn't seem to mean him any harm."
   not capable of being wounded or defeated

2. Write an original sentence for each of the italicized words in Exercise 1.
   Accept all reasonable answers.

WORD ATTACK CHECK TEST

▶ Use context clues to define the *italicized* words in the sentences below.
  a. "The snake raised his head but made no attempt to strike or even to rattle. In captivity, rattlers often grow *sluggish* and can be handled with comparative impunity."
  b. "Hunters have been *mauled* by wounded elephants and lived to tell about it, but no one survives a body bite from a big cobra."
  c. They tied a *tourniquet* around her finger to stop the venom from entering her system.
  d. The snake *sloughs* off its dead skin by rubbing against rocks.

ANSWERS TO WORD ATTACK CHECK TEST

▶ a. dull; not active
  b. mangled
  c. a bandage wrapped around a limb
  d. cast off a layer of skin

ABOUT THE AUTHOR

Daniel Mannix studied zoology and journalism in college. He then worked as a magician and sword-swallower in carnivals, establishing a world record for swallowing the longest sword (23½"). He has written books about his carnival experiences and about his adventures with animals—his own childhood pets included a rabbit, skunk, raccoon, and alligator. His book *The Fox and the Hound* received the Dutton Animal Book Award in 1967.

The Dying Detective

MICHAEL and MOLLIE HARDWICK
(Adapted from a short story by ARTHUR CONAN DOYLE)
pp. 122–139

Summary   In this play, Sherlock Holmes feigns illness in order to extract a murder confession from Culverton Smith.

BEFORE READING

Have students turn to p. 122. Read the title of the play and the authors' names aloud. Have one student read the cast of characters aloud. Then assign students for each of the roles. Assign one student to act as narrator and read the stage directions aloud.

Glossary Words

*agitate
  (agitated, p. 124, b, 5)
*carafe (p. 122, a, 1)
 colleague (p. 125, b, 12)
*corroborate (p. 133, b, 10)
 delirious (p. 128, b, 12)
 ghastly (p. 134, b, 5)
 incubation (p. 125, a, 12)
 invalid (p. 134, a, 6)

irksome (p. 133, a, 7)
methodical (p. 128, b, 8)
*pathological (p. 125, b, 12)
prolific (p. 128, b, 14)
recumbent (p. 130, b, 6)
remonstrance (p. 126, a, 3)
stealthily (p. 126, b, 3)
*vindictive (p. 134, b, 3)
writhe
  (writhing, p. 132, b, 3)

TEACHING THE GLOSSARY WORDS

Write the glossary words on the chalkboard. Say each word aloud and have the students repeat it after you. Then write the following sentences on the board and have students use context clues to figure out the meaning of each <u>underlined</u> word.

"I knew his <u>vindictive</u> nature, and I was certain he would come to gloat over his handiwork."

"There are many problems of disease, many <u>pathological</u> possibilities, peculiar to the East."

"Now he'll pretend I've said anything he cares to invent that will <u>corroborate</u> his insane suspicions."

"But he got so <u>agitated</u>—almost shouted that he wouldn't allow any doctor on the premises."

". . . on which stands a <u>carafe</u> of water and a glass . . ."

Have students check their answers in the glossary. Have them look up the remaining words for homework and write the definitions in their notebooks. (Word Attack: Dictionary, Context)

CHECK TEST

(T)   1. Holmes refuses to allow Mrs. Hudson to send for a doctor.
(F)   2. Watson claims to be a specialist on the Black Formosa Corruption.
(F)   3. Culverton Smith is a respected doctor.
(T)   4. Smith's cousin contracted an out-of-the-way Asiatic disease in London.

(F)   5. Holmes's real reason for asking Smith to turn up the light is that he doesn't want to die in the dark.

AFTER READING

Ask students to imagine they work for a casting agency. Have them name real actors they would cast in the roles in this play. Tell them to choose actors who are like these characters (e.g., look like them, have similar mannerisms). (Relationships: Comparison/Contrast)

CLOSE UP (Comprehension Questions)

1. **The first scene sets up the problem: Sherlock Holmes is dying from an exotic tropical disease. Why didn't Mrs. Hudson send for Dr. Watson as soon as she learned of Holmes's illness?** (Relationships: Cause/Effect)
   Holmes said that he wouldn't allow Watson to see him.

2. **(a) Why does Holmes tell Watson that he has no confidence in Watson's medical ability?** (Relationships: Cause/Effect)
   Holmes can't afford to have Watson examine him—Watson will discover he's not really ill.
   (b) How does Watson interpret this remark? (Inferences)
   Watson is hurt. He coldly replies that such a remark merely shows what a state Holmes's nerves are in.

3. **Holmes sends Watson for Mr. Culverton Smith. (a) Why does Smith have knowledge of this tropical disease?** (Relationships: Cause/Effect)
   Smith owns a plantation in the tropics—where there is a scarcity of medical knowledge. An outbreak of Tapanuli Fever caused him to study the disease.
   (b) At the end of Scene Two, what else does Holmes ask Watson to do?
   Holmes asks Watson to get Smith to come, but to make certain that he returns before Smith, he instructs Watson to "make any excuse so as not to come with him."

4. **(a) What is Watson's reason for hiding behind the head of the bed?**
   Watson wants "to hear every word of this so-called medical expert's opinion."
   (b) What is Holmes's real reason for having Watson hide there?
   Holmes needs a witness to Smith's confession.

5. **It turns out that Holmes has faked his illness in order to trap Smith into confessing to the murder of Victor Savage. (a) What steps did Holmes take to make himself look ill?** (Relationships: Cause/Effect)
   Holmes fasted for three days and used vaseline to produce a glistening forehead, belladona to make his eyes water, rouge on his cheekbones to make his cheeks look feverish, and a crust of beeswax around his lips (to make his lips appear crusted and dry).
   (b) Find three statements he made that convinced others he was delirious. (Inferences)
   (1) "I wonder how a battery feels when it pours electricity into a

nonconductor?" (2) ". . . you can put them (your half-crowns) in your watch pocket—and all the rest of your money in your left trouser pocket. It will balance you so much better that way." (3) "No, I really can't think why the whole ocean bed isn't one solid mass of oysters . . . . They're so prolific, you know."

CONFLICT (Literature Skill Questions)

1. **Sherlock Holmes wants to prove that Smith killed Victor Savage. (a) What does Smith want?**
   Smith wants to kill Holmes before he proves it.
   (b) How does Smith plan to accomplish this goal?
   He sends Holmes a box that is rigged with a sharp, poisoned spring. (Upon opening the box, Holmes will be injected with the fatal poison.)
2. **Smith laughs and says, "I don't see you in any witness-box, Holmes. Quite another shape of box, I assure you." What does this statement mean?** (Inferences)
   Smith envisions Holmes in a coffin. (He is convinced Holmes is dying from the poison; he is gloating over the apparent success of his plan.)
3. **Because of his elaborate trick, Holmes wins this conflict. (a) What personality traits does this trick reveal about Holmes (for example, cleverness)?**
   It shows that Holmes is cunning, a master planner, a convincing actor, and a man of great perseverance and discipline.
   (b) What personality trait causes Smith to fall into Holmes's trap?
   A spiteful desire to rejoice in his own cleverness proves to be Smith's undoing. Holmes explains, "I knew his vindictive nature, and I was certain he would come to gloat over his handiwork."

ADDITIONAL ACTIVITIES

1. Make a list of characteristics you think a good detective should have.
2. Select one scene in the play and draw the stage plan for it. Show where the furniture is placed and where each character is located.

TEACHING RELATIONSHIPS (Reading Skill)

Read the explanatory material in the book aloud while the students read it silently. Then have them complete the skill exercises and check their answers.

RELATIONSHIPS (Reading Skill Exercises)

Understanding Contrast Relationships

1. **Find the word or words that signal a contrast relationship in each of the following items.**

a. **Although he was not a doctor, Culverton Smith was the one person who knew everything about the disease.**
   although
b. **Holmes was delirious; however, he was not dying.**
   however
c. **Smith bore a grudge against Holmes. Still, he came at Holmes's request.**
   still
d. **Victor was a strong, hearty fellow; yet he died on the fourth day of his illness.**
   yet
e. **Holmes was healthy in spite of his appearance.**
   in spite of

2. **Answer the question following each of the lettered items.**
   a. **Although Victor lived in the heart of London, he contracted a rare tropical disease.**
      Where would you expect someone who contracted a tropical disease to live?
      in the tropics
   b. **Three days ago Holmes was perfectly hale and healthy; yet today he is weak and delirious.**
      How was Holmes's health three days ago different from his health today?
      He was in good health then.

TEACHING WORD ATTACK

Write the words *hit, tap,* and *book* on the chalkboard. Ask the students to volunteer as many different definitions for each as they can think of. Then have them read the explanatory material in their books and complete the skill exercises. Check their answers.

WORD ATTACK (Exercises)

Finding the Meaning That Fits the Context

1. **Read each sentence below. Then, for each *italicized* word, choose the meaning that fits the context.**
   a. **"Mrs. Hudson bristles at this form of *address.*"**
      (1) the place where a person lives
      (2) speech directed to an individual
      (3) the writing on an envelope
         (2)
   b. **"By the way, Inspector, you might add the attempted murder of one Sherlock Holmes to that *charge.*"**
      (1) accusation
      (2) the price of something
      (3) an attack
         (1)

c. "As you know, my *correspondence* is a varied one.
   (1) similarity
   (2) agreement
   (3) mail; letters or packages received and sent
   (3)

d. "I wonder how a *battery* feels when it pours electricity into a nonconductor?"
   (1) object used to knock down a wall
   (2) the pitcher and the catcher
   (3) a connected group of cells carrying an electrical charge
   (3)

e. "Such a remark, coming from you, merely serves to tell me what *state* your nerves are in."
   (1) condition
   (2) a political body
   (3) position in life
   (1)

2. For each *italicized* word below, write an original sentence.
   a. *address,* meaning "the writing on an envelope"
   b. *charge,* meaning "the price of something"
   c. *correspondence,* meaning "mail"
   d. *battery,* meaning "a connected group of cells carrying an electrical charge"
   e. *state,* meaning "condition"
   Students' answers will vary.

WORD ATTACK CHECK TEST

▶ Select the correct definition for each *italicized* word in the sentences below.
   a. "What sort of *game* is this, then . . . ?"
      (1) poultry
      (2) contest or sport
   b. "I was just taking my lamp to go to my bed on Wednesday night when I heard a *faint* knocking at the street door."
      (1) light; barely audible
      (2) swoon; loss of consciousness
   c. "You'll *ring* if I can be of help."
      (1) sound a bell
      (2) piece of jewelry for the finger
   d. "Whether you like it or not, I'm going to examine you and *treat* you."
      (1) reward
      (2) care for or cure
   e. "You can just see, if you look at it sideways, where the sharp *spring* emerges as you open it."
      (1) coiled wire that gives under pressure and returns to its normal shape once the pressure is removed
      (2) a flow of water

ANSWERS TO WORD ATTACK CHECK TEST

▶ a. (2)   d. (2)
   b. (1)   e. (1)
   c. (1)

ABOUT THE AUTHORS

Michael and Mollie Hardwick have adapted several Sherlock Holmes stories for BBC (British Broadcasting Corporation) television and radio. Their books include *The Sherlock Holmes Companion; The Charles Dickens Companion; The Man Who Was Sherlock Holmes; Four Sherlock Holmes Plays; Sherlock Holmes Investigates; Writer's House: A Literary Journey in England;* and *Alfred Deller; A Singularity of Voice.*

Sir Arthur Conan Doyle (1859–1930) took up writing to supplement the income from his poor medical practice. He modeled his most famous character, Sherlock Holmes, on a teacher at the Edinburgh University Medical School. Holmes first appeared in *A Study in Scarlet,* Doyle's first novel, which was published in *Beeton's Christmas Annual* in 1887. Three more Holmes novels and fifty-six Holmes stories followed. The stories were published monthly in *Strand* magazine. They were an instant success, and Doyle soon retired from medicine altogether to concentrate on writing. Doyle wanted to be acknowledged as a writer of serious literature, but Holmes overshadowed his more serious literary efforts. Because of this, he killed off the detective in 1893, in a story called "The Final Problem." There were such cries of public indignation, however, that Doyle finally relented and resurrected the character a few years later.

The Adventure of the Dying Detective

ISAAC ASIMOV

Arthur

OGDEN NASH

The Old Lady from Dover

CAROLYN WELLS
p. 141

Summaries   Three amusing limericks.

BEFORE READING

Since most students will be familiar with limericks, ask them to bring in a limerick and read it to the class. Then select students to read aloud the limericks in this book.

ABOUT THE AUTHORS

Isaac Asimov (1920–   ) is best known for his science-fiction works. His short stories appear in *Analog, Galaxy,* and other leading science-fiction magazines and have been collected in several books, including *The Early Asimov, The Bicentennial Man and Other Stories,* and *Before the Golden Age.* His novel *The Gods Themselves,* published in 1972, won both the Nebula Award and the Science Fiction Achievement Award (or the Hugo Award). He has edited several anthologies, including *The Hugo Winners, 1962* and *Nebula Award Stories Eight,* and publishes his own science-fiction magazines, *Isaac Asimov's Science Fiction Magazine* and *Asimov's SF Adventure Magazine.* Asimov is a great fan of Sherlock Holmes. He is an active member of the Baker Street Irregulars (a Sherlock Holmes fan club), and wrote *Asimov's Sherlockian Limericks,* which contains a limerick for each of the sixty Holmes stories.

Ogden Nash (1902–1971) was a brilliant writer of comic verse. Nash had a passion for puns, and once called himself a "worsifier" (a pun for versifier—a perfect description, since he used the best as well as the worst rhymes he could dream up). A frequent contributor to *The New Yorker* and other leading American magazines, Nash enjoyed giving lectures and readings of his works.

Carolyn Wells (187?–1942) was an American anthologist and a writer of mystery and detective stories. A victim of scarlet fever, she was left deaf at the age of six. Her novels include *Murder Will In* and *Who Killed Caldwell?* She frequently contributed poems to American periodicals and to *Punch,* a British magazine.

Big Red

JIM KJELGAARD
pp. 143–153

Summary In this tense, exciting story, Danny and his dog, Red, stalk Old Majesty, a killer bear. While trying to save Danny from the bear, Red is gravely injured. To save Red, Danny willingly places his own life in danger—he bravely runs up to the bear, places the muzzle of his gun within two feet of its ear, and fires. He then nurses Red back to health.

BEFORE READING

Write the following lines on the chalkboard.

> Life that dares send
> A challenge to his end,
> And when it comes, say, Welcome,
>   friend!
> (Richard Crashaw)

Ask students why someone would welcome a challenge. Do they think that a challenge must be faced, or is it something that you can walk away from? Why?

Then tell students they are going to read an excerpt from a novel. A huge bear called Old Majesty has been terrorizing the people. Danny feels he must accept the bear's challenge and go into the mountains to fight the bear on its own ground. Have them read the story to find out how this encounter turns out. (Judgments; Flexibility: Setting a Purpose)

Glossary Words

*avert
  (averted, p. 144, a, 1)
*breech (p. 148, a, ℓ. 1)
*copse (p. 144, b, 1)
*eddy
  (eddied, p. 144, b, 1)
*erratic (p. 146, b, 2)
*hackles (p. 145, b, 1)
*proffer
  (proffered, p. 144, b, ℓ. 2)

*quail
  (quailed, p. 144, a, ℓ. 1)
*quarrelsomely (p. 150, b, 1)
*reckoning (p. 144, a, 2)
*ruff (p. 148, a, 1)
*scud
  (scudded, p. 146, a, 2)
*sheathe
  (sheathed, p. 143, a, 1)
*stance (p. 147, b, 1)

TEACHING THE GLOSSARY WORDS

Write the glossary words on the chalkboard. Say each word aloud and have the students repeat it after you. Assign each student one word from the list of glossary words. Have the students look up their words and then use them in original sentences. Tell the students to use context clues in their sentences that will help the other students figure out the meaning of the glossary word. Then have all or selected students read their original sentences and have the other students try to define the glossary words from the context clues in the original sentences. (Word Attack: Dictionary, Context)

CHECK TEST

(T) 1. Old Majesty has killed one of Danny's dogs and wounded Danny's father.

(F) 2. Red is the best trailing dog in the county.

(T) 3. Danny and Red are hunting Old Majesty, but Old Majesty is also hunting them.

(T) 4. As far as Danny knows, this is the first time anyone has stalked Old Majesty by night.

(F) 5. At the end of the story, Danny's father comes to his rescue.

AFTER READING

In many ways, this is a coming-of-age story. Ask students to compare and contrast it with other stories in this book that tell how someone faces a challenge and becomes an adult. (Relationships: Comparison/Contrast)

CLOSE UP (Comprehension Questions)

1. **(a) What are the four reasons Danny gives for going into the Wintapi wilderness to fight Old Majesty?** (Relationships: Cause/Effect)
   Danny feels he must fight Old Majesty because (1) the bear killed Asa, a hound dog; (2) he hurt Ross, Danny's father; (3) he would probably hurt or kill other men; and (4) he asserted supremacy over the whole Wintapi area by attacking Ross.
   (b) Which reason do you think is the most important? (Judgments)
   Students' answers will vary. The second and third reasons are the most important, since they involve human safety.
2. **Danny thinks that how he will face bears in the future depends on how he faces Old Majesty now. What do you think the bear represents, or stands for, to Danny?** (Figurative Language)
   The bear is a personal challenge to Danny. It is "his fight"—his job to do. If he avoids facing it, he will lose self-respect and his father's respect as well. Also, Old Majesty is both daring and cunning, so he represents a challenge

to Danny's skill as a hunter. He also seems to represent life's problems and responsibilities.

3. **Danny uses both scientific woodcraft and his wits to track Old Majesty. (a) How does Danny find the bear's trail?** (Relationships: Cause/Effect)
Danny realizes that Old Majesty, having failed in his attempt to raid the farms, would have to take his living from the wilderness. At that time of year, "grubs were the most plentiful and easiest-to-get food." Danny reasons that Old Majesty has gone across the two mountains, where the grubs are most plentiful. Instead of wasting days trying to work out the bear's old trail, Danny is able to find a fresh trail.
(b) Why does Danny think Old Majesty is not too far from this spot?
There are plenty of grub-infested logs lying about. There are fresh bear tracks (less than two hours old)—Old Majesty couldn't have found a better resting place. There are no signs that Old Majesty knows he is being pursued.
Danny figures that the bear, after eating his fill of grubs, is resting close by.

4. **Danny knows that the bear is near when he feels Red stiffen. (a) What does Danny realize the bear is doing?**
When Red slowly swings his body around in a complete circle, Danny realizes that the bear must be circling them. He also realizes that the bear is hunting *them*—"selecting (the) fight to his own advantage."
(b) Why is it a good time for the bear to do this? (Inferences)
The darkness is the best time for the bear to make his move; it conceals him. He then has time to prepare himself and choose the best method of attack.

5. **(a) How does Red save Danny's life?**
Old Majesty charges Danny and is about to kill him. Red charges the bear in the nick of time and diverts his attention from Danny.
(b) How does Danny save Red's life?
Danny fires the fatal shot at the bear from less than two feet away. Then he carries Red back to where he left the pack, dusts the gaping wound with sulfa powder, and gives him his jacket for a soft bed.

6. **At the end of the story, how has Danny changed?**
Danny has gained confidence and self-respect. He is now sure of his skill, courage, and reliability. The new Danny Pickett is "able to do what he never could have done before."

CONFLICT (Literature Skill Questions)

1. **How has Old Majesty proclaimed supremacy over all the Wintapi?**
Old Majesty has proclaimed supremacy by wantonly attacking a man and killing his dog.

2. **What three risks does Danny take when he sets out to fight Old Majesty?**
Danny risks (1) killing or hurting his dog, Red, whom he loves most in all the world, next to his father; (2) ruining the hours of training Red underwent to become a partridge-hunting dog; and (3) hurting himself.

3. **(a) At what point in the story does it seem as though Old Majesty may win?**
When Danny repeatedly shoots Old Majesty and the bear keeps coming toward him and Red, it seems as though the bear may win.

(b) How does Danny finally win?

Danny holds the gun within two feet of Old Majesty's ear and shoots.

4. **Danny thinks of the bear as "a fallen king." (a) Why is Danny glad that Red does not molest, or disturb, the fallen enemy?**

As former ruler of the wilderness, the bear is entitled to dignity after death.

(b) What does he think this proves about Red?

It proves that Red is not only beautiful, courageous, and strong, as Danny thought, but noble as well.

5. **Do you think Old Majesty is a good name for the bear? Why or why not?** (Main Idea)

Students' answers will vary, but most will agree that the bear is well-named. He is majestic—he is ruler of the wilderness (he has asserted his supremacy over the Wintapi); he is bigger and fiercer than any other bear; Danny refers to the dead bear as "a fallen king."

ADDITIONAL ACTIVITIES

1. Continue this story. Tell what you think happened when Danny and Red got back to the cabin. How did Red spend his remaining years?
2. Write the words that might have been spoken between Ross and Danny when Danny returned to the cabin.
3. Suppose that Ross and Danny wanted to place a marker at the spot where Old Majesty had been killed. What might they have written on the marker?
4. Imagine Danny ten years in the future. What kind of work would he be doing? How would he dress? Would he have pets? Would he have gone to college?

TEACHING RELATIONSHIPS (Reading Skill)

Ask the students to describe where they are in relation to various objects or people in the room (e.g., to the right of the door, under the ceiling, next to the wall). Write some of the words that indicate spatial order on the chalkboard. Then have the students read the explanatory material in their books and complete the skill exercise. Check their answers.

RELATIONSHIPS (Reading Skill Exercise)

Understanding Spatial Order

▶ **Read each item from the story and answer the questions that follow.**
   a. **"Danny climbed the mountain where he and Ross had taken a snarling, spitting fisher from a cave two years before, and walked to its east slope to stand directly under what had been a fine chestnut tree."**
   (1) In what direction did Danny walk?
   east
   (2) Where did Danny end up in relation to the tree?
   directly under it
   b. **"The wind was almost straight out of the west, blowing gently but steadily. Clouds scudded across the sky, and the feathered tips of the pine trees bent."**

(1) From what direction was the wind coming?
the west

(2) In what direction were the trees bent?
toward the east

c. "Danny sat beneath the chestnut stub, an arm about Red's neck and the rifle resting where he could instantly reach and bring it into play."

(1) Where was Danny in relation to Red?
right beside him

(2) Where was Danny in relation to his rifle: eight to ten yards away or no more than arm's length away?
no more than arm's length away

d. "Red turned his head, and held it poised while he remained rooted in his tracks. Slowly he swung his body about, facing up the ridge now instead of into the valley. Inch by inch he continued to turn, facing down the other side of the razor-backed ridge, and swinging until he had made a complete circle and was staring into the valley again."

(1) Where was Red facing at the very beginning of this description?
into the valley

(2) Where was Red facing at the end of this description?
into the valley

(3) All the time, Red was facing the bear. How had the bear moved?
in a circle

TEACHING WORD ATTACK

Read the explanatory material in the book aloud while the students read it silently. Then have them complete the skill exercises and check their answers.

WORD ATTACK (Exercises)

Finding Root Words

1. **Find the root in each of the words below. Then use that root to figure out the meaning of the new word. Check the meaning in a dictionary.**

   a. **supremacy**
   supreme

   b. **proffer**
   offer

   c. **mysterious**
   mystery

   d. **renewal**
   new

   e. **burial**
   bury

   f. **realization**
   real

   g. **proclaim**
   claim

   h. **reckoning**
   reckon

2. **Write an original sentence for each of the words above.**
   Accept all grammatically correct sentences.

3. **Find the root in each of the words below. Then use that root to figure out the meaning of the new word. Check the meaning in a dictionary.**

a. **relation** relate	f. **monstrous** monster
b. **unashamed** shame	g. **metallic** metal
c. **beautiful** beauty	h. **scientific** science
d. **courageous** courage	i. **lonesome** lone
e. **reality** real	j. **meaningless** mean

Check answers against dictionary definitions.

4. **Write an original sentence for each of the words above.**
Students' answers will vary.

5. **The root *anima* means "the soul or mind." Use your dictionary to find five words built from the root *anima*.**
Students' answers will vary.

WORD ATTACK CHECK TEST

► Identify the root word in each of the words below.

a. remembrance	f. instantaneous
b. happiness	g. redesign
c. entitled	h. softened
d. reclaim	i. steadily
e. perfection	j. forested

ANSWERS TO WORD ATTACK CHECK TEST

► a. memory	f. instant
b. happy	g. design
c. title	h. soft
d. claim	i. steady
e. perfect	j. forest

ABOUT THE AUTHOR

Jim Kjelgaard (1910–1959) based his first book, *Forest Patrol*, on his experiences as a forest ranger. He wrote two books about the American frontier: *Rebel Siege* and *Buckskin Brigade*. He is best known for his dog stories. His books about dogs are *Big Red*, *Irish Red*, *Outlaw Red* (about Irish setters), and *Stormy*, *Lion Hound*, *Desert Dog*, and *Snow Dog*.

The Wall

NOËL MURCHIE
pp. 154–169

Summary   Even though she is paired with Gunner Benner, a world-famous mountain climber, Josephine is terrified during the first part of her climb up the great Wall. However, when Gunner is in trouble and starts to fall, she forgets her fear and works swiftly and automatically to brake his fall. In gratitude for saving his life, Gunner gives Josephine his climbing hat, which has always been a good-luck charm for him.

BEFORE READING

Eleanor Roosevelt once said: "You gain strength, courage, and confidence by every experience in which you really stop to look fear in the face. You are able to say to yourself, 'I lived through this horror. I can take the next thing that comes along' . . . You must do the thing you think you cannot do."

Ask students to discuss the meaning of this statement. Then ask them if they agree with it. Why or why not? Have them read "The Wall" to find out how Jo faces her fear. (Main Idea; Flexibility: Setting a Purpose)

Glossary Words

*agile (p. 156, a, 2)
*agility (p. 163, a, 7)
 arduous (p. 162, b, 5)
 concerto (p. 160, b, 1)
 diaphragm (p. 160, a, 4)
 dishevel
    (disheveled, p. 157, b, 2)
*exhilaration (p. 156, a, 1)
 loathe (p. 162, b, 6)
 lug (p. 158, a, 14; p. 160, a, 7)
 niche (p. 162, a, 5)

pedometer (p. 157, a, 3)
piton (p. 159, b, 2)
rucksack (p. 159, b, 2)
skeptically (p. 157, b, 8)
taut (p. 162, a, 9)
*topographical (p. 160, b, 7)
*traipse
    (traipsing, p. 161, a, 7)
traverse
    (traversing, p. 165, b, 6)
*void (p. 162, a, 10)

TEACHING THE GLOSSARY WORDS

Write the glossary words on the chalkboard. Say each word aloud and have the students repeat it after you. Then write the following sentences on the board. Have students look up the starred glossary words to decide which word best fits in each blank.

"So I awaited for my parents to notice that I was coordinated, _____, and keenly interested." (agile)

"At last we were _____ single file up a steep trail, through trees whose leaves were the brilliant color of flames." (traipsing)

"From Indian Bluff, I graduated to the spindly, terrifying fire tower, where I rappelled eighty feet off the concrete platform so many times that the sour taste of fear vanished from my mouth and I finally knew the _____ of propelling myself through free space." (exhilaration)

"There was a lone man standing with a _____ map in his hands when we drove into the meadow that lay in the shadow of Mount Adams." (topographical)

"When I opened them again I looked down between my legs. Space fell away in an awesome, limitless _____." (void)

"As I scaled the next pitch, I found the natural rhythm of climbing. Energy and _____ were automatic." (agility)

For homework, have students look up the remaining words and write their meanings in their notebooks. (Word Attack: Dictionary, Context)

CHECK TEST

(F)   1. Jo's brother is her partner for the climb up the wall.
(T)   2. When Jo looks at the Wall, she feels frightened.
(F)   3. Experienced climbers use their knees to hoist themselves from ledge to ledge.
(T)   4. After she saves him from a fall, Gunner gives Jo his hat.
(T)   5. At the end of the story, Jo's mother tells her that she is very proud of her.

AFTER READING

In this story, Jo wants to get to know her mother and win her respect. Ask students if they think Jo accomplishes this goal. Why or why not?

CLOSE UP (Comprehension Questions)

1. **Jo is happy when her parents decide it's time to take her on a difficult climb. (a) What is the Wall?**
The Wall is a series of cliffs stacked on top of one another under the north face of Mount Adams.
(b) How much climbing experience does Jo have?
Jo has already learned the system of technical climbing (scrambling up, belaying, tying secure knots, splicing, and efficient coiling) at Indian Bluffs and has graduated to rappelling eighty feet off the fire tower.
2. **Jo sees a photograph of her mother standing on a mountaintop. (a) What does Jo want to find out about her mother?**

She wants to know what it would be like to stand on a summit with her because she wants to "discover the secret of knowing her."

(b) Why do you think she wants to climb with her mother? (Inferences)
Jo looks up to her mother and wants her approval. Her mother often gives the impression of dealing with Jo absent-mindedly.

3. **Jo's parents ask Gunner Benner to be her climbing partner. How does their choice show that they want her climb to be successful?** (Inferences)
Gunner is an Austrian who climbs all over the world and lectures and gives clinics on technical climbing. Also he is a man who conquered his own fear of heights but still experiences tremendous fears. He will be a very understanding and sympathetic partner for Jo.

4. **(a) Why does Jo feel she has disgraced her parents during the first part of the climb?** (Relationships: Cause/Effect)
Jo feels that she has disgraced her parents by sobbing in uncontrollable terror while clinging to the cliff.

(b) What does she then say about climbing?
She says, "I loathe this sport. I wish I'd never heard of mountains."

5. **(a) How does Jo save Gunner's life?** (Relationships: Cause/Effect)
She reacts instantly, automatically, and correctly to his cry "Falling!" by jamming her right hand down to the rope between her thighs to break his fall.

(b) How does Jo know that she has won her mother's respect? (Inferences)
Her mother says, "I don't think I could have held him as well as that, Jo. Good job."

6. **How is Jo like the wild violets that cling to the rock?** (Figurative Language)
She describes the violets as "delicate wild violets, somehow clinging and surviving." Jo is also surviving.

CONFLICT (Literature Skill Questions)

1. **At first, Jo is happy when her parents ask her to climb the Wall. How does she feel when she leans over the railing and imagines herself swinging down the Wall?** (Relationships: Time Order)
She shivers at the thought of the icy winds and the possibility of hurtling to her death.

2. **Why is Jo frightened when she learns about Jack Holmes's accident?**
If even very experienced climbers have accidents, she wonders, what will become of her?

3. **During the first part of the climb, Jo is overcome by fear and begins to sob uncontrollably. What does Gunner tell her that helps her overcome her fear?**
Gunner tells her that he still experiences tremendous fears.

4. **(a) How does Jo prove her courage?** (Relationships: Cause/Effect)
Jo proves her courage by reacting promptly to save Gunner's life even though it leaves her "suspended over the lip of the edge with nothing but air"

beneath her. Even though the rope cuts cruelly into her skin, she doesn't flinch. She even insists "It's not that bad" when the extent of her rope burn is noticed.

(b) Why does Gunner give her his courage bird? (Relationships: Cause/Effect)

Gunner gives her the pin—given to him by villagers for avalanche rescue work—because he is grateful that she has saved his life and because she has shown courage on her first real climb. He hopes it will be an omen of good luck for her, as it has been for him; obviously he feels that she has a long career of climbing ahead of her.

ADDITIONAL ACTIVITIES

1. Create a different title for this selection.
2. Imagine this family ten years in the future. What has happened to Jo and to Will?

TEACHING RELATIONSHIPS (Reading Skill)

Ask the students to volunteer the names of different makes of automobiles. Put the names on the chalkboard and point out that they have compiled a list of automobile makes. Ask them what other kinds of lists could be compiled. Have them discuss the different purposes of compiling lists. Then have them read the explanatory material in their books and complete the exercises by referring to the story. Check their answers.

RELATIONSHIPS (Reading Skill Exercises)

Understanding Listing

1. **Jo says that her mother's dressing table is an odd combination of corner drugstore and fancy boutique. (a) List all of the items on the dressing table that would fall into the category *corner drugstore*.**
   Absorbine horse liniment, Sloan's rubbing mixture, tubes of chapped-lip and glacier creams, salt tablets, suntan lotions, little mounds of moleskin, a pedometer.
   (b) List all of the items that would fall into the category *Fancy Boutique*.
   French perfume, jars of rose-scented cold cream, monogrammed silver-backed hairbrushes and matching mirror, a pale-blue satin pincushion, a fountain pen with a solid gold point, a Wedgwood knick-knack box.
2. **List all the books on the shelf that would fall into the category *mountaineering books*.**
   Volumes on how to use a compass, surviving in the mountains in winter, first aid and identifying birds and flowers in the Alps, and an encyclopedia of mountain climbing terms.
3. **List the objects in the mountain closet. Then divide this list in two, with one list for clothing and one list for equipment.**
   Mountain Closet: ropes, summit packs, rucksacks, frames, karabiners, thick down parkas, Levi jackets, bandannas, sweaters, slings, boots, prickly

crampons, flashlights, portable stoves, tents, sleeping gear, ice axes, hammers, pitons, a bag labeled "Survival Gear."

Clothing: thick down parkas, Levi jackets, bandannas, sweaters, boots.

Equipment: ropes, summit packs, rucksacks, frames, karabiners, prickly crampons, flashlights, portable stoves, tents, sleeping gear, ice axes, hammers, pitons, slings.

4. **List all of the items that would fit into the category *gorp*.**
   dried fruit, lemon drops, beef jerky, nuts.

5. **Imagine you are going on a camping trip. List ten items you would include in your backpack. Arrange these items from most important to least important.**
   Students' answers will vary.

6. **List ten items you have on the top of your bureau or chest of drawers. Arrange these items from biggest to smallest.**
   Students' answers will vary.

7. **Imagine you are either Jo or Gunner. List five presents you would like to receive for your birthday. Arrange these items from least expensive to most expensive.**
   Students' answers will vary.

TEACHING WORD ATTACK

Have the students read the explanatory material in their books. Then ask them for as many examples of jargon as they can think of. Write some of their examples on the chalkboard. Finally, have them complete the exercise.

WORD ATTACK (Exercise)

Understanding Jargon

▶ **Use a dictionary to find the meaning of each of the following mountaineering terms.**
   a. orography—the study of the physical geography of mountains
   b. slings—looped ropes used for hoisting something
   c. chock—heavy metal fitting through which cables may be run
   d. belay—to secure a rope on a rock or other protuberance
   e. gaiter—covering for the leg, extending from the knee to the instep
   f. piton—metal spike fitted at one end with a ring through which a rope is passed
   g. timberline—the altitude in mountainous regions beyond which trees do not grow
   h. escarpment—a steep slope or cliff
   i. flume—a narrow gorge
   j. bushwhack—to make one's way through thick woods by cutting away brush

ABOUT THE AUTHOR

Noël Murchie frequently contributes short stories to *Redbook*, where her popular stories "Easy Riders" and "The Wall" first appeared in print.

REVIEW QUIZ

ON THE SELECTIONS

p. 170

1. **In "You Can't Take It with You," how does the family's stinginess backfire on them?** (Relationships: Cause/Effect)
   They refuse to spend the money to buy Basil a better coffin and so cremate the coffin he had lined with all his money.

2. **In "The Promised Visit," why are there white crosses along the highway?** (Relationships: Cause/Effect)
   The white crosses mark the sites of fatal accidents.

3. **How does the young man feel when he sees the girl standing along the side of the highway?** (Inferences)
   He is surprised and frightened to see an object by the roadside in the dark.

4. **In "Say It with Flowers," what is Teruo's problem?**
   Teruo cannot bear to lie to customers about the freshness of the flowers. If he does not lie, he will lose his job.

5. **In "A Running Brook of Horror," what is Grace Wiley's special talent?**
   Grace Wiley can handle poisonous snakes.

6. **After Grace is bitten by the cobra, why does she ask for an injection of strychnine?** (Relationships: Cause/Effect)
   Strychnine is a stimulant to the nervous system and so would temporarily counteract the poison, which depresses the nervous system.

7. **In "The Dying Detective," why is the little box that came through the mail important?** (Relationships: Cause/Effect)
   The box has been rigged to infect Holmes with the tropical disease.

8. **Why does Holmes ask Smith to turn up the light?** (Relationships: Cause/Effect)

   Turning up the light is the signal to Inspector Morton, the Scotland Yard detective, who is waiting in the street below.

9. **In "Big Red," the dog does not molest the bear after it has fallen. Why does this make Danny feel proud?** (Inferences)

   It shows the dog has intrinsic nobility—it won't attack a "fallen enemy."

10. **In "The Wall," Jo learns that Jack Holmes, an experienced climber, has had a serious accident. Why does this knowledge make her feel afraid?** (Relationships: Cause/Effect)

    If even experts have accidents, she thinks, what chance do beginners like her have?

ON RELATIONSHIPS

p. 171

1. **In "You Can't Take It With You," why do the family think that Uncle Basil can't hear what they say about him?**

   Uncle Basil pretends to be hard of hearing. The family believe he is deaf.

2. **In "Say It with Flowers," at first Teruo likes his job. What does he learn later that makes him change his mind?**

   When he learns that he has to lie to the customers, he changes his mind.

3. **(a) In "The Dying Detective," where is Watson when Smith confesses to the murder?**

   Watson is behind Holmes's bed.

   (b) Where is Inspector Morton?

   Inspector Morton is in the street below, waiting for the signal.

4. **Think about "The Wall." (a) Write three sentences showing how Jo and her brother are alike.**

   Accept all reasonable answers. Here is a sample answer: They both like adventure—Will in stories, Jo in real life. They both desire praise from their mother. They both show jealous hostility toward each other.

   (b) Write three sentences showing how they are different.

   Accept all reasonable answers. Here is a sample answer: Will is older than Jo. He is sickly and stays indoors a lot, while she is healthy and active. Jo is interested in mountain climbing, but Will is not.

5. **Make a list of equipment Jo needs to climb the Wall.**

hooks	portable stoves
ropes	tents
summit packs	sleeping gear
rucksacks	ice axes
frames	hammers
karabiners	pitons
flashlights	"survival gear"

COMPOSITION (Exercise)

Sentence Combining

p. 172

▶ **Combine each pair of sentences below by using the signal word contained in parentheses after the second sentence. (If a punctuation mark appears in the parentheses, use this too.)**

a. **When I looked at her I almost drove off the road.**
   She was the prettiest girl I had ever seen. (because)
   When I looked at her, I almost drove off the road because she was the prettiest girl I had ever seen.

b. **The family planned to inherit Basil's money.**
   Basil had other plans. (; however)
   The family planned to inherit Basil's money; however, Basil had other plans.

c. **He stopped the car.**
   He saw the girl standing by the side of the road. (when)
   He stopped the car when he saw the girl standing by the side of the road.

d. **Teruo sold the fresh flowers.**
   Mr. Sasaki had asked him to sell the older ones. (, although)
   Teruo sold the fresh flowers, although Mr. Sasaki had asked him to sell the older ones.

BEFORE GOING ON

p. 173

Skateboarding

KAREN FOLGER JACOBS
pp. 175–183

Summary This is an interview with fourteen-year-old Kim Milburn, a skateboarding champion from San Diego, California.

BEFORE READING

Ask the students to volunteer any experiences they have had with skateboarding. Then have them compare and contrast the skills needed for skateboarding with the skills needed for surfing, skiing, swimming, tennis, and horseback riding. (Relationships: Comparison/Contrast)

Glossary Words

*acrobatic (p. 180, a, 3)
*asphalt (p. 175, b, 5)
*fiberglass (p. 177, a, 1)
*frustrate
   (frustrating, p. 176, a, 6)
*idolize (p. 179, b, 1)
*inertia (p. 183, b, 2)

*mogul (p. 177, a, 6)
*paralyze
   (paralyzed, p. 181, a, 3)
*pivot (p. 176, a, 1)
*suspension (p. 176, b, 6)
*trampoline (p. 181, a, 3)

TEACHING THE GLOSSARY WORDS

Write the glossary words on the chalkboard. Say each word aloud and have the students repeat it after you. Then have them locate each word in the selection and write the sentence in which they find each word in their notebooks. Tell them to write the definitions of each word under each sentence. (Word Attack: Dictionary, Context)

TEACHING FLEXIBILITY (Reading Skill)

Read the explanatory material in the book aloud while the students read it silently. Then ask them to close their books and recall the steps for scanning in their proper order from memory. You may want to give them several minutes to study before they recite the steps from memory. Finally, have them complete the skill exercise and check their answers.

FLEXIBILITY (Reading Skill Exercise)

Scanning for Facts

▶ Use these steps to help you find the following information.

  a. **Where does Kim Milburn do most of her skateboarding? (Look for a place name as you scan.)**
    She does most of it at Bay Park School.

  b. **What is the first trick Kim learned? (Scan for the key words, "first trick.")**
    The first trick she learned was a handstand with a backbend that leaves her feet resting on her head (later referred to as "the spider").

  c. **What are "nose wheelies" and "tail wheelies"? (Scan for those names.)**
    They are tricks involving standing on one end of the board and coasting on the back wheels only.

  d. **How many degrees is the skateboard swung after each end-over? (Scan for the key word, "degrees.")**
    It is swung 180 degrees.

  e. **What are skateboards made of? (Scan for names of types of woods, metals, etc.)**
    They are made of plywood, fiberglass, aluminum, or combinations of those materials.

f. **What does Kim wear in competitions? (Scan for the key words, "wear" and "competitions.")**
    She wears shorts and a shirt.
g. **How much does it cost to skate in a skateboard park? (Scan for prices.)**
    It costs from $2.25 to $3.00.
h. **Why is it good to be on a team? (Scan for the key word, "team.")**
    Teams are formed by manufacturers who "buy you everything for practice and contests." Also, "they help you practice, and you get more publicity."
i. **When might skateboarding be an Olympic sport? (Scan for the key word, "Olympics," and a date.)**
    It might be in 1980.

ABOUT THE AUTHOR

Karen Folger Jacobs (1941–   ), a Ph.D. and former teacher at Berkeley, is very active in sports. She has written two books, *Ward 81* (with photographer Maty Ellen Monk) and *GirlSports*. The latter book consists of interviews with fifteen young girls who play sports traditionally restricted to boys.

READING SKILLS UNIT TEST (Profiles)

1. **Identify the words in each of the following sentences that signal time order.**
    a. **After Kim Milburn learned to do a handstand, she practiced other tricks.**
        After
    b. **Before Sherlock Holmes let Culverton Smith into his room, he made sure Dr. Watson was hidden within hearing distance.**
        Before
    c. **As the bear circled, Ted turned with him.**
        As
    d. **Grace Wiley calmed the cobra. Then she picked it up.**
        Then
    e. **Kim Milburn trains hard before she enters a competitive event.**
        before
2. **Identify the word or words in each sentence below that signal a cause-and-effect relationship.**
    a. **Holmes pretended he was dying, so that Culverton Smith would confess to him.**
        so that
    b. **Grace Wiley died as a result of the cobra's venom.**
        as a result of
    c. **She was the prettiest girl he had ever seen. Accordingly, he fell in love with Susan Billy.**
        Accordingly

d. **Both Mother and Father loved mountain climbing; therefore, they wanted their children to love it too.**
therefore

e. **Since my word is as good as yours, Holmes, you have no proof!**
Since

3. **Identify the cause and the effect in the following sentence:**
    Because she is a champion, Kim Milburn has no trouble finding a sponsor for her skateboarding activities.
    "Kim Milburn has no trouble finding a sponsor for her skateboarding activities" is the effect; "she is a champion" is the cause.

4. **Tell whether each statement below is a comparison or a contrast.**
    a. **The hounds were brave fighters, but they were no match for Old Majesty.**
    contrast

    b. **Red and Old Majesty were cunning, proud, and ready to fight to the finish.**
    comparison

    c. **You're alive, young man, but Susan Billy has been dead for ten years.**
    contrast

    d. **The difference between Smith and Holmes is the difference between evil and good.**
    contrast

    e. **Snakes are like people; they strike out when they are frightened or angry.**
    comparison

5. **Identify the word or words in each sentence below that indicate spatial order.**
    a. **Kim Milburn does a handstand with a backbend on her skateboard.**
    on

    b. **Sherlock Holmes told his friend Dr. Watson to hide himself behind the head of the bed.**
    behind

    c. **Jo stood shivering and gazing at Mount Adams, which loomed above.**
    above

    d. **Teruo went up front to complete the sale.**
    up front

6. **List each of the characters named below under the appropriate category title:**
    "The Wall"   "Big Red"   "The Dying Detective"
    Characters: Danny, Jo, Dr. Watson, Will, Old Majesty, Sherlock Holmes, Gunner, Old Mike, Culverton Smith, Red, Inspector Morton

"The Wall"	"Big Red"	"The Dying Detective"
Jo	Danny	Dr. Watson
Will	Old Majesty	Sherlock Holmes
Gunner	Old Mike	Culverton Smith
	Red	Inspector Morton

7. **Arrange the following steps for scanning in their proper order.**

a. Make notes as you read.
b. Make a list of all the facts you want to find.
c. When you locate a key word, read around it to find the fact you are searching for.
d. Start at the beginning of the selection. Let your eyes sweep across and down each page, looking for key words.

The proper order is b, d, c, a.

PERSPECTIVES

SELECTION	TYPE	LITERATURE SKILL	READING SKILL	WORD ATTACK SKILL
Alone on the Hilltop by Lame Deer and Richard Erdoes pp. 186–195	non-fiction	Point of View. Understanding first-person narration in nonfiction	Judgments. Distinguishing between primary and secondary sources	Context. Using direct context clues
The Contest by Paul Darcy Boles pp. 197–205	fiction	Point of View. Understanding first-person narration in fiction	Judgments: Identifying statements of fact and statements of opinion	Figurative Language. Understanding figurative expressions
I Love All Gravity Defiers by Lillian Morrison p. 207	poetry	Poetry. Understanding figurative language		
Night Rider by Steven Otfinoski pp. 208–217	fiction	Point of View. Understanding first-person narration in fiction	Judgments. Identifying mixed statements of fact and opinion	Context. Understanding context
The Sin of Madame Phloi, by Lilian Jackson Braun pp. 219–229	fiction	Point of View. Understanding third-person narration (limited to one character)	Judgments. Recognizing stereotypes	Structure. Understanding negative prefixes
Catalog by Rosalie Moore pp. 230–231	poetry	Poetry. Understanding imagery		

SELECTION	TYPE	LITERATURE SKILL	READING SKILL	WORD ATTACK SKILL
How the Leopard Got Its Spots by Forbes Stuart pp. 233–239	fiction	Point of View. Understanding third-person narration (omniscient)	Judgments. Identifying loaded words	Context. Using context clues
Review Quiz pp. 240–241				
Composition. Narration p. 242				
Before Going On p. 243			Flexibility. Skimming	
Further Reading *The Fastest Woman on Earth* by Phil Bowie pp. 244–249	non-fiction			

Alone on the Hilltop

LAME DEER AND RICHARD ERDOES
pp. 186–195

Summary   Lame Deer must undergo a Sioux ritual of meditation and vision-seeking to prove he is a man. During this ritual, he has a vision that tells him he will become a medicine man.

BEFORE READING

Tell students that most cultures mark the transition or change from childhood to adulthood by means of a ceremony. Ask students to list ceremonies in American culture that mark this transition (confirmation, bar mitzvah, graduation). Ask them why these ceremonies are important. Do they think it important that youngsters know they have passed a test that proves them capable of taking on adult responsibilities? Do they think it important that youngsters know the community supports them?

Then have students turn to p. 186. Have students read the selection to find out how Lame Deer's passage from childhood to adulthood is marked. (Flexibility: Setting a Purpose)

Glossary Words

CHECK TEST

(T)   1. Lame Deer is left on the hilltop for four days and nights.
(F)   2. Lame Deer's parents make sure he has a lot to eat during the four days.
(T)   3. Lame Deer's grandmother had made him a star blanket.
(T)   4. Smoking the pipe helps Lame Deer get rid of his fears.
(F)   5. Lame Deer decides to go to school to learn to be a medicine man.

AFTER READING

Lame Deer says that the Sioux believe there is something inside people that controls them. This "something" helps them know what to do with their lives. In American society, we say someone has a vocation if he or she feels a calling toward a certain career. Ask students what types of jobs would be vocations rather than occupations (e.g., ministry, nursing, art).

CLOSE UP (Comprehension Questions)

1. **Lame Deer's experience on the hilltop is part of a Sioux ritual. What is the purpose of this ritual?** (Main Idea)
   It is a meditation and vision-seeking ritual. It marks the boy's transition to adulthood. If the boy has a vision, he will become a medicine man.

2. **Lame Deer tells you that the Sioux family is very close. (a) In what two ways does Lame Deer's grandmother help him feel her nearness during his first *hanblechia*?**
   She makes him a blanket with a star on it to use on his first *hanblechia*. She cuts forty small squares of flesh from her arm to put in the ceremonial gourd [she underwent pain to "help (him) pray and make (him) strong-hearted"].
   (b) Why does the pipe make him feel that he is not alone?
   Smoke from the peace pipe goes straight into the spirit world; power also flows down from the spirit world through the smoke. Also, the pipe belonged to his father and grandfather. He would pass it on to his son. "As long as we had the pipe there would be a Sioux nation."

3. **Why is Lame Deer worried that he will not receive a vision?** (Relationships: Cause/Effect)
   If he does not receive a vision, he cannot become a *yuwipi*, a medicine man or healer, which is his ambition.

4. **(a) When Lame Deer has his vision, what do the birds tell him?**
   They tell him that he will become a medicine man, and that he will belong to the nation of the birds and will never harm them but will always understand them. They conclude: "A man's life is short. Make yours a worthy one."
   (b) What does his great-grandfather tell him?
   The boy understands that his great-grandfather, Lame Deer, wishes him to take his name. This makes him "glad beyond words."

5. **(a) What is *nagi*?** (Word Attack)
   Nagi means something like soul, spirit, or essence, "something within us that controls us."
   (b) Why does Lame Deer know he will become a medicine man when he discovers he has *nagi*? (Relationships: Cause/Effect)
   He realizes that he does have the special power it takes to be a medicine man.

POINT OF VIEW (Literature Skill Questions)

1. **(a) How does Lame Deer feel immediately after he is left alone in the vision pit?** (Relationships: Time Order)
   He feels scared.
   (b) How do you know how he feels?
   He says, ". . . let me tell you, I was scared. I was shivering and not only from the cold." (This was the first time he was ever alone, since Indian children are always accompanied by relatives.)

2. **(a) Why is the experience of being in the vision pit important to Lame Deer?**
His future as a medicine man hinges on whether or not he has a vision.
Also, being in the vision pit makes him feel close to his ancestors, as well as close in spirit to living people like his grandmother.
(b) How does he feel about himself after this experience?
He weeps for happiness at the realization that he will become a medicine man.

3. **(a) Could anyone else accurately tell you what Lame Deer's feelings during his vision were like? Why or why not?**
No, because Lame Deer was alone. Also, feelings are an internal and personal experience. Therefore, the person experiencing them is best able to describe them.
(b) Do you think this story would have been less convincing if someone else had told it? Why or why not? (Judgments)
Yes. The story is about a personal experience—it would be less compelling if told by an uninvolved, or a third, party.

TEACHING JUDGMENTS (Reading Skill)

Read the explanatory material in the book aloud while the students read it silently. Ask volunteers to relate a short experience as primary sources. Ask other volunteers to relate a short experience as secondary sources. Then have them complete the skill exercise and check their answers.

JUDGMENTS (Reading Skill Exercise)

Using Direct Context Clues

▶ **Answer each of the questions below.**
   a. **Lame Deer tells you how the Sioux crossed the Missouri two hundred years ago. Is he a primary or a secondary source?**
   secondary source
   b. **Lame Deer says, "I felt feathers or a wing touching my back and head. This feeling was so overwhelming that it was just too much for me. I trembled and my bones turned to ice." Is he a primary or a secondary source?**
   primary source
   c. **Lame Deer says, "I know a lady who had a butterfly sitting on her shoulder. That butterfly told her things." Is he a primary or a secondary source of information about the lady's experience?**
   secondary source
   d. **Lame Deer says, "Besides the pipe, the medicine man had also given me a gourd. In it were forty small squares of flesh which my grandmother had cut from her arm with a razor blade. I had seen her do it." Is he a primary or secondary source of information about this event?**
   primary source

TEACHING WORD ATTACK

Read the explanatory material in the book aloud while the students read it

silently. Then have them complete the skill exercise and check their answers.

WORD ATTACK (Exercise)

Using Direct Context Clues

▶ Use direct context clues to find the definition of each of the *italicized* words below.

a. "I wanted to become a medicine man, a *yuwipi,* a healer carrying on the ancient ways of the Sioux nation."
a medicine man or a healer

b. "That would make me at once into a *heyoka,* a contrariwise, an upside-down man, a clown."
a clown

c. "The medicine man had also left a peace pipe with me, together with a bag of *kinnickinnick*—our kind of tobacco made of red willow bark."
tobacco

d. "We call it *nagi,* what other people might call soul, spirit, or essence."
soul, spirit, or essence

e. "Now I knew for sure that I would become a *wicasa wakan,* a medicine man."
a medicine man

WORD ATTACK CHECK TEST

1. Use direct context clues to define each of the *italicized* words in the sentences below.

a. "I sat there in the *vision pit,* a hole dug into the hill, my arms hugging my knees . . . ."

b. "My grandmother had made it especially for this, my first *hanblechia,* my first vision-seeking."

c. "If *Wakan Tanka,* the Great Spirit, would give me the vision and the power, I would become a medicine man . . . ."

d. "I had never been in a *sweat lodge* before. I . . . sat in the little beehive-shaped hut made of bent willow branches and covered with blankets to keep the heat in."

e. "I knew that *hanhepiwi* had risen, the night sun, which is what we call the moon."

ANSWERS TO WORD ATTACK CHECK TEST

▶ a. a hole dug into the hill
  b. vision-seeking
  c. the Great Spirit

  d. a little beehive-shaped hut
  e. the night sun, or the moon

ABOUT THE AUTHOR

Lame Deer is a Sioux and a holy man of the Lakota tribe. He was born over seventy years ago on the Rosebud Reservation in South Dakota. He is a storyteller of the history and folklore of the Sioux. During his lifetime he has been a rodeo clown, painter, sheepherder, and policeman.

The Contest

PAUL DARCY BOLES
pp. 197–205

Summary Joey loves music, but his stepfather feels it is a waste of time. When Joey wins the contest, he proves his talent to himself and the values of his talent to his stepfather.

BEFORE READING

Ask students if they have ever cared so much about doing something, that it seemed they could do nothing else—that it was a part of them (e.g., dancing, playing music, sketching)? Then ask them to define the word *talent*. Is it easy for a person to hide, or deny, his or her talent? Why or why not? Tell them they are going to read a story about a talented musician whose stepfather thinks that music is a waste of time. Have them read the story to find out how Joey, the musician, resolves the conflict.

Glossary Words

catapult
  (catapulted, p. 197, b, 1)

*embouchure (p. 199, a, 2)
sardonic (p. 197, a, 3)

TEACHING THE GLOSSARY WORDS

Write the glossary words on the chalkboard. Say each word aloud and have the students repeat it after you. Tell them that one word has a direct connection with music. Have them look up the words in the glossary to find out which word this is. (Word Attack: Dictionary; Context)

CHECK TEST

(F) 1. Joey's stepfather is a professional musician.
(F) 2. Joey's stepfather refuses to attend the contest.
(T) 3. Joey boards with a woman whose son has died in Viet Nam.

(F)   4. When Joey stands on the stage, he is sure he will lose the contest.

(T)   5. At the end of the story, Joey calls Rob "Dad."

AFTER READING

Throughout this story, Joey has refused to call Rob "Dad." Ask students to discuss why he does this at the end of the story. (Inferences)

CLOSE UP (Comprehension Questions)

1. **(a) How does Joey's stepfather feel about the trumpet contest?**
He doesn't approve. He'd prefer that Joey didn't go. He feels that horn-playing is a frivolous pursuit and that it will interfere with Joey's schoolwork ("You'll have to make up the schoolwork you're missing").
(b) How does Joey think his real father would have felt? (Relationships: Cause/Effect)
His real father would have encouraged his horn-playing: "He'd played around in ricky-tick bands when he was (Joey's) age and knew how it was."

2. **Neither Joey nor his stepfather voices his feelings, but both are aware of tension between them. (a) Why does Joey resent his stepfather's suggesting things "for his own good"?** (Relationships: Cause/Effect)
He feels Rob doesn't know him well enough to be able to tell what's good for him. ("How did he *know* my own good," he thinks.)
(b) What does Joey mean when he says that his stepfather looks as though "he'd like to roll up all the trouble—which hadn't even come out in the open—in his hands and toss it at me like a snowball"? (Figurative Language)
Things are so tense that Rob looks as though he'd like to clear the air and "get things off his chest."

3. **When Joey reaches the house where he will spend the night, he goes upstairs and practices. (a) How does the music make him feel?**
He feels that "the world was still going to be fresh and wonderful and its true self." The music revitalizes him, cheers him up, and makes him forget his problems.
(b) What does this tell you about the importance of music in his life? (Inferences)
Music has the power to lift his spirits and cure his depression. Obviously he cares a lot about music—it is not just a "frivolous pursuit" to him.

4. **Joey wants to become a professional musician. (a) Why is it difficult for his stepfather to understand this?** (Relationships: Cause/Effect)
His stepfather says he "was raised strictly. Overstrictly. Entertainers, the arts, these were things to stay away from; hard work, a profession, that was the thing to cultivate."
(b) What happens that makes his stepfather realize how important music is to Joey? (Relationships: Cause/Effect)
He and Joey's mother attend the contest. When Rob sees and hears Joey play, he realizes how serious Joey is about music and how talented he is.

5. Earlier on the train, Joey told Sue, "It's just . . . sometimes things *do* get lost, and I don't want them to." **(a) Why does Joey give the old woman his medal?** (Inferences)

Joey had just won Rob's approval. As he is leaving the house, he looks into the front room, "the one with the doilies, the TV, and the silver-framed picture of the little old lady's grandson." He realizes how little she has left in life and decides that he will give her his medal. (". . . I wanted her to have the medal because it, by itself, couldn't mean as much to me as it could if I gave it to her.")

(b) Why does he come to feel that nothing gets lost at all? (Inferences)

Joey's real father was proud and supportive of him. After the contest, Rob also proves to be proud and supportive of him.

POINT OF VIEW (Literature Skill Questions)

1. **(a) Who is the author of this story?**
   The author is Paul Darcy Boles.
   (b) Who is the narrator, the character who tells the story?
   The narrator is Joey.
2. **There are two important characters, Joey and his stepfather, Rob. About whose feelings do you learn more? Why?**
   We learn more about Joey's feelings, because he narrates the story, or tells it from his point of view.
3. **Does the narrator tell you mostly about something that happened to him or about something that happened to someone else?**
   Joey describes experiences that happened to him.
4. **Rob asks Joey if he'll be back Thursday night. (a) What does Joey think his stepfather means by this statement?**
   Joey thinks Rob disapproves of the trip—that, if Rob had his way, Joey wouldn't be going at all.
   (b) Do you think Joey is correct? Why or why not? (Inferences)
   Students' answers will vary. Joey thinks the "little line of worry across (Rob's) forehead" indicates that Rob disapproves of his going to the contest. Rob may just be worried about Joey's being on his own away from home.

ADDITIONAL ACTIVITIES

1. **Composition.** Imagine Joey ten years in the future. What is he like? What does he do for a living? Did he go to college? Is he married?
2. **Composition.** Imagine that Joey later has a son who isn't interested in music. What might Joey say to him to get him interested?
3. Does the author of this story know much about high-school students?

TEACHING JUDGMENTS (Reading Skill)

Read the explanatory material in the book aloud while the students read it

silently. Ask them to volunteer statements of fact. Then ask them to volunteer statements of opinion. Have them tell why each statement they make is a fact or opinion. Then have them complete the skill exercise and check their answers.

JUDGMENTS (Reading Skill Exercise)

Identifying Statements of Fact and Statements of Opinion

▶ Read the items below. Decide whether each statement is a statement of fact or a statement of opinion.

    a. "She didn't look like a flutist, or even a flautist, which is what fancy people call flutists; matter of fact, she was pretty beautiful."
    opinion

    b. "I was third on the program."
    fact

    c. "He'd been married to my mother for three months . . . ."
    fact

    d. "He was a fine man, not handsome, just quiet and tough."
    opinion

    e. "The dog had been killed by a car about two years later.
    fact

    f. ". . . eating just before playing makes you feel like a stuffed duck . . . ."
    opinion

    g. "There were nine other contestants from schools around Illinois."
    fact

    h. "The first contestant was a lot taller than I . . . ."
    fact

    i. "He did very well on the first section . . . ."
    opinion

    j. ". . . this will never be a waste of your time."
    opinion

TEACHING WORD ATTACK

Read the explanatory material in the book aloud while the students read it silently. Then have them complete the skill exercises and check their answers.

WORD ATTACK (Exercises)

Understanding Figurative Expressions

1. Identify the figurative expressions in the sentences below.
    a. "For half a second I, in turn, wanted to tell him to go ahead and get it off his chest."
    get it off his chest
    b. "In the train, when I'd settled down with a paperback and then tired of it . . ."
    settled down

c. "She thanked me for the book but said she was too keyed up to read."
   keyed up
d. "I still had the same feeling when I peeled off and went to the house where I was supposed to sleep that night."
   peeled off
e. "You have to know what you're doing, know where you're going, but the rest of it is riding a wave."
   riding a wave

2. **Replace the figurative expressions in the sentences above with words that keep their basic meanings.**
   Students' answers will vary. The following are sample answers.
   a. talk about it; get it out in the open
   b. got comfortable with; relaxed with
   c. nervous or excited; wound up; on edge
   d. turned or veered off
   e. a cinch; easy ("a piece of cake")

3. **Write the meaning of each of the following *italicized* figurative expressions. Check your answers in the dictionary by looking up the word that is a part of the body.**
   a. **His stepfather liked to keep his feelings to himself; he didn't *wear his heart on his sleeve*.**
      tell everyone his private thoughts or emotions (the heart is thought of as the center of one's emotions)
   b. **Things didn't always work out as she planned, but *her heart was always in the right place*.**
      she had the best of intentions
   c. **When he saw her, he fell *head over heels* in love.**
      rolling or somersaulting
   d. **I have so much work to do, I'm having trouble *keeping my head above water*.**
      surviving; keeping out of trouble (not getting "drowned," or overwhelmed, with work)
   e. **During the contest, he *put his best foot forward*.**
      made a good start or a fine first impression
   f. **My mother *put her foot down* about late hours.**
      insisted on having her way in the matter (the act of stomping, or putting one's foot down, implies aggression or assertiveness—it is a strong, forceful action)
   g. **She had the answer *on the tip of her tongue*.**
      almost expressed, but not yet quite recalled
   h. **They had *their hands full* running the contest.**
      were fully occupied (unable to carry anything else—unable to take on any more tasks)
   i. **The noise had gotten *out of hand*.**
      out of control
   j. **He knew his parents were angry, and he didn't want *to face the music*.**

to accept the consequences (to face the "noise" they'd make)

WORD ATTACK CHECK TEST

▶ Identify the figurative expressions in the sentences below.
  a. I was so angry I thought I would blow my top.
  b. The music was so loud and grating that my hair stood on end.
  c. His smile was deep as a well.
  d. Rob had to eat humble pie when he realized that Joey really was talented.
  e. She was walking on air over winning second place.
  f. That note was a mile high and clear as a bell.

ANSWERS TO WORD ATTACK CHECK TEST

▶ a. blow my top   d. eat humble pie
  b. hair stood on end   e. walking on air
  c. deep as a well   f. a mile high, clear as a bell

ABOUT THE AUTHOR

Paul Darcy Boles (1919–   ) received the Georgia Writer's Association
Literary Achievement Award for fiction in 1969. He wrote the novels
Deadline and *Parton's Island* (self-illustrated) and the books *A Million
Guitars and Other Stories* and *I Thought You Were a Unicorn and Other
Stories*. His short stories are anthologized in the books *Best Post Short
Stories, 1961* and *Seventeen's Stories, 1958*.

I Love All Gravity Defiers

LILLIAN MORRISON
p. 207

Summary   A short poem extolling people who have the courage to "stand
straight and stay alive."

BEFORE READING

Have students list occupations that seem to defy gravity. Then read the
poem aloud to the students.

CLOSE UP (Comprehension Questions)

1. **Find at least five gravity defiers listed in this poem.**
   Correct answers are: vaulter, trapeze artist, kids on swings, ski-jumpers,

broad and high jumpers, somersaulters, boxers "up at the count of nine," springboard athletes, and "people who stand straight and stay alive."

2. **Reread lines 17–20. Why does the poet admire gravity defiers?**
The poet admires gravity defiers because they try.

3. **Someone who defies gravity will not be pulled or held down. Reread lines 25–28. Do you think this poem is really about all people who have the courage to defy life's problems? Why or why not?** (Figurative Language)
This poem is about all people who have the courage to defy life's problems. The poet says she admires "people who stand straight and stay alive."

ABOUT THE AUTHOR

Lillian Morrison wrote *The Sidewalk Racer*, a volume of poetry, and the highly acclaimed *Sprints and Distances*, an anthology of sports poetry. She is the Coordinator of Young Adult Services at the New York Public Library.

Night Rider

STEVEN OTFINOSKI
pp. 208–217

Summary   A truck driver named Jake picks up a hitchhiker who says his name is Jake too. The hitchhiker is really an alien from the planet Astrax who has crashed his spaceship on the Earth. When the truck driver discovers this, he helps the alien to get past the roadblocks and return to his ship.

BEFORE READING

Have students turn to p. 208. Ask one student to read the title, the author's name, and the headnote aloud. Then have them study the photograph. Does the photograph lead them to think that the story will be humorous or mysterious? Why? Have them read the story to answer the following questions.

1. Where does the hitchhiker come from?

2. What is the hitchhiker's real name?

3. How does the hitchhiker gain Jake's trust?

4. How does Jake feel about the hitchhiker after he is gone?

(Flexibility: Setting a Purpose)

Glossary Words

CHECK TEST

(F) 1. Jake often picks up riders along Route 109.

(F) 2. The truck driver believes that the hitchhiker's name is Jake.

(T) 3. When the truckers begin talking about flying saucers, the hitchhiker runs away.

(T) 4. The hitchhiker tells Jake that he comes from the planet Astrax.

(F) 5. XT-115 uses his blue light to escape from the police.

AFTER READING

Ask students what they would have done if they had been in the truck driver's place. Would they have helped XT-115 escape? Would they have reported him to the police?

CLOSE UP (Comprehension Questions)

1. **At the beginning of the story, the truck driver feels there is something odd about the hitchhiker. Find three things about the hitchhiker that seem unusual.** (Relationships: Comparison/Contrast)
   The hitchhiker's eyes are unusually blue. There is something strange about the way he talks: he says *automobile* instead of *car*. He shakes hands, "but it (isn't) natural." Also, his hand feels strangely warm for someone who has been standing out in the night air.

2. **(a) At what point in the story does the truck driver suspect that the hitchhiker is from outer space?** (Relationships: Time Order)
   The truck driver suspects it when the hitchhiker runs out of the diner (the other truckers are talking about the object that fell out of the sky). He is convinced of it when he sees two beams of light coming from the hitchhiker's eyes. (The hitchhiker averts an accident by destroying a boulder with the light beams.)
   (b) Why does the truck driver follow the hitchhiker after he leaves the diner? (Relationships: Cause/Effect)
   The driver becomes suspicious and wants some straight answers from the hitchhiker.

3. **What do the truck driver and the hitchhiker do for each other that establishes their friendship?** (Relationships: Cause/Effect)
   The hitchhiker saves Jake's life by destroying a giant boulder in the truck's path. Jake distracts the attention of the troopers at the roadblock long enough for the hitchhiker to reach and repair his spaceship.

POINT OF VIEW (Literature Skill Questions)

1. **(a) What is the truck driver's first reaction when he sees the hitchhiker?**
The driver's first reaction is to keep driving—he is already behind schedule delivering his load of vegetables.
(b) Why does he finally decide to give him a ride?
He stops because he feels sorry for the hitchhiker. Since Route 109 is an old road that is hardly used anymore, it will be difficult for the hitchhiker to find a ride.

2. **Find two paragraphs in which the truck driver tells you what the hitchhiker looks like.** (Imagery)
Possible answers are:

> "I looked him over. He was just a kid—sixteen, maybe seventeen at the oldest. He was tall, thin, and very pale. He looked like any one of a thousand kids I've seen hitchhiking. And yet there was something different about him. I couldn't put my finger on it." (p. 210, column a, paragraph 1)

> "I expected him to get mad, but he didn't. He just turned two big, blue eyes on me and spoke very calmly. I'd never seen eyes that blue. They looked like the sea on a sunny day." (p. 210, column a, paragraph 3)

> " 'But my name really is Jake,' he insisted, turning those unearthly blue eyes on me again." (p. 210, column b, paragraph 6)

> "The nightmare that every trucker dreams about happened. In the moment my eyes had left the road, and turned to face those bright blue ones that sat next to me, the truck jumped off the road. Ahead of us was a giant boulder. I spun the wheel to miss it, but it was too late. In another second we would both be dead. Or so I thought." (p. 212, column b, paragraph 1)

3. **At the diner, Charley tells the truck driver, "There's been an accident up in the mountains near Bakerville. Something fell out of the sky a few hours ago." What do you suspect, that the truck driver does not yet suspect?** (Inferences)
At this point you probably suspect that the hitchhiker is from outer space.

4. **How do you think this story would have been different if XT-115 had told it?** (Judgments)
Probably you would have learned his true identity at the beginning of the story. Human beings would be the aliens. XT-115 probably would have examined and commented upon their strange customs and behavior. You would probably have learned something about XT-115's powers, home planet, and race. You would also have learned his feelings.

ADDITIONAL ACTIVITIES

1. Draw a picture of the spaceship XT-115 was flying as you imagine it looked.
2. If you were a television producer and this story were offered to you, would you buy it and produce it as a television drama? Explain your answer.

3. If this story were produced as a television drama and had to be interrupted by two commercials, where would you insert the commercials? Explain your answer.

TEACHING JUDGMENTS (Reading Skill)

Read the explanatory material in the book aloud while the students read it silently. You may want to provide some additional explanation or answer their questions if they have any. Then have the students complete the skill exercise and check their answers.

JUDGMENTS (Reading Skill Exercise)

Identifying Mixed Statements of Fact and Opinion

▶ **In each sentence below, decide which part contains a statement of fact and which part contains a statement of opinion.**
  a. Route 109 was an old road (fact), but it was more fun to drive on than the interstate (opinion).
  b. The night was scary because (opinion) there was no moon in the sky (fact).
  c. Truckers know the best places to eat, so (opinion) Lou's parking lot was filled with trucks (fact).
  d. Jack switched on his CB radio (fact), the best invention ever made for truckers (opinion).
  e. The state troopers were on the scene (fact), making all motorists feel a lot safer (opinion).
  f. Jake ran from the restaurant without even touching (fact) the best cup of coffee in the state (opinion).

TEACHING WORD ATTACK

Read the explanatory material aloud while the students read it silently. Ask them to supply examples of jargon they are familiar with. Then have them complete the skill exercise and check their answers.

WORD ATTACK (Exercise)

Understanding Jargon

▶ **Write the meaning for each of the *italicized* phrases below.**
  a. "I was *tooling* down Route 109 doing about fifty."
     driving
  b. "Maybe I figured he'd be standing out there all night waiting for the next *set of wheels* to come along."
     truck
  c. " 'Do I have a *copy*?' '*Ten-four* on that, Bronco Bill,' I answered.
     Copy means understanding. *Ten-four* means yes.
  d. "Not a *Smokey* in sight . . . ."
     state trooper

e. "All's clear up here. *Over and out.*"
   end of message

WORD ATTACK CHECK TEST

▶ Identify the field or occupation associated with the jargon in each of the following sentences.
  a. She drilled the ball through the hoop for another two points.
  b. Oil change, new filter, and lube job in fifteen minutes.
  c. We're going to spin a few more from the top ten.
  d. Her serve was high and wide—love–fifteen.
  e. Two pars and a birdie—not bad for the first three holes.

ANSWERS TO WORD ATTACK CHECK TEST

▶ a. basketball   d. tennis
  b. service station   e. golf
  c. disc jockey

ABOUT THE AUTHOR

Steven Otfinoski is the author of several books, including *The World's Darkest Days, The Third Arm, Sky Ride, High Fliers, Village of Vampires,* and *Monsters to Know and Love.*

The Sin of Madame Phloi

LILIAN JACKSON BRAUN
pp. 219–229

Summary   The man next door lures Madame Phloi and Thapthim onto his window ledge with a saucer of milk and deliberately causes Thapthim to fall to the pavement below. Madame Phloi uses the man's tactics to get revenge. The very next day she lures him onto the ledge, which crumples under his weight.

BEFORE READING

Have students turn to p. 219. Ask one student to read the title of the story and the author's name aloud. Then have a student read the first two paragraphs aloud. Who do they think Madame Phloi is? Why? Have them finish reading the story to discover what her "sin" is. (Inferences; Flexibility: Setting a Purpose).

Glossary Words

*aperture (p. 223, a, 1)
*condescend
     (condescended, p. 220, b,
     ℓ. 8)
*dispassionately (p. 221, a, 3)
*emanate
     (emanated, p. 221, b, 10)
*falsetto (p. 222, b, 1)
*fastidious (p. 222, b, 3)
*furtively (p. 226, a, 1)
*guttural (p. 224, b, ℓ. 5)
*impeccable (p. 219, b, 5)
*innovation (p. 224, a, 4)
*insipid (p. 222, a, 8)
*interminable (p. 221, b, 1)

*lethargic (p. 223, b, 1)
*mince
     (mincing, p. 223, b, 1)
*oblivious (p. 224, b, ℓ. 3)
*overture (p. 220, b, 1)
*rebuff
     (rebuffed, p. 225, b, ℓ. 2)
*sally (p. 224, a, 4)
*saunter
     (sauntered, p. 222, b, 5)
*strident (p. 221, b, 1)
*svelte (p. 223, b, ℓ. 3)
*uncouth (p. 219, a, 3)
*unsavory (p. 219, a, 1)

TEACHING THE GLOSSARY WORDS

Write the glossary words on the chalkboard. Say each word aloud and have the students repeat it after you. Then have them find each word in the following game. Tell them the words may read from left to right, from right to left, from top to bottom, from bottom to top, or diagonally. After they find each word, have them look up its meaning in the glossary.

F G A C O N D E S C E N D I D
A U K E P D O P Q U M J I N E
S T R P A N H E P C A O S N A
T T H T U O C N U R N R P O Y
I U F O I N P L S K A E A V F
D R C A M V S E A M T T S A I
I A O G L R E A T A E S S T O
O L N L A S Y L V C H A I I B
U S T O S R E V Y O K F O O L
S V E L T E A T W F R C N N I
A T L I S N A A T N H Y A J V
L B R E B U F F D O O O T C I
L A R I M P E C C A B L E I O
Y H S I D H S T L P E R L G U
S A U N T E R I K E C N Y R S
S V E S D I N Q U R O E L A T
T N O I U E L T A T U R M H A
H C R P C R E S O U T U R T M
O T M I N C E R U R H S G E E
R E H D E R U T R E V O R L A
I N T E R M I N A B L E I C N

CHECK TEST

(F) 1. Madame Phloi obeys all the apartment rules.
(T) 2. Thapthim is very friendly and comes when called.
(F) 3. The fat man loves cats and is a regular admirer of Thapthim.
(F) 4. Thapthim accidentally falls from the window ledge to his death.
(T) 5. The fat man falls as he reaches for Madame Phloi.

AFTER READING

Ask students if they think that telling this story from the cat's point of view was effective. Why or why not? (Judgments)

CLOSE UP (Comprehension Questions)

1. **Madame Phloi treats Thapthim with a great deal of love, even though they have different personalities. In what ways is Thapthim different from Madame Phloi?** (Relationships: Comparison/Contrast)
Thapthim is drowsy and unambitious; Madame Phloi is sensitive and spirited. He gobbles his food; she is dainty. He is lovable, amiable, tender, and trusting; she considers such openness "uncatly" and lacking in proper character. He obeys the rules of the house; she considers it "a matter of integrity to violate" a rule.

2. **(a) Why do people adore Madame Phloi?** (Relationships: Cause/Effect)
They adore her independence, her clever methods of getting her own way, her unusual appearance, and her charm.
(b) Why do they adore Thapthim? (Relationships: Cause/Effect)
They appreciate his good nature—his obedience, his friendliness, his rolling over, purring, and looking soulful.

3. **(a) Why does Madame Phloi try to get through the screens?**
She regards every aperture, no matter how small, as a temptation. She has to prove that she can wiggle through any tight space.
(b) Later, after the screens have been repaired, Madame Phloi still manages to get out onto the ledge. What does this tell you about her personality? (Inferences)
It shows that she is enterprising and able to surmount obstacles. She doesn't let anything stand in the way of her goals.

4. **At first, Madame Phloi waits for Thapthim to return. (a) When does she realize what has happened to him?** (Relationships: Time Order)
She senses it after searching in vain for him day and night. (Also, when she goes out on the ledge the next day and approaches the spot where Thapthim disappeared, she recognizes danger.)
(b) By what clever method does she trap the neighbor and take revenge? (Relationships: Cause/Effect)
She alternately creeps toward the saucer of milk and retreats diagonally—"half toward home and half toward the dangerous brink." By so doing, she lures the fat man onto the ledge, which crumbles under his weight.

POINT OF VIEW (Literature Skill Questions)

1. **Since this story is told from the cat's point of view, you get a slightly different slant on life. Find three details that show that the way Madame Phloi sees the world is different from the way a human being sees the world. (For example, because Madame Phloi likes to sit in laps, she thinks people without laps are useless.)** (Relationships: Comparison/Contrast)

   She likes or dislikes people according to their smell or the musical or gentle qualities of their voices. She values disobedience and condescension and disdains gratitude and "following the rules." She considers the apartment hers, thinks that her companions (the humans) have no names (probably because they have no occasion to call each other), and doesn't know what they are doing when they quietly turn the pages of books (reading). She considers watching and listening her official work. She thinks violin music is "unbearable screeching."

2. **What does Madame Phloi think is proper cat behavior?**

   She thinks all cats should be haughty, independent, defiant, dignified, and manipulative.

3. **Because Madame Phloi is a cat, she cannot tell anyone about what happened to Thapthim. (a) Why do you know what really happened to him?**

   You see the events in this story through Madame Phloi's eyes. She knows that Thapthim was swept off the ledge by the man's long black box (violin case).

   (b) Would you know this if one of Madame Phloi's owners had told the story? Why or why not? (Judgments)

   No, because they didn't view the incident. They have no way of knowing that the fat man was involved.

ADDITIONAL ACTIVITIES

1. **Composition.** How is Madame Phloi like or unlike cats you have known? Write a paragraph explaining your answer.
2. Some people say that people and their pets begin to resemble each other. Do one of the following: Find a photograph in a magazine or newspaper of (a) a person who looks like his or her pet (e.g., a rich, thin aristocratic woman with a Russian wolfhound); (b) a person who looks completely different from his or her pet (e.g., a short, tough-looking man with a French poodle).

TEACHING JUDGMENTS (Reading Skill)

Ask the students to describe their idea of an athlete. List their descriptions on the chalkboard. Ask them if they can think of any athletes whom their descriptions do not fit. Help them to see that an athlete cannot be described as a type without using stereotypes. Then have them read the explanatory material in their books and complete the skill exercises, and check their answers.

JUDGMENTS (Reading Skill Exercises)

Recognizing Stereotypes

1. **Which of the following statements are stereotypes?**
   a. All heavyset people dislike animals.
   b. All ailurophobes are afraid of cats.
   c. Cats know by instinct how to clean themselves.
   d. Cats are nasty and haughty creatures.
   e. All people who own cats are genial and good-natured.
   f. All musicians are moody.
   g. All janitors take care of the buildings where they work.
   h. Violin players like birds, but they dislike cats.
   Statements a, d, e, f, and h are stereotypes.

2. **Find advertisements in magazines or newspapers. Bring into class any that you think present people as stereotypes.**
   Review the students' selections with them.

3. **Which of the following statements are stereotypes?**
   a. All truck drivers enjoy hockey and football.
   b. All secret agents are young, sophisticated, handsome men who enjoy fast cars and sophisticated gadgetry.
   c. All doctors have medical degrees.
   d. All nurses are young, beautiful women.
   e. All college professors are absent-minded.
   f. All college professors have graduated from one or more colleges.
   g. All waiters serve food.
   h. All private eyes are tough, quick-talking men of action.
   i. All actors are temperamental.
   j. All lawyers practice the law.
   Statements a, b, d, e, h, and i are stereotypes.

TEACHING WORD ATTACK

Read the explanatory material in the book aloud while the students read it silently. Then ask them to supply words they know that have negative prefixes. Have them complete the exercise and check their answers.

WORD ATTACK (Exercise)

Understanding Negative Prefixes

▶ The words with negative prefixes in the sentences below are printed in *italics*. Write the definition of each of these words.
   a. "From the very beginning Madame Phloi felt an instinctive *distaste* for the man who moved into the apartment next door."
   distaste—dislike

b. "And with the long black box he was carrying, the fat man lunged at the *impeccable* Madame Phloi, who sat in her corner, flat-eared and tense."
impeccable—without any fault; flawless

c. "This drowsy, *unambitious,* amiable creature—her son—was a puzzle to Madame Phloi, who was sensitive and spirited herself."
unambitious—not ambitious, or greatly desirous of success

d. "His wise parent *disapproved* this *uncatly* conduct; it indicated a certain lack of character, and no good would come of it."
disapproved—did not approve; had an unfavorable opinion of
uncatly—not like a cat

e. "She was respected for her *independence,* admired for her clever methods of getting her own way . . . ."
independence—lack of dependence; freedom

f. "Until the fat man and his black box moved in next door, Madame Phloi had never known an *unfriendly* soul."
unfriendly—not friendly; hostile or disagreeable

g. "They strutted, searched their feathers, and ignored the Madame, who sat on the sill and watched them *dispassionately* but thoroughly through the window screen."
dispassionately—without any passion, or strong feeling; impersonally

h. "An *interminable* screech was coming out of that wall, like nothing the Madame had ever heard before."
interminable—never-ending

Have the students check their definitions against a dictionary.

Catalog

ROSALIE MOORE
p. 230

Summary   An appealing poem describing how a cat moves.

BEFORE READING

Tell students that as they read this poem they should look for words and phrases that create a vivid image of how a cat moves. (Imagery)

ABOUT THE AUTHOR

Rosalie Moore (1910–   ) wrote *The Grasshopper's Man and Other Poems*, a volume of poetry. Her poetry is anthologized in *The Golden Treasury of Poetry* (edited by Louis Untermeyer) and in *New World Writing, 100 Best Modern Poems*.

How the Leopard Got Its Spots

FORBES STUART
pp. 233–239

Summary This African folk tale describes how the leopard got its spots, the zebra got its stripes, and the hyena got its spotted coat.

BEFORE READING

Write the following words on the chalkboard: *leopard, zebra, hyena*. Ask the students to describe the physical appearance of each. Then tell them to read the selection to find out the explanation an African legend gives for the appearance of these animals. (Flexibility: Setting a Purpose)

Glossary Words

*derisively (p. 235, b, 4)   succulent (p. 235, b, 1)
*diabolically (p. 233, b, 2)   swagger
*plaintively (p. 233, b, 1)   (swaggered, p. 234, a, 3)

TEACHING THE GLOSSARY WORDS

Write the glossary words on the chalkboard. Say each word aloud and have the students repeat it after you. Ask them to identify the three adverbs. Which suffix tells them that these words are adverbs? Then have them look up these words and decide which adverb best fits in each sentence below.

He mocked the tortoise behind his back and spoke _____ (derisively) about him.

He begged the tortoise to make him beautiful. "Paint my coat, too," he said _____ (plaintively).

The wicked creature laughed _____ (diabolically), and then, with an evil grin, left the turtle in the tree.

Have students look up the remaining words in the glossary and write sentences using them. (Word Attack: Structure, Glossary, Context)

CHECK TEST

(T) 1. The tortoise asks the hyena for help because he can't reach the fruit in the tree.

(F) 2. Later, the hyena comes back to help the tortoise.

(F) 3. The leopard helps the tortoise only after the tortoise promises him a reward.

(T) 4. The leopard is pleased by the black spots the tortoise paints on his coat.

(T) 5. At the end of this legend, the hyena is ashamed of his coat.

AFTER READING

For thousands of years, people have invented legends to explain things in nature. In part, this desire to explain is a desire for knowledge. Write the following quotation on the board and have students discuss its meaning.

"For all knowledge and wonder (which is the seed of knowledge) is an impression of pleasure in itself." (Francis Bacon)

CLOSE UP (Comprehension Questions)

1. **What has the leopard done to make the tortoise eager to improve the leopard's appearance?** (Relationships: Cause/Effect)
The leopard has rescued the tortoise from the tree (where the hyena had placed him). Out of gratitude, the tortoise offers to paint black spots on the leopard to make him "admired throughout the jungle."

2. **Why does the hyena want his coat painted?** (Relationships: Cause/Effect)
The hyena is jealous of the attention that the zebra's new striped coat is receiving from the animals.

3. **Why does the tortoise make a fool of the hyena?** (Relationships: Cause/Effect)
He wants to get even with the hyena for leaving him in the tree. (He does so by painting a splotched and muddy pattern on the hyena's coat—all the animals in the jungle laugh and jeer derisively when they see it.)

4. **Why is the hyena's cry "a sad and lonely moan"?** (Inferences)
To avoid being mocked, the hyena dares show his face only at night, when most animals are asleep. Therefore, "when he raises his head to the moon, his cry is a sad and lonely moan."

POINT OF VIEW (Literature Skill Questions)

1. **Although the tortoise is the main character, you learn how all the other char-**

acters think and feel, too. (a) **How do the leopard and the zebra feel after the tortoise paints their coats?**

The leopard and zebra are proud and delighted when they see their new coats.

(b) How do the other animals react to the appearance of the leopard and the zebra?

The other animals are dazzled by the new paint jobs.

2. **The narrator takes time out from the action of the story to comment on, or explain, certain events. (a) According to the narrator, why do all zebras kick up their heels and gallop away when they see human beings?**

They prefer "the dangers of the jungle to sharing man's love with the goats, chickens, turkeys, geese, and ducks." (In the story, the zebra's beautiful new coat makes people want to capture him and domesticate him. Although flattered, he kicks up his heels and gallops away, "as zebras have been doing ever since.")

(b) Why do all hyenas come out only at night, when the other animals are asleep?

They want to avoid being mocked (most other animals sleep at night).

ADDITIONAL ACTIVITY

▶ Make a list of characteristics animals have that help them protect themselves—for example, the turtle's shell, the cat's claws, and the elephant's tusks.

TEACHING JUDGMENTS (Reading Skill)

Read the explanatory material in the students' book aloud while the students read it silently. Then work through the items in the skill exercise one at a time, checking the answer for each before attempting the next item. You may also want to have the students identify the loaded words and substitute other words that convey nearly the same meaning.

JUDGMENTS (Reading Skill Exercise)

Identifying Loaded Words

▶ **For each of the sentences below, tell whether the author is trying to make you admire the character, dislike the character, or feel sorry for the character.**

a. **"Proud and handsome in his beautiful coat, the hyena went *loping* through the jungle."**
admire

b. **"Then he leaped down again, laughing *diabolically* at the tortoise's plight before disappearing into the jungle."**
dislike

c. **"Afraid to move, *clinging* to the branch, the tortoise stayed up there for hours . . . ."**
feel sorry for

d. "Every time he looked down at the ground far below, he felt dizzy and terrified . . . ."
   feel sorry for

e. "The leopard *leaped gracefully* into the tree . . . ."
   admire

f. ". . . when the leopard *swaggered* through the jungle . . ."
   dislike

g. ". . . he shouted to them, *strutting* and *prancing* in his pride . . . ."
   dislike

h. "Ashamed, with his shoulders *drooping,* his head hanging down and his tail *trailing in the dust,* the hyena *slunk* away into the jungle."
   feel sorry for

i. "*Seizing* the tortoise between his strong teeth . . ."
   dislike (the hyena is taking advantage of the tortoise)

TEACHING WORD ATTACK

Write the following sentence on the chalkboard:

> The huge *pachyderm* stomped through the jungle, lifting his trunk, and trumpeting at every monkey he saw.

Ask the students to identify the context clues that help them figure out the meaning of the word *pachyderm*. Then have them read the explanatory material in their books and complete the skill exercise. Check their answers.

WORD ATTACK (Exercise)

Using Context Clues

▶ The words *italicized* in the sentences below may be unfamiliar to you. Try substituting the more familiar words in the list under them until you find one that means about the same thing.

a. "Suddenly he stopped, gazing down at the tortoise who stood in his way looking up at him *plaintively.* 'Hyena, I am in need of your help.' "
   pitifully

b. "Then he leaped down again, laughing *diabolically* at the tortoise's *plight* before disappearing into the jungle."
   devilishly
   difficulty

c. "At last, with darkness falling and despair growing, the tortoise saw a leopard *padding* past the tree and cried for help."
   walking softly

d. "If you let me paint black spots all over your *tawny* coat, you will be admired throughout the jungle."
   yellow-brown

e. "The zebra was *enchanted* by what he saw, a *transformation* as complete

as the leopard's, and went frisking through the jungle to show off his new coat.''

delighted

change

WORD ATTACK CHECK TEST

▶ Each sentence below has a word missing. Use context clues to help you replace each missing word with a word from the list under the sentences.

a. ''Ashamed, with his shoulders drooping, his head hanging down, and his tail trailing in the dust, the hyena _____ away into the jungle.''

b. ''When the hyena burst into the clearing where the animals stood, he shouted to them, strutting and prancing in his _____, 'Look at this coat!' ''

c. ''Come in the morning, when the sun gives us _____.''

d. ''The gray zebra was so impressed by the change in the leopard's appearance that he _____ as fast as he could to the tortoise . . . .''

e. ''Although _____ by this praise, the zebra kicked up his heels and galloped away . . . .''

(1) galloped   (4) pride

(2) flattered   (5) slunk

(3) light

ANSWERS TO WORD ATTACK CHECK TEST

▶ a. (5) slunk   d. (1) galloped

   b. (4) pride   e. (2) flattered

   c. (3) light

ABOUT THE AUTHOR

Forbes Stuart (1924–   ) is a former writer of documentary and educational films. He was born and raised in South Africa, but moved to London in the sixties to pursue a career in public relations. He is now a fulltime writer and college lecturer. *Horned Animals Only, The Boy on the Ox's Back,* and *Magic Horns* are collections of his African stories. Some of his other books are *A Medley of Folk Songs, Stories of Britain in Song,* and *The Witch's Bridle and Other Occult Tales.*

ON THE SELECTIONS

p. 240

1. **In "Alone on the Hilltop," why does Lame Deer spend four days and nights in a hole dug into the hill?** (Relationships: Cause/Effect)
    He is undergoing a coming-of-age ritual. He is hoping to have a vision that will tell him he will become a medicine man.

2. **What will happen to Lame Deer if he has a vision?** (Relationships: Cause/Effect)
    If he has a vision, he will be a medicine man.

3. **In "The Contest," why does Joey's stepfather think that Joey's trumpet playing is a waste of time?**
    Joey's stepfather was raised to believe in hard work and to consider the arts a "frivolous pursuit." ("For wrong or right I was raised strictly. Overstrictly. Entertainers, the arts, these were things to stay away from; hard work, a profession, that was the thing to cultivate.")

4. **How do Joey's mother and stepfather feel when he tells them that he has given the medal away?**
    After Joey explains how he felt, they agree fully with his decision.

5. **In "Night Rider," why does the hitchhiker run from the diner?** (Inferences)
    The truckers are discussing an unknown object that fell from the sky, which is actually his spacecraft. He is frightened that they will realize he is the alien who was operating the spacecraft.

6. **How does the hitchhiker save the truck driver's life?** (Relationships: Cause/Effect)
    He uses beams of light from his eyes to destroy a boulder and thus avert an otherwise fatal accident.

7. **In "The Sin of Madame Phloi," the cat is the official listener and watcher for the household. What sounds does Madame Phloi hear that the humans do not hear?** (Relationships: Comparison/Contrast)
    She hears termites chewing, pipes sweating, plaster cracking, and the ghosts of generations of deceased mice.

8. **How does Madame Phloi wake up each of the members of the family?**
    She stares intently at their foreheads.

9. **In "How the Leopard Got Its Spots," why does the tortoise ask the hyena for help?** (Relationships: Cause/Effect)
    The tortoise wants the hyena to shake some fruit loose from a tree bough for him.

10. **How does the tortoise get even with the hyena?**
    The tortoise paints a muddy, splotched pattern upon the hyena's coat.

ON JUDGMENTS

p. 241

1. **Is Lame Deer a primary or a secondary source of information when he tells about his first *hanblechia*? Why?**

Lame Deer is a primary source of information because he experienced the *hanblechia* firsthand.

2. **Which of the following are statements of fact and which are statements of opinion?**
   a. **Joey is the best trumpet player in the state.**
      opinion
   b. **Joey won the trophy at the state trumpet contest.**
      fact
   c. **Joey wants to become a professional trumpet player.**
      fact
   d. **Joey will become a professional trumpet player.**
      opinion

3. **Which part of the following sentence is a statement of fact and which part is a statement of opinion? The hitchhiker came from the planet Astrax and thousands like him will follow to take over the earth.**
   "The hitchhiker came from the planet Astrax" is a statement of fact. "Thousands like him will follow to take over the earth" is a statement of opinion.

4. **Which of the following statements is a stereotype?**
   a. **All truck drivers are talkative.**
   b. **All truck drivers need a driver's license.**
      Statement *a* is a stereotype.

5. **Identify the loaded word in each pair below.**
   a. **doctor—sawbones**
      sawbones
   b. **lawyer—mouthpiece**
      mouthpiece
   c. **whine—cry**
      whine
   d. **criticize—attack**
      attack
   e. **discriminating—finicky**
      finicky
   f. **blab—tell**
      blab
   g. **ruler—tyrant**
      tyrant
   h. **save—hoard**
      hoard
   i. **old—antique**
      antique
   j. **slave—work**
      slave

ON POINT OF VIEW

p. 241

▶ **Decide whether the following statements are true or false.**

a. The narrator is the person who tells the story.
   true
b. The narrator is always the main character in the story.
   false
c. When a story is told in the first person, the narrator refers to himself or herself with the pronoun *I*.
   true
d. An omniscient narrator is able to tell you about only one character.
   false

BEFORE GOING ON

p. 243

The Fastest Woman on Earth

PHIL BOWIE
pp. 244–249

Summary Kitty O'Neil suffered a complete loss of hearing at the age of 5 months. This article tells how she overcame her handicap and grew up to be the most sought-after stunt woman in Hollywood.

BEFORE READING

Ask students to dicuss movies and television shows they have seen that have contained fantastic stunts. What qualities do they think people who perform stunts need to have? What training do they need? Then have them read the selection to find out how Kitty O'Neil became a stunt woman. (Flexibility: Setting a Purpose)

Glossary Words

agility (p. 246, a, 2)
concurrently (p. 246, b, 1)
concussion (p. 247, b, ℓ. 9)
defiantly (p. 247, b, 2)
endeavor (p. 248, a, 1)
grueling (p. 248, b, 1)
impediment (p. 246, b, ℓ. 1)

orient
  (oriented, p. 247, b, ℓ. 12)
resonant (p. 246, b, 3)
subdue (p. 244, a, 1)
unanimously (p. 249, b, 2)
unscathed (p. 246, a, 1)
velocity (p. 247, a, 4)

TEACHING THE GLOSSARY WORDS

Write the glossary words on the chalkboard. Say each word aloud and have the students repeat it after you. Then have them look up each word in the glossary and write a sentence using it. (Word Attack: Dictionary: Context)

TEACHING FLEXIBILITY (Reading Skill)

Read the explanatory material in the book aloud while the students read it silently. After reading the six steps, ask the students to recall as many as they can from memory. Give them time to study the steps until they, or most of them, can recall the steps in correct sequence. Then have them complete the skill exercises and check their answers.

FLEXIBILITY (Reading Skill Exercises)

Skimming

1. **Skim "The Fastest Woman on Earth" according to the steps listed above. Then decide whether each of the statements below is true or false.**
   a. **Kitty O'Neil is a dramatic actress.**
      false
   b. **Kitty O'Neil is deaf.**
      true
   c. **Kitty was never able to excel in sports.**
      false
   d. **Kitty succeeded without the help of either parent.**
      false
   e. **Kitty's only sports are swimming and diving.**
      false
   f. **Kitty gets her jobs because she is the best-qualified person.**
      true

2. **List all the information you remember after just skimming.**
   Students' answers will vary.

READING SKILLS UNIT TEST (Perspectives)

1. **Tell whether each of the statements described below is from a primary or a secondary source.**
   a. **Kitty O'Neil tells what it feels like to be deaf and to compete in a motorcycle race.**
      primary
   b. **The tortoise tells how proud the leopard is with his new spots.**
      secondary
   c. **The hyena tells how sorry he is that he was mean to the tortoise.**
      primary
   d. **Lame Deer says, "I sat there in the vision pit . . . my arms hugging my knees . . . ."**
      primary

e. Jake tells how XT-115 raced to his spacecraft, repaired it, and took off for Astrax.
   secondary
f. Kitty O'Neil's swimming coach tells how much it hurt Kitty each time she dived into the water wrong.
   secondary
g. Joey tells his mother and stepfather that he enjoyed giving his medal to the lady who lost her grandson in Vietnam more than he would have enjoyed keeping it.
   primary

2. Tell whether each of the statements below is a statement of fact or a statement of opinion.
   a. "Kitty doesn't look like the most sought-after stunt woman in Hollywood."
      opinion
   b. "Kitty was born in Corpus Christi, Texas."
      fact
   c. "At sixteen, Kitty moved to Anaheim to study with Dr. Lee."
      fact
   d. "The pipe would someday pass to my son and, through him, to my grandchildren."
      opinion
   e. "But it seemed to have made my brains empty. Maybe that was good, plenty of room for new insights."
      opinion
   f. " 'Turn my coat into a spotted masterpiece like the leopard's.' "
      opinion
   g. " 'No . . . spots are not for you.' "
      opinion
   h. "He was bulky, uncouth, sloppily attired."
      opinion
   i. "Thapthim was lovable, to be sure."
      opinion
   j. "He had a face like a beautiful flower . . . ."
      opinion

3. Identify the sentences below that are mixed statements of fact and opinion.
   a. "The nearest human being was many miles away, and four days and nights is a long, long time."
      mixed statement
   b. "It was a beautifully designed quilt, white with a large morning star made of many pieces of brightly colored cloth."
      mixed statement
   c. "As long as we had the pipe there would be a Sioux nation."
   d. "It was snowing, fresh and full of enchantment, by the time I got to the trumpet-registration building."
      mixed statement

e. "She had dyed gray-blue hair and sad eyes like the basset hound I'd been given by my father and mother for my eighth birthday."
mixed statement

f. "It had a big TV set in it and a lot of lace doilies, along with a picture of a soldier in a silver frame."

g. "I was all alone on the hilltop."

4. Identify the sentences below that contain loaded words.
   a. "He was fat, and his trouser cuffs had the unsavory odor of a fire hydrant."
   yes

   b. " 'GET that cat away from me,' the fat man roared . . . ."
   yes

   c. " 'Don't you like animals?' asked the gentle voice at the other end of the leash."
   yes

   d. " 'They never leave the apartment except on a leash.' "
   no

   e. " 'Joey,' he said, 'I didn't know.' "
   no

   f. "He did very well on the first section, but in the second he lost his place and just flurried around for a while, hitting a few prize clinkers."
   yes

5. Identify the loaded words in each of the relevant sentences in Question 4.
   a. unsavory   c. gentle
   b. roared   f. flurried; prize clinkers

6. Which of the following statements reflect stereotypes?
   a. "The Madame deplored fat men."
   stereotype

   b. "They met for the first time in the decrepit elevator as it lurched up to the tenth floor of the old building . . . ."

   c. "I took out the mouthpiece and held it cupped in my hand to keep it warm while I waited."

   d. "Kitty doesn't look like the most sought-after stunt woman in Hollywood."
   stereotype

   e. "For months she wore ugly pie-size bruises, but she shrugged off the punishment."

   f. " 'Don't you like animals?' asked the gentle voice at the other end of the leash."
   'Filthy, sneaky beasts,' the fat man said with a snarl."
   stereotype

7. Decide whether the following statements are true or false.
   a. Skimming is a good skill to use with material being learned for a test.
   false

   b. The title of a selection may give a good clue to the content of the selection.
   true

c. Knowing the beginning and ending of a selection may give many clues to the content in between.

true

d. In skimming, the index finger should be run down the middle of each page faster than the eyes can follow it.

false

e. One step in skimming is to pause after every page or two to recall some of the information on that page or those pages.

true

WINTER THUNDER

SELECTION	TYPE	LITERATURE SKILL	READING SKILL	WORD ATTACK SKILL
Winter Thunder by Mari Sandoz pp. 250–281	fiction	Reading a novel	Reading a long selection	
Part 1 pp. 250–265		Understanding plot development Understanding motivation Understanding characterization Understanding conflict	Inferences Relationships: Understanding cause and effect	
Part 2 pp. 266–281		Understanding plot development Understanding motivation Understanding characterization	Relationships: Understanding cause and effect Inferences Judgments Relationships: Understanding comparison and contrast	

Winter Thunder

MARI SANDOZ
pp. 250–281

Summary   In this short novel based on a true story, a young schoolteacher and a group of children are stranded during a violent snowstorm. After surviving the bitter cold for eight days, they are rescued by a search party.

BEFORE READING

Have students turn to p. 250. Ask one student to read the title of the story, the author's name, and the headnote aloud. Then have them read this short novel to find out if the group survives. (Flexibility: Setting a Purpose)

Glossary Words

condescend
  (condescending, p. 274, a, 2)
delirious (p. 271, a, 3)
gaunt (p. 273, a, 1)

incomprehensible (p. 262, a, 4)
instinct (p. 267, b, 1)
ominous (p. 255, a, 2)
pneumonia (p. 273, a, 3)

TEACHING THE GLOSSARY WORDS

Write the glossary words on the chalkboard. Say each word aloud and have the students repeat it after you. Then have the students look up the words in the glossary and write sentences using them. (Word Attack: Dictionary, Context)

CHECK TEST

(T)   1. Aside from Lecia, the oldest person in the group is Chuck, who is sixteen.
(F)   2. Lecia wants the children to separate so that each can look for shelter.
(T)   3. Olive is calm because she is certain her father will rescue her.
(T)   4. Lecia buries Maggie's feet in the snow to stop the inflammation from spreading.
(F)   5. Chuck hikes back to town and finds help.

AFTER READING

The rescuers seem amazed that everyone survived. Ask the students to discuss the reasons why the group stayed alive. (Relationships: Cause/Effect)

CLOSE UP (Comprehension Questions)—Part 1

1. **(a) Why is the teacher, Lecia Terry, in a hurry to get the children out of and away from the bus?** (Inferences)
Lecia is afraid that the bus will explode.
(b) What supplies does she manage to save from the bus?
She and Chuck manage to salvage the lunches and some blankets.

2. **(a) How does Lecia prevent the children from getting separated and lost?** (Relationships: Cause/Effect)
She ties the empty left coat sleeve of each child to the right arm of the child in front.
(b) Why does she place herself at the front of the line of children and Chuck at the back? (Relationships: Cause/Effect)
She places herself at the front and Chuck at the back in order to enclose the group. She wants to ensure that none of the children get separated and lost during the blizzard.

3. **Why does Lecia think that the storm will last a long time?** (Inferences)
Three things indicate this: lightning, snow thunder, and cattle drifting about.

4. **(a) How does Lecia build the shelter in the willow clumps?**
Lecia and Chuck use the buckles of their coats to tie the longer brushy tops of the two clumps of willows together. Then they fasten blankets across the gap between the willows.
(b) What does she do to keep the wind from cutting through the blankets that form the walls of the shelter? (Relationship: Cause/Effect)
She reinforces the blanket walls by placing behind them the bushier portion of the willow branches she has gathered. She works other branches, long as fish poles, into a sort of lattice inside the blankets.

5. **Although Lecia is often frightened, she acts calmly and decisively. (a) What decision does she make about the food?**
In order to make the food last for several days, she decides that everyone must share his or her food. Once she gathers the food together, she hangs it high, in plain view, so that no one can secretly make off with any of it. She also decides that the thermos bottles of milk must be saved for anyone who gets sick and can't eat solid food.
(b) Find two other instances where she acts calmly and decisively. (Inferences)
Students' answers will vary. Some will cite the following examples. Lecia gets all the children out of the smoke-filled bus. She remembers to salvage the lunches and some blankets. Instead of panicking in the storm, she remembers and heeds her grandfather's warning, "Never get separated and never stop moving." Instead of wandering blindly, she looks for a wire fence that might lead to a ranch. She takes the precaution of setting poles into the snowbanks by the shelter to prevent getting lost while gathering wood. She has the children pack snow around the shelter to make a wickiup.

6. **Chuck and some of the children rebel against Lecia's authority. (a) How does Lecia regain control of the group?** (Relationships: Cause/Effect)
She does not make a scene in front of the children. She engages Chuck in a

"silent, incomprehensible struggle." She reestablishes her control with a stare—"commanding at first, then changing to something else in spite of herself, into a sort of public test."

(b) Find two reasons why she wants Chuck to stay with the group.
She knows that if Chuck goes off by himself, he might die. Also, she needs Chuck to help forage for the rapidly diminishing clumps of wood.

7. **(a) Why does Lecia try to make the children aware of the danger of the storm?** (Inferences)
She knows that in order to stop their petty bickering, she needs to inject some fear. She believes and tells the children that "not one of us will get out of here alive unless we keep working together."

(b) Why does she also try to assure them that they will be all right? (Inferences)
She doesn't want them to panic or to give up trying and working to survive.

CLOSE UP (Comprehension Questions)—Part 2

1. **When Lecia awakens in the middle of the night, she hears cattle bawling. Why does this frighten her?** (Relationships: Cause/Effect)
She knows this means that the cattle are stampeding in a blind panic. Since they cannot see the shelter, they may trample it and its inhabitants.

2. **Lecia's knowledge of woodcraft helps her to face two crises. (a) Why does she place Maggie's legs in two deep holes in the snow wall?** (Relationships: Cause/Effect)
She hopes the snow will retard the spread of gangrene and reduce Maggie's pain and delerium.

   (b) Why does she give Joanie and Eddie a drink make from willow bark? (Relationships: Cause/Effect)
Lecia remembers that the early settlers used willow bark tea to break a fever.

3. **Why does Lecia feel hopeless after Chuck deserts the group?** (Inferences)
She has kept the children alive for five days, but some are so ill as to be close to death. Chuck's desertion makes her feel totally alone. She fears she cannot keep the fire going by herself. She knows she cannot leave the children alone, yet she must go out and search for wood.

4. **Why does Chuck change his mind and come back to the group?** (Inferences)
Students' answers will vary, but many will say that Chuck has come to feel responsible for the well-being of the group. He cannot desert the children and leave them to die. Once he finds the small calf head, he wants to bring it to the group so that the children can have food.

   (b) Do you think this decision shows that he has matured? Why or why not? (Judgments)
Students' answers will vary, but many will feel that his decision to take responsibility for the well-being of the group and place their needs before his own shows that he has matured.

5. **Composition. After eight days the group is rescued. Select one character and write a paragraph telling how this character changed during the eight days.** (Relationships: Comparison/Contrast)
Students' answers will vary.

ABOUT THE AUTHOR

Mari Sandoz (1901–1966) won the *Atlantic Monthly* prize in 1935 for her first book, *Old Jules* (a biography of her father). She was one of the country's leading historians on life in the old west. Her nonfiction books are *The Buffalo Hunters, Love Song to the Plains, These Were the Sioux,* and *The Beaver Men.* Her novels include *The Horsecatcher, Christmas of the Phonograph Records,* and *The Story Catcher.* The latter won the Levi Straus Award in 1963 for best novel on the West.

VISTAS

SELECTION	TYPE	LITERATURE SKILL	READING SKILL	WORD ATTACK SKILL
Beware of the Dog by Roald Dahl pp. 285–297	fiction	Setting. Seeing place as an important element of setting	Inferences. Making inferences based on evidence	Context. Understanding words used as nouns and verbs
Otero's Visitor by Manuela Williams Crosno pp. 298–307	fiction	Setting. Visualizing setting	Inferences, Making inferences about characters	Context. Using context to understand words from Spanish
The Sea by James Reeves p. 309	poetry	Poetry. Understanding metaphors		
Back There by Rod Serling pp. 310–327	drama	Setting. Seeing place as an important element of setting	Inferences. Making inferences about a character's feelings	Imagery. Understanding adverbs
Storm Ending by Jean Toomer	poetry	Poetry. Understanding metaphors and imagery		
Nocturne by Gwendolyn Bennett p. 329	poetry			
Crime on Mars by Arthur C. Clarke pp. 330–339	fiction	Setting. Understanding how setting affects plot	Inferences. Making inferences about realistic and fantastic details	Context. Using context clues

SELECTION	TYPE	LITERATURE SKILL	READING SKILL	WORD ATTACK SKILL
Avalanche by Robb White pp. 341–357	fiction	Setting. Understanding how setting can affect characters	Inferences. Making inferences about future actions and events	Structure. Understanding compound words
Crow Call by Lois Lowry pp. 358–367	fiction	Mood. Understanding mood— happiness	Inferences. Identifying valid inferences	Dictionary. Using a dictionary to break words into syllables
Crows by David McCord	poetry	Poetry. Understanding mood in poetry		
Haikai II by Sadakichi Hartmann	poetry			
Cynthia in the Snow by Gwendolyn Brooks	poetry			
One Alaska Night by Barrett Willoughby pp. 371–383	fiction	Mood. Understanding mood—terror	Inferences. Making inferences about past events	Figurative Language. Understanding similes
The Night the Ghost Got In by James Thurber pp. 384–391	non-fiction	Mood. Understanding mood—humor	Inferences. Making inferences about tone	Figurative Language. Understanding figurative expressions
Review Quiz pp. 392–393				
Composition. Description p. 394				

SELECTION	TYPE	LITERATURE SKILL	READING SKILL	WORD ATTACK SKILL
Before Going On p. 395			Flexibility and Main Idea: Outlining	
Further Reading *How People Flew Before Airplanes Were Invented* by Robert Miller pp. 397–401	non-fiction			

Beware of the Dog

ROALD DAHL
pp. 285–297

Summary   During World War II, Peter Williamson, a wounded British pilot, bails out of his plane over the English Channel. When he wakes up in the hospital, he believes he is in England, but mounting evidence forces him to conclude he is really in enemy-occupied France.

BEFORE READING

Before students read this story, make sure they understand some basic facts about World War II. First show them a map of Europe. Point to each country as you mention it. Tell students that Nazi Germany invaded Poland in 1939, which forced Britain and France to declare war on Germany. About seven months later, Germany invaded Denmark and Norway and then Luxembourg, Belgium, and the Netherlands. Then on June 5, 1940, Germany overran France. Paris fell on June 14. This left only Great Britain to fight Germany. The English Channel separated Great Britain from its enemy. Germany then sent its air force to bomb Britain as a preliminary to invading the island. The British retaliated by bombing German targets and shooting down German planes.

Have students turn to p. 285. Have one student read the title of the selection and the author's name aloud. Have another student read the headnote aloud. Ask them what they think the title could mean. Have them read the story to find out the significance of the title. (Flexibility: Setting a Purpose).

Glossary Words

*delirious (p. 290, a, 5)   *undulate
*dispersal (p. 294, a, 1)   (undulating, p. 285, a, 1)
*obsession (p. 291, b, 2)

TEACHING THE GLOSSARY WORDS

Write the glossary words on the chalkboard. Say each word aloud and have the students repeat it after you. Have the students look up each word in the glossary. Then write the following sentences on the chalkboard.

"Down below there was only a vast, white, _____ sea of cloud." (undulating)

"Perhaps I am imagining things. Perhaps I am a little _____." (delirious)

"The idea became an _____ with him, and soon he could think of nothing except the window." (obsession)

"It was a sentence which Johnny, the Intelligence Officer of his squadron, always repeated to the pilots every day before they went out. He could see Johnny now, leaning against the wall of the _____ hut with his pipe in his hand, saying, 'And if they get you, don't forget, just your name, rank, and number.' " (dispersal)

Have students decide which word best fits in each blank. (Word Attack: Dictionary, Context)

CHECK TEST

(F)   1. Peter's plane is shot down over the English Channel.
(F)   2. The Germans try to make Peter believe that he has lost his memory.
(T)   3. When Peter wakes up, the nurse tells him he is in Brighton.
(F)   4. Peter is reassured when members of his squadron come to visit.
(T)   5. The nurse makes a mistake when she complains about the hard water.

AFTER READING

Point out that this story was told entirely from Peter's point of view. Ask students if this technique helped make the story more effective. Did it make it more suspenseful? Why or why not? (Judgments)

CLOSE UP (Comprehension Questions)

1. **Peter Williamson fights to remain calm and alert while flying back to base. Do you think his thoughts show that he is really calm or do they show that he is frightened and confused? Why?** (Inferences)
His thoughts show that he is in a state of shock. They are a confused mixture of rational and irrational thoughts, fears, and imaginings. The recurring theme is indifference to the loss of his leg, which is an attempt to blot out the reality.

2. **(a) Why does Peter decide to bail out of the plane?** (Relationships: Cause/ Effect)
He decides to bail out because he realizes that he is about to lose consciousness.
(b) Why does he turn the Spitfire over on its back? (Relationships: Cause/ Effect)
He turns the plane over so that he can fall out of it. In his condition, he can't jump.

3. **When Peter wakes up, he thinks that he is in a hospital in Brighton. (a) Why does the sound of the Junkers 88 overhead make him suspicious?** (Inferences)

The Junkers 88 is a German plane. Why, he wonders, would it be flying over England in daylight, with no air-raid sirens and no antiaircraft artillery trying to shoot it down?

(b) Why are Peter's suspicions further aroused when the nurse complains about the hard water? (Relationships: Cause/Effect)

Peter went to school in Brighton, and he knows that the water there is soft.

4. **(a) Where does Peter begin to suspect he is?** (Inferences)

   Peter begins to suspect that he is behind enemy lines.

   (b) What finally confirms his suspicions? (Inferences)

   His suspicions are confirmed when he crawls to the window. He sees a sign in French: *Garde au chien* ("Beware of the dog").

5. **(a) Why do the nurse and doctor lie to Peter?** (Inferences)

   They want him to think that he is among his compatriots. He will be more likely to reveal valuable information if he thinks he is among friends.

   (b) Why does Peter tell the Wing Commander only his name, rank, and serial number? (Inferences)

   He wants the Wing Commander to know that he has not been fooled and that he will not cooperate. (It is standard procedure for prisoners of war to reveal only their name, rank, and serial number.)

SETTING (Literature Skill Questions)

1. **The time of this story is during World War II. Use a dictionary or an encyclopedia to find out when World War II occurred.**

   The dates for World War II are 1939–1945.

2. **How does the fact that Peter bails out over the Channel keep you uncertain about the place of the story?**

   He could be on either side of the English Channel—either in England or in France.

3. **List the setting details that make Peter believe he is in Brighton. For example, when Peter wants a cigarette, the nurse gives him a package of Players, a brand of cigarettes popular in England.** (Inferences)

   The staff speak English and presumably wear British uniforms. The doctor wears British ribbons from World War I. The nurse says her brother is in the Royal Air Force. The Wing Commander wears a British flying medal.

4. **List the setting detail that convinces Peter he is really in France.** (Inferences)

   He is convinced when he sees the sign in French ("Garde au chien") from his window. (When he hears unfamiliar or definitely German planes overhead, he first becomes suspicious. Also, the water is hard, but it shouldn't be in Brighton. When he sees the sign, his suspicions are confirmed.)

ADDITIONAL ACTIVITIES

1. At what point in the story did you begin to suspect that Peter was not in a hospital in England?

2. Explain what you think happened to Peter after the story ended.
3. Make a list of the many different kinds of jobs that must be done in the wartime military. Compare your list with the lists of other students.

TEACHING INFERENCES (Reading Skill)

Write the following sentence on the chalkboard:

Ramon stood on the beach, dripping wet and breathing hard.

Have the students read the explanatory material in their books and tell what they can infer from the sentence on the chalkboard. (Ramon has been swimming.) Ask them what evidence in the sentence supports their inference. Then have them complete the skill exercises and check their answers.

INFERENCES (Reading Skill Exercises)

Making Inferences Based on Evidence

1. **Use evidence from the story to help you answer each of the following questions.**
   a. **Why does Peter take some quick, deep breaths from his oxygen mask before he bails out of the plane?**
      He wants to clear his head.
   b. **The doctor tells Peter that some lads from his squadron have called and asked about him. Why does the doctor also say that he told them to wait a few days before coming to visit?**
      He doesn't want Peter to get suspicious. This way, Peter won't find it odd that he has no visitors—he'll think it's doctor's orders.
   c. **Peter falls asleep thinking about the JU-88's and the hardness of the water. Why does his room feel unfriendly to him when he wakes up the next day?**
      He suspects that he might not be in England after all.
   d. **When Peter crawls back into bed after reading the sign that says, *"Garde au chien,"* his leg throbs painfully. Why doesn't he tell the nurse about the pain?**
      He suspects that she is part of the enemy plot. (He doesn't want anyone to know that he has been out of bed.)
   e. **Why does the Wing Commander ask Peter the name of his squadron?**
      He hopes to extract valuable military information.

2. **The author does not tell you how much time Peter spends in the hospital before he regains consciousness. Reread the last paragraph on p. 286. Find evidence that shows that at least several days have passed.**
   Although he does not see things clearly, he can distinguish periods of white (daytime) and black (nighttime). These periods alternate several times.

3. **Find evidence that shows that the nurse is part of the enemy's plan to get information from Peter.**

She lies to Peter, telling him that he is safe in England, that he is wrong in his identification of the German planes, and that her brother is in the Royal Air Force. When he mentions that he went to school in Brighton, she "looks up quickly." Her movements are "too sharp and nervous" to go well with the casual manner in which she speaks. There is something "uneasy" about her eyes—"they never (look) at anything for more than a moment, and they (move) too quickly from one place to another in the room." (All of these actions suggest a person who is afraid of being "found out.")

TEACHING WORD ATTACK

Read the explanatory material in the book aloud while the students read it silently. Write the following words on the chalkboard: *run, hit.* Ask them to think of the game of baseball and to use each word in a sentence as a noun and in a different sentence as a verb. (Examples: Run around the bases. He scored a run. She hit the ball. It was a solid hit.) Then have them complete the skill exercise and check their answers.

WORD ATTACK (Exercise)

Understanding Words Used as Nouns and Verbs

▶ Read each sentence below. First decide if the word in *italics* is used as a noun or as a verb. Then find its meaning in your dictionary. Write this meaning on a separate piece of paper.

a. After landing, Peter would *taxi* in and turn off the engine.
   verb
b. Peter planned to go everywhere in a car or in a *taxi.*
   noun
c. He did not *voice* his fears to the nurse.
   verb
d. He wanted to make his *voice* sound ordinary.
   noun
e. Peter noticed the *rivet* in the engine cowling of the plane.
   noun
f. The words on the sign *rivet* his eyes.
   verb
g. Parachute jumpers sometimes *somersault* in the air.
   verb
h. Peter jumped from the plane and did a *somersault.*
   noun
i. Each movement would *jar* his leg and cause him pain.
   verb
j. There was a *jar* of medicine on the table.
   noun
k. Peter held on to the *edge* of the windowsill.
   noun
l. Peter tried to *edge* forward.
   verb

m. The Wing Commander wanted Peter to fill out a combat *report.*
noun

n. Peter would *report* only his name, his rank, and his serial number.
verb

o. He attempted to *hoist* himself up onto the bed.
verb

p. They used a *hoist* to load the plane.
noun

Accept any appropriate definitions.

WORD ATTACK CHECK TEST

▶ Identify each word in *italics* below as either a noun or a verb.

a. He hoped he would be *landing* the plane soon.

b. Because of the clouds he couldn't see any place for a *landing.*

c. "*Jump,*" a voice pounded in his head. "*Jump!*"

d. He was in a hospital. The *jump* must have been successful.

e. Peter was so happy to be alive he didn't *notice* everything at first.

f. From his window he could see the *notice* on a post in the garden.

g. All I will give is my *name,* rank, and serial number.

h. Would you *name* your squadron, please?

ANSWERS TO WORD ATTACK CHECK TEST

▶ a. verb   e. verb
   b. noun   f. noun
   c. verb   g. noun
   d. noun   h. verb

ABOUT THE AUTHOR

Roald Dahl (1916–   ) twice received the "Edgar" (the Edgar Allan Poe Award of Mystery Writers of America). He wrote the novels *Charlie and the Chocolate Factory* and *James and the Giant Peach.* Some books of his collected short stories are *Over to You; Kiss, Kiss; Someone Like You;* and *Selected Stories of Roald Dahl.* He contributes short stories to the *New Yorker, Esquire, Town and Country,* and *The Saturday Evening Post.* He also wrote a play, "The Honeys," and the screenplays for "Chitty Chitty Bang Bang" and the James Bond movie "You Only Live Twice."

Otero's Visitor

MANUELA WILLIAMS CROSNO
pp. 298–307

Summary A stranger asks Don Adolfo Otero to hide a small wooden box for him, but Otero dies before the stranger calls for it again. Otero's ghostly footsteps repeatedly pace the room where the box is hidden, until the stranger returns to claim his property, and Otero honorably discharges his trust.

BEFORE READING

Have students turn to p. 298. Ask one student to read the title of the story, the author's name, and the headnote aloud. Then have them look at the illustration. On the basis of these clues, ask them what type of story they think this is (a ghost story). Where do they think it takes place (New Mexico)? Do they think it occurs in the past, the present, or the future (the past)? Then have them read the story to find out if their predictions are correct. (Inferences; Flexibility: Setting a Purpose)

Glossary Words

*abate (p. 300, b, ℓ. 7)
*agitate
   (agitation, p. 300, b, 1)
*assuage (p. 302, b, 3)
*disconsolate (p. 304, a, 2)
*hospitality (p. 300, a, 1)
*implore
   (implored, p. 302, a, 1)

*perturb
   (perturbed, p. 302, b, 1)
*reverie (p. 300, b, 1)
   (Also spelled revery)
*smolder
   (smoldering, p. 300, b, ℓ. 6)
*vitality (p. 300, b, 1)

TEACHING THE GLOSSARY WORDS

Write the glossary words on the chalkboard. Say each word aloud and have the students repeat it after you. Then have them use the glossary to find the answers to the following puzzle.

ACROSS
1. to beg
2. to ease or abate
3. welcome or greeting
4. to upset or disturb

DOWN
2. to excite or perturb
5. disappointed
6. strength, energy
7. to smoke
8. daydream
9. to lessen

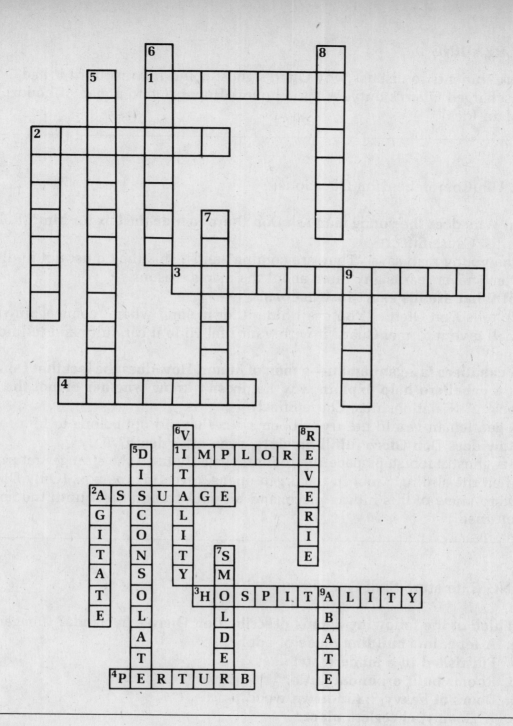

Crossword solution:

1 (Across) IMPLORE
2 (Across) ASSUAGE
3 (Across) HOSPITALITY
4 (Across) PERTURB

5 (Down) DISCONSOLATE
6 (Down) VITALITY
7 (Down) SMOLDER
8 (Down) REVERIE
9 (Down) ABATE
2 (Down) AGITATE

CHECK TEST

(T)   1. The Otero family originally came from Spain.
(F)   2. People stay away from the Otero hacienda because it is a place of gloom.
(F)   3. The stranger tells Don Otero that the box contains secret documents.
(T)   4. Reyes is Otero's oldest son.
(F)   5. Reyes takes the box from its hiding place and returns it to the stranger.

AFTER READING

Ask students to discuss why Otero's ghost could not rest until it had discharged Otero's duty. What is honor? How is Otero a man of honor? (Main Idea)

CLOSE UP (Comprehension Questions)

1. **(a) Why does the young man ask Don Otero to hide the box for him?** (Relationships: Cause/Effect)
   The young man says "They are coming" and "This they must not find!" Don Otero never learns any more about the man's reasons.
   (b) What are his exact instructions?
   He tells Don Otero: "You shall hide it for me and when I come again you shall give it to me! Guard it with your life! Hide it carefully and tell no one!"
2. **A caballero is a gentleman—a man of honor. How does the fact that Don Otero is a caballero help explain why he doesn't know whether or not the box is locked?** (Relationships: Cause/Effect)
   A gentleman would not try to open a box that did not belong to him.
3. **How does Don Otero fulfill his duty, even after death?**
   His ghostly footsteps pace the room repeatedly until the stranger returns. Then the sliding panel in the organ opens, revealing the box. (Only Don Otero knew of this hiding place, and his soul couldn't rest until the box was returned.)

SETTING (Literature Skill Questions)

1. **Which of the following details describe Don Otero's hacienda?** (Imagery)
   a. **A long, low building made of adobe.**
   b. **Furnished in a modern style.**
   c. **Rooms built around a patio.**
   d. **Doors of heavy, hand-hewn wood.**
   e. **A gloomy, cheerless place.**
   f. **Lace curtains on the windows.**
   Details *a*, *c*, *d*, and *f* describe Don Otero's hacienda.
2. **This passage creates a vivid impression of the setting:**
   "Now this is a country of many winds. Sometimes the soft winds blow from the southwest and travel close to the ground. They are the winds that sing songs in the yucca and grasses that grow on the mesa."
   Find three other statements that help you to picture the setting and feel as though you are there. (Imagery)
   Students' answers will vary. (For example, p. 300, column b, paragraph 2 and p. 302, column b, paragraph 3.)

ADDITIONAL ACTIVITIES

1. **Composition.** Imagine that you were a guest at one of Adolfo Otero's fiestas. Write a diary entry telling about the fiesta.
2. **Composition.** Write a short eulogy to be read at the funeral service for Adolfo Otero.

TEACHING INFERENCES (Reading Skill)

Read the material in the book aloud while the students read it silently. Then write the following passage on the chalkboard and ask the students what they can infer about Jason from it.

> On Saturday, Jason got up early and ran ten miles. After showering, he worked until noon on repairing his bike so that he could get in shape for the race tomorrow. (Students should be able to infer that Jason is athletic.)

Then have them complete the skill exercises and check their answers.

INFERENCES (Reading Skill Exercises)

Making Inferences About Characters

1. **To answer the following questions, use evidence from the story to make inferences about Don Otero.**
   a. **Do you think Don Otero is an unhappy man or a contented man? Why?**
   He is a contented man because he has wealth, good health, and a good family life. His house is known as a place of laughter and music.
   b. **Do you think Don Otero's word is respected in his community? Why or why not?**
   Yes, it is. The stranger considers him completely trustworthy without ever having met him.
   c. **Do you think Don Otero's children honor and respect him? Why or why not?**
   Yes, they do. His oldest son follows his example. (He also honors the days when Don Otero was alive.)
   d. **Do you think Don Otero values his Spanish heritage? Why or why not?**
   Yes, he does. He builds and furnishes his hacienda in the Spanish style, observes the Spanish customs of his youth, and remains a true caballero to the end.
   (Accept any reasonable explanations.)
2. **The stranger who comes for the box makes an inference about Reyes. He says, "A son of Adolfo Otero could not be other than trustworthy." On what knowledge or evidence does he base his inference?**
   He bases it on the knowledge that Adolfo Otero was the most trustworthy of men and on the assumption that he would have raised his son to act accordingly.

TEACHING WORD ATTACK

Have the students read the explanatory material in their books and complete the skill exercise. Check their answers.

WORD ATTACK (Exercise)

Understanding Words from Spanish

▶ Use context clues to match the *italicized* Spanish words in the sentences below with the definitions under them. (There is one extra answer.)

a. "Handsome were the *señors* and beautiful the *señoritas.*"
   (5), (7)
b. "The walls of the long, low building were made of *adobe* and were four feet thick."
   (2)
c. "They are the winds that sing songs in the yucca and grasses that grow on the *mesa.*"
   (4)
d. "It was curiously carved, but whether or not it was locked, Otero never knew, for he was a Spanish gentleman—a *caballero!*"
   (1)
e. "For days at a time, however, the hacienda would ring with the laughter of young people and of old, when Reyes would call them there for a *fiesta* to honor the old days."
   (3)

   (1) a gentleman
   (2) sun-dried brick used for building houses
   (3) a feast or big party
   (4) plateau or flat land with steep walls of rock
   (5) men
   (6) a large state
   (7) women

WORD ATTACK CHECK TEST

▶ Use context clues to match the *italicized* words in the sentences below with the definitions under them.
a. Pedro and Arturo sat on the *patio,* letting the sun warm their bodies.
b. Hernandez turned, waved, and shouted *"Adios"* before he rode away.
c. *"Mi amigo,"* Conchita whispered in the ear of her beloved doll.
d. He laughed, took the huge *sombrero* from his head, and sailed it high into the air.

   (1) hat with a wide brim
   (2) goodbye
   (3) yard outside a house for dining or recreation
   (4) my friend

ANSWERS TO WORD ATTACK CHECK TEST

▶ a. (3)   c. (4)
  b. (2)   d. (1)

ABOUT THE AUTHOR

Manuela Williams Crosno graduated and later earned an MA degree from New Mexico State University. Now a retired junior high school teacher, Mrs. Crosno is a writer who pursues several hobbies, including drawing pastel portraits and designing latchhook tapestries. Her poems *Chant* and *March Melody* have appeared in the poetry quarterly *Rose Chalice* and her short stores "Tulita's Daughter" and "Martinez' Treasure" have appeared in *New Mexico* magazine. Her short story "Otero's Visitor," which won honorable mention in O'Brien's *Best Short Stories* (1937), first appeared in print in the *New Mexico Quarterly*.

The Sea

JAMES REEVES
p. 309

Summary   A short poem comparing the sea to a hungry dog.

BEFORE READING

Tell students that a metaphor is an implied comparison between two essentially unlike things. It does not contain the words *like* or *as*. Ask them to look for the metaphor as they read "The Sea." (Figurative Language; Flexibility: Setting a Purpose)

CLOSE UP (Comprehension Questions)

▶ **Make a list of things the sea and a dog have in common.** (Figurative Language)
They are hungry (for stones or bones); they are giant and gray; they roll on the beach all day; they moan for their food; they lick their extremities (shore or paws); they make sniffing sounds; they shake water off; they howl at night; they are quiet in warm weather.

ABOUT THE AUTHOR

James Reeves (1909–   ) is editor of several anthologies, including *Poet's World*, *The Rhyming River* (four volumes), and *The Cassell Book of English*

Poetry. He has written several books of poetry, including *The Imprisoned Sea; The Password, and Other Poems;* and *Collected Poems, 1929–1959.* Some of his novels are *The Shadow of the Hawk, The Ballad,* and *Quest and Conquest.*

Back There

ROD SERLING
pp. 310–327

Summary   This compelling episode from "The Twilight Zone" is about a young man who travels back in time and tries to prevent John Wilkes Booth from assassinating Abraham Lincoln.

BEFORE READING

Tell students that some people think there is a fifth dimension known as time through which we may one day be able to travel. Ask students if they think time travel will one day be possible. Why or why not? Then have them read the play to find out what happens to a young man who is transported back in time. (Flexibility: Setting a Purpose)

Glossary Words

abyss (p. 312, a, 5)	*miscreant (p. 317, a, 2)
benefactor (p. 319, b, 2)	*palaver (p. 323, b, 8)
*composure (p. 320, b, ℓ. 1)	*premonition (p. 319, b, 12)
*cordon (p. 317, b, 8)	*proffer
deference (p. 312, b, 11)	(proffered, p. 319, a, 6)
*demented (p. 318, b, 11)	*remand
disheveled (p. 317, a, 2)	(remanded, p. 318, a, 6)
disposition (p. 317, a, 2)	skein (p, 324, b, 4)
*incarcerate	*staccato (p. 323, a, 2)
(incarcerated, p. 318, a, 4)	theoretical (p, 312, b, 4)
inventory (p. 315, b, 9)	thesis (p. 324, b, 4)

TEACHING THE GLOSSARY WORDS

Write the glossary words on the chalkboard. Say each word aloud and have the students repeat it after you. Then have students look up the starred words and write the meanings in their notebooks. Have them match the words with their meanings.

1.	miscreant	a.	nonsense talk
2.	premonition	b.	to put in jail
3.	composure	c.	a group forming a barrier
4.	incarcerate	d.	to hand over
5.	cordon	e.	a forewarning
6.	staccato	f.	crazy, insane
7.	remand	g.	a wrongdoer
8.	demented	h.	to extend or hold out
9.	palaver	i.	a series of sharp, short noises
10.	proffer	j.	calmness of mind

(Answers: 1. g; 2. e; 3. j; 4. b; 5. c; 6. i; 7. d; 8. f; 9. a; 10. h)

Have students look up the remaining words for homework and write their meanings in their notebooks. (Word Attack: Dictionary)

CHECK TEST

(F) 1. At the beginning of this play, Corrigan believes in time travel.

(T) 2. Corrigan becomes upset when he learns that Lincoln will be at Ford's Theater.

(F) 3. The police captain believes Corrigan when Corrigan tells him Lincoln will be shot.

(T) 4. Wellington drugs Corrigan in order to prevent him from interfering with his plan to assassinate Lincoln.

(F) 5. At the end of this play, Corrigan finds that it is impossible to alter the past.

AFTER READING

Read the last paragraph of this play aloud. Ask students if they agree or disagree with the narrator's conclusion. Why? (Judgments)

CLOSE UP (Comprehension Questions)

1. **Millard claims that if people could go back in time, they would be able to alter the course of history. Why does Corrigan disagree with Millard?**
Corrigan believes that the events of history are fixed and cannot be altered.

2. **Corrigan leaves the club on the night of April 14, 1965. (a) List three things that occur as he stands outside the Club that make you think Corrigan has traveled back in time.** (Inferences)
The light wavers and becomes a gas light. Corrigan's wristwatch has disappeared, and there is a fringe of lace at his wrist. The plaque in front of his club no longer reads "The Washington Club, Founded 1858" but rather "Washington Club."

(b) How does the attendant's behavior support this idea? (Inferences)
The attendant, who is half undressed, says the club is now closed. Also, the attendant doesn't recognize Corrigan and doesn't know who William (the attendant of 1965) is.

3. **Before renting a room to him, Mrs. Landers asks Corrigan if he is an army veteran. Which army does she mean?** (Inferences)
She means the Union Army in the War Between the States.

4. **Why is Corrigan upset when he learns that President Lincoln will attend Ford's Theater that night?** (Relationships: Cause/Effect)
Corrigan realizes that Lincoln will be shot at that performance.

5. **(a) What reason does Wellington give the police for taking Corrigan into his custody?** (Relationships: Cause/Effect)
Wellington convinces the police that he is concerned about their new, strange prisoner, and that he may be able to help him.
(b) What is his real reason? (Relationships: Cause/Effect)
Wellington is really John Wilkes Booth, and he wants to get Corrigan out of the way so that he can proceed with his assassination plans.

6. **Peter Corrigan isn't able to change history in a large way by saving President Lincoln. How is he able to change history in a small way?**
He changes William's history. Corrigan returns to the present (1965) to find that William is no longer a deferential attendant but a millionaire and fellow member of the club. He has inherited his wealth from his great-grandfather, who turns out to be the young and sympathetic police officer Corrigan encountered in the past. (The police officer became famous trying to warn people of the impending assassination—because of the publicity, he was able to rise in life and make a fortune.)

SETTING (Literature Skill Questions)

1. **The place where the events in this play occur is Washington, D.C. (a) When do the events in Act One, Scene 1 occur?** (Relationships: Time Order)
The events in Act One, Scene 1 occur on April 14, 1965.
(b) When do the events in Act One, Scene 2 occur? (Relationships: Time Order)
The events in Act One, Scene 2 occur on April 14, 1865.

2. **Corrigan tells Mrs. Landers that her house is the oldest building in this section of town. (a) Why does she think that this statement is strange?** (Inferences)
In 1865 Mrs. Landers' building isn't significantly older than any of the other buildings in the area. That distinction is appropriate to the building only in 1965.
(b) Find one other statement Corrigan makes to Mrs. Landers that shows he is from another time. (Inferences)
Corrigan says he is not used to wearing a hat. (Hats were an important part of a man's wardrobe in 1865.)

3. **Imagine that you are going to record this play as a radio drama. (a) List the sound effects you would use to indicate the present.**
Sound effects from the present might include: noises associated with

motorized traffic (the revving of engines, the honking of horns, the sound of ambulance or police sirens); sounds of appliances inside the club (dishwashers, heaters); the sound of an airplane flying overhead, etc.

(b) List the sound effects you would use to indicate the past.

Sound effects from the past might include: the click of horses' hooves or the sound of carriage wheels on cobblestones; the rustle of long dresses (with petticoats); the sound of chimes from a steeple clock, etc.

ADDITIONAL ACTIVITIES

1. Read two or three of Corrigan's speeches as you think a professional actor would read them.
2. If this play were presented on television, which three scenes do you think would be most effective? Explain your answer.
3. **Composition.** Imagine you are a radio announcer. What kind of announcement would you make for this play if it were produced as a radio drama? Write out your announcement and practice reading it until you sound professional.

TEACHING INFERENCES (Reading Skill)

Read the explanatory material in the book aloud while the students read it silently. Then have them complete the skill exercise and check their answers.

INFERENCES (Reading Skill Exercise)

Making Inferences About a Character's Feelings

▶ **Read each of the following passages. Pay special attention to clues to feelings. Then make an inference about how Corrigan feels in each passage.**

a. **"Corrigan backs away from the door, goes down to the sidewalk, stands there, looks up at the gas light, then up and down the street, starts at the sound of noises . . . . He takes a few halting, running steps out into the street. He bites his lip, looks around."**
He feels confused, surprised, and disbelieving.

b. **"He stops suddenly and begins to waver. He reaches up to touch the bruise over his head."**
He feels faint and is in pain.

c. **"(Corrigan) waves a clenched fist at her. He still holds the handkerchief. (He says,) 'Don't tell me there is no one here by that name. He brought me here. He lives in this room.'"**
He feels angry.

d. **"He stops abruptly, suddenly caught by something he sees on the handkerchief. His eyes slowly turn to stare at it in his hand."**
He feels surprised and absorbed.

e. **"Corrigan rises weakly and goes to the window, staring out at the night and listening to the sounds of a nation beginning its mourning. He closes his**

eyes and puts his head against the windowpane, and with fruitless, weak-
ened smashes, hits the side of the window frame as he talks."
He feels tired, angry, frustrated, and depressed.

TEACHING WORD ATTACK

Read the explanatory material in the book aloud while the students read it
silently. Write the following words on the chalkboard and ask the students
to make –ly adverbs from them and to use them in original sentences:

sad   skillful   wicked

Then have them complete the skill exercise and check their answers.

WORD ATTACK (Exercises)

Understanding Adverbs

1. **Use a dictionary to find the meaning of each of the *italicized* adverbs
   below.**
   a. **William answers Corrigan's questions *deferentially*.**
   b. **The door was *partially* closed.**
   c. **Mrs. Landers looked at Corrigan *suspiciously*.**
   d. **She glanced at his hat *expectantly*.**
   e. **Corrigan pounded on the door *intently*.**
   f. **The captain glanced *inquiringly* toward the officer.**
   g. **Wellington was dressed *elegantly*.**
   h. **The police captain slammed his fist on the desk and spoke *impatiently*.**
   i. **Corrigan tried *desperately* to focus his eyes.**
   j. **Wellington smiled *apologetically* at him.**
   Check answers against dictionary definitions.

2. **Read each sentence above, but leave out the adverbs. How do the sentences
   change?**
   You know less about the actions in each sentence. You don't know *how* the
   action was carried out.

3. **For each sentence in Exercise 1, replace the *italicized* adverb with an adverb
   that means the opposite, or nearly the opposite.** (Note: Tell students they may
   use a dictionary.)
   Students' answers will vary. Some sample answers are:
   a. disrespectfully   f. innocently
   b. totally   g. shabbily
   c. trustingly   h. patiently
   d. unexpectantly   i. calmly
   e. absently   j. defiantly

WORD ATTACK CHECK TEST

▶ Identify the adverb in each sentence below.
   a. The captain of police was incorruptibly dense.

b. Sympathetically, the young police officer tried to help Corrigan.
c. William helpfully held the door open for Corrigan.
d. Corrigan generously pressed a bill into William's hand.

ANSWERS TO WORD ATTACK CHECK TEST

▶ a. incorruptibly
   b. sympathetically

   c. helpfully
   d. generously

ABOUT THE AUTHOR

Rod Serling (1924–1978) created, wrote for, and acted as narrator for the popular television series *The Twilight Zone*. He won an Emmy four times, once for his play, *Requiem for a Heavyweight*. Other stories from the Twilight Zone are anthologized in *Stories from the Twilight Zone*, *More Stories from the Twilight Zone*, and *New Stories from the Twilight Zone*.

Storm Ending

JEAN TOOMER

Nocturne

GWENDOLYN BENNETT
p. 329

> **Summaries** Two short poems describing the end of a storm and a cool night in summer.

BEFORE READING

Ask students to jot down words and phrases that create a vivid picture of the end of a storm. Then ask them to jot down words and phrases that describe a cool night in summer. Tell them that as they read "Storm Ending" and "Nocturne," they should look for words and phrases that create vivid images. (Imagery; Flexibility: Setting a Purpose)

CLOSE UP (Comprehension Questions)

1. **In "Storm Ending," the poet creates a vivid picture of thunder by comparing it to bell-like flowers. How is the sound of thunder like the sound of a bell?** (Figurative Language)
Both are loud, hollow, and resounding.

2. **Lightning is followed by thunder. Why do you think the poet describes thunder as blossoming into flowers?** (Figurative Language)
Just as lightning is followed by thunder, blossoms are followed by flowers. Also, the word *blossom* creates the image of something breaking out, just as thunder seems to break out of the skies.

3. **(a) Find four lines that give you a vivid picture of rain.** (Imagery)
Lines 6–9
(b) How does this picture help you to know that the storm is ending, rather than beginning? (Imagery)
Line 6 tells us that the sun is appearing. Line 8 tells us the storm has subsided so that now the sky is only "dripping rain."

ABOUT THE AUTHORS

Jean Toomer (1894–1967) was a leader of the Harlem Renaissance in the 1920s. In 1923, he published *Cane,* a collection of stories, sketches, and poems about Southern black life.

Gwendolyn Bennett (1902–   ) is a well known artist and poet. Her poems have appeared in *The Book of American Negro Poetry* and *The Poetry of the Negro.*

Crime on Mars

ARTHUR C. CLARKE
pp. 330–339

Summary   Danny Weaver almost succeeds in stealing the Siren Goddess—Mars' greatest art treasure—but he makes a crucial mistake about time and is captured. Inspector Rawlings then tries to capture Mr. Maccar, Danny's accomplice, with whom Rawlings is returning to Earth.

BEFORE READING

Write the term *International Date Line* on the chalkboard. Ask students to explain what it means. If they do not know, tell them it is an imaginary line corresponding to 180° longitude. By international agreement, to the east of this line, the calendar date is one day earlier than to the west. This line passes through the Pacific Ocean.

Ask the students to imagine that the International Date Line passes through a city. What problems could it cause? Then have them read this story to find out what problems a burglar has when he tries to plan a crime in a Martian city on the International Date Line. (Flexibility: Setting a Purpose)

Glossary Words

*aboriginal (p. 332, b, 1)
*antiquity (p. 332, a, 5)
*artifact (p. 333, b, 3)
*bas-relief (p. 333, b, 3)
 cleave (p. 334, a, ℓ. 2)
*controversy (p. 332, a, 6)
 crag (p. 330, a, 2)
*discreet (p. 334, b, 5)

*inconspicuous (p. 334, a, ℓ. 15)
*inquisitive (p. 333, b, 2)
 meridian (p. 330, b, 1)
 presumably (p. 330, b, 2)
*reconnoiter
 (reconnoitering, p. 332, b, 3)
 surveillance (p. 334, b, 5)

TEACHING THE GLOSSARY WORDS

Write the glossary words on the chalkboard. Say each word aloud and have the students repeat it after you. Then have them look up the words *aboriginal, antiquity, artifact,* and *bas-relief* and write sentences using these words. Have the students look up the remaining words. Then write the following sentences on the chalkboard and have the students decide which word fits in each blank.

The discovery of the Siren Goddess caused much _____ among scientists. (controversy)

Danny hoped it would be years before some _____, or curious, expert discovered that the real statue had been stolen. (inquisitive)

Danny planned to _____, or check out, the museum on Saturday. (reconnoiter)

Then ask students to find the two words on the list that have closely related meanings (*discreet—inconspicuous*). Have them find the sentences in the story in which these words appear and copy these sentences in their notebooks. (Word Attack: Dictionary, Context)

CHECK TEST

(F)   1. The narrator of this story is Danny Weaver.
(F)   2. The aboriginal Martians are very similar in appearance to human beings.
(T)   3. Danny plans to replace the Siren Goddess with a souvenir replica.
(F)   4. When Danny escapes from the museum, he finds the streets completely empty.
(F)   5. Danny is sentenced to a long jail term on Earth.

AFTER READING

Ask the students to tell when they first suspected Mr. Maccar was Danny's accomplice. What clues led them to believe this? (Inferences)

CLOSE UP (Comprehension Questions)

1. **Inspector Rawlings tells the narrator and Maccar about the crime. Why does he mention the fact that an art collector had paid Danny Weaver to steal the Siren Goddess?** (Inferences)

   Maccar *is* an art collector. The Inspector suspects him and is casually trying to "feel him out."

2. **(a) What is the Siren Goddess?**

   The Siren Goddess is Mars' greatest art treasure. It is a statue of the head of a young woman, slightly Oriental-looking, only eight or nine inches high.

   (b) Why is the statue a puzzle to archeologists? (Relationships: Cause/Effect)

   They cannot explain how "a perfectly human head" dating back to aboriginal times was discovered on Mars: after all, aboriginal Martians "never came near to achieving space flight, and their civilization died before men existed on Earth."

3. **(a) How did Weaver plan to get away with the theft?**

   Weaver planned to hide himself in the museum on Saturday evening, spend all day Sunday removing the Goddess, and leave among the crowd on Monday morning.

   (b) What mistake did he make?

   He didn't realize that since the museum is in the eastern half of the city, it was still Saturday there, a normal working day. (The city is called Meridian City because it is exactly on longitude one hundred eighty degrees. Therefore, the International Date Line runs through it.)

4. **(a) What happens to Weaver?**

   Weaver's "sentence" is to become the night watchman for the museum.

   (b) Why is this ironic, or just the opposite of what he had planned? (Inferences)

   Now it is his job to stop others from attempting to steal any of the museum's treasures.

5. **At the end of the story, why does the narrator think he is going to have an interesting trip home?** (Inferences)

   The cat-and-mouse game between the Inspector and Maccar, who is obviously now under suspicion as the mastermind of the ill-fated operation, will intensify. Probably, Maccar will be arrested.

SETTING (Literature Skill Questions)

1. **How did Meridian City get its name?**

   Meridian City is exactly on longitude one hundred eighty degrees. It is bisected by the International Date Line.

2. **Danny checked into a hotel on Friday afternoon. (a) Where was the hotel located?** (Relationships: Spatial Order)
Danny's hotel was in Meridian West (the western half of the city).
(b) Where was the museum located? (Relationships: Spatial Order)
The museum was in Meridian East (the eastern half of the city).

3. **Why didn't the museum have a night watchman or burglar alarms?**
There aren't such things on Mars because they aren't needed. Every city on Mars is a closed little world beneath the force field that protects it from the freezing near-vacuum outside. That makes law enforcement very easy.

4. **(a) Why was Danny surprised when the museum's doors were unbarred and the staff walked in?** (Relationships: Cause/Effect)
Danny was shocked to see the museum open on what he thought was a Sunday.
(b) How did the location of the museum upset Danny's plan? (Relationships: Spatial Order)
The location of the museum on the eastern side of the International Date Line meant that it was Saturday there. (Therefore the museum was open as usual.)

ADDITIONAL ACTIVITIES

1. Create Martian names for a game like baseball, a tall building, and a school.
2. If a Martian were making his or her first trip to Earth, what would you want him or her to be sure to see?

TEACHING INFERENCES (Reading Skill)

Read the explanatory material aloud while the students read it silently. Ask them if they can name any stories, books, characters, movies, or television programs that are more fantastic than real. Ask them if there are any elements of realism in those stories, books, characters, etc. For example, the Incredible Hulk and Frankenstein's monster wear clothing and come in contact with real people in real settings. Then have them complete the skill exercises and check their answers.

INFERENCES (Reading Skill Exercises)

Making Inferences About Realistic and Fantastic Details

1. **Which of the following sentences contain fantastic details?**
   a. "The ferry rocket that had brought us up from Mars had left ten minutes ago and was now beginning the long fall back to the ocher-tinted globe hanging there against the stars."
   b. "It bore the certificate of the Mars Bureau of Antiquities, guaranteeing that 'this full-scale reproduction is an exact copy of the so-called Siren Goddess, discovered in the Mare Sirenium by the Third Expedition, A.D. 2012 (A.M. 23).'"
   c. "'You know how absolutely dead a Martian city gets on Sunday, when

everything closes down and the colonists stay home to watch the TV from Earth.' "

d. " 'Danny spent the day going over the museum, exactly like any other tourist determined to get his money's worth.' "

e. "I'd been thinking in terms of Earth, forgetting that every city on Mars is a closed little world of its own beneath the force field that protects it from the freezing near-vacuum."

f. " 'He was going to cut through the base of the cabinet and substitute one of those souvenir replicas for the genuine Goddess.' "

g. " 'It took most of the night to slice out the trapdoor, and it was nearly dawn when he relaxed and put down the saw.' "

h. " 'And Gallery Three, which houses the Goddess, is particularly unsettling. It's full of bas-reliefs showing quite incredible animals fighting each other; they look rather like giant beetles, and most paleontologists flatly deny that they could ever have existed.' "

Sentences a, b, c, e, and h contain fantastic details.

2. **Make a list of ten fantastic details in this story.**
   Students' answers will vary.

TEACHING WORD ATTACK

Have the students read the explanatory material in their books and complete the skill exercise. Check their answers.

WORD ATTACK (Exercise)

Using Context Clues

► Use context clues to help you select the correct definition for the *italicized* word in each sentence below.

a. "Although I'd never seen the original, like most departing tourists I had a *replica* in my baggage. It bore the certificate of the Mars Bureau of Antiquities, guaranteeing that 'this full-scale reproduction is an exact copy of the so-called Siren Goddess . . . .' "
   (1) perfect copy of the original

b. "Beyond those electronic shields is the utterly *hostile* emptiness of the Martian Outback, where a man will die in seconds without protection."
   (3) unfriendly; threatening

c. " 'The main item was a *microsaw* no bigger than a soldering iron; it had a wafer-thin blade . . . .' "
   (1) a very small saw

d. " 'Danny set to work on that cabinet as carefully as any diamond cutter preparing to *cleave* a gem.' "
   (2) cut

WORD ATTACK CHECK TEST

▶ Each of the sentences below contains an *italicized* word that is made up. Use context clues to help you determine the meaning of each made-up word.

   a. New Day on Mars is like Christmas on Earth. The children are given *semples* in brightly colored paper to open on New Day morning.
   Semples must be _____.

   b. The Martian week is much like a week on Earth. The first day of each week, *Roaken*, is a holiday for most Martians.
   Roaken must be like _____.

   c. Martians wear heavy *clanders* to protect their feet from the many sharp rocks on Mars.
   Clanders must be _____.

   d. Many Martians enjoy playing a game like poker. They shuffle a deck of *plokars* and deal five *plokars* to each player.
   Plokars must be _____.

   e. Some Martian museums are free. A big sign on the front of these museums says, "No *Blasten*."
   An English word for *blasten* would be _____.

ANSWERS TO WORD ATTACK CHECK TEST

▶ a. gifts or presents
   b. Sunday
   c. shoes or boots

   d. cards
   e. admission charge

ABOUT THE AUTHOR

Arthur C. Clarke (1917–   ) has written almost forty books of fiction and nonfiction. He is a member of several scientific organizations, and, in 1962, he was awarded the Kalinga Prize for science writing by UNESCO. His short story, "The Sentinel," inspired the movie "2001: A Space Odyssey." His short stories are collected in several books, including *The Nine Billion Names of Gods, Childhood's End,* and *Tales of Ten Worlds.*

Avalanche

ROBB WHITE
pp. 341–357

Summary   Thousands of dollars' worth of television cameras and crews are waiting for Marick to ski down the mountain. Because there are signs of an avalanche coming, Scotty, a guide, urges him to turn back. However, Marick is determined to proceed. The avalanche comes, and both get buried alive. Scotty manages to tunnel out of the snow, rescue Marick, and get him back to the village.

BEFORE READING

Write the following quotation on the chalkboard.

"For fools rush in where angels fear to tread."
(Alexander Pope)

Ask the students to discuss what this statement means. Then ask students if they think caution is a virtue. Why or why not? Can a cautious person be brave or is caution synonymous with cowardliness? Why? What is the difference between bravery and foolhardiness? Then have students read "Avalanche" to determine whether Scotty is a brave man or a coward. (Main Idea; Flexibility: Setting a Purpose)

Glossary Words

*aerosol (p. 343, a, 3)
*apprehension (p. 352, b, 2)
*cohesion (p. 348, a, 5)
*consolation (p. 348, b, 2)
*contour (p. 344, a, 7)
*desolate (p. 351, a, 7)
*erupt
   (erupted, p. 346, a, 4)
*fanatical (p. 342, a, 5)
*flail (p. 346, b, 2)
*inevitable (p. 348, b, 1)
*jubilation (p. 347, b, 1)

*mantle (p. 344, a, ℓ. 7)
*monitor
   (monitored, p. 349, b, 5)
*obscure
   (obscured, p. 351, a, ℓ. 4)
*onslaught (p. 347, a, 3)
*porous (p. 350, a, 2)
*precede
   (preceding, p. 350, b, 1)
*profound (p. 347, a, 1)
*terrain (p. 350, b, 1)
*tranquility (p. 342, a, 8)

TEACHING THE GLOSSARY WORDS

Write each of the glossary words on the chalkboard. Say each word aloud and have the students repeat it after you. Then have students look up each word in the glossary in order to prepare for a game of Password.

To play Password follow these steps.
1. Divide the class into two teams.
2. Divide each team into pairs. Each odd-numbered person on each team is the clue-giver in the pair and each even-numbered person is the answerer.
3. Have the first pair from each team start the game. Give a card with one of the glossary words written on it to the clue-giver on both teams.

4. Tell the clue-giver on team A to give a one-word clue to the answerer to help him or her guess the word. If the answerer guesses the word, team A gets 10 points.

5. If the answerer on Team A does not guess the word, the clue-giver on team B gives a one-word clue to his or her partner. If the answerer guesses the word, team B gets 9 points.

6. If the answerer on team B does not guess the word, team A gets another chance for 8 points.

7. Repeat this procedure until someone guesses the word or there are no points left.

8. Then the second pair in each team becomes the contestants. Give them a card containing a new word and have them repeat steps 4–7. (Have team B start the game this time.)

9. Repeat this procedure for each word on the glossary list. The team with the highest score wins. (Word Attack: Dictionary)

CHECK TEST

(F) 1. Scotty has a great deal of respect for Marick.

(F) 2. Scotty persuades Marick to give up his attempt to outrace the avalanche.

(T) 3. The red dust on the gray snow helps Scotty to locate Marick.

(T) 4. When Scotty digs Marick out of the snow, he finds that Marick's leg is broken.

(F) 5. The next morning, several newspapers carry pictures of Marick outskiing the avalanche.

AFTER READING

Marick tells Scotty, "Kid, when you try to accomplish big things, you've got to take big risks." Ask students to discuss whether they agree or disagree with this statement. (Judgments)

CLOSE UP (Comprehension Questions)

1. **(a) Why has Scotty lost respect for Marick?** (Relationships: Cause/Effect)
Scotty feels that Marick is risking his life—and Scotty's—for a trivial reason: fame and publicity. "To get his picture on TV and his name, in small print, in a paperback book of records, this man was climbing straight into an avalanche."
(b) Why is Marick angry with Scotty? (Relationships: Cause/Effect)
Marick hired Scotty as a guide, and he resents Scotty's efforts to make him abandon the project for which he has been planning and training for years.

2. **(a) What signs warn Scotty of the avalanche?** (Inferences)
The vast amount of snow on the mountain, the ten-degree rise in temperature in the last hour, the hot wind, and the sunballs (globes of

snow—some of them the size of basketballs) rolling down the mountain all warn Scotty of an impending avalanche.

(b) How does Marick interpret each of these signs? (Relationships: Comparison/Contrast)

Marick totally disregards all these warning signals. He is chiefly concerned about whether the TV cameras will manage to catch his descent. (Also, he says that the snow is why he is there: this is the first time that there has been enough snow on that mountain for a person to ski down it. In fact, he continues, he *wants* to ski in front of an avalanche.)

3. **(a) Why does Scotty head for the black stone ridge?** (Relationships: Cause/Effect)

When Marick pushes off toward his starting point, Scotty looks for anything that will give him even a little protection from an avalanche. The low black ridge is the only thing he sees that would afford him any measure of safety.

(b) Why does he throw away his ice axes? (Relationships: Cause/Effect)

When the avalanche starts, he throws the axes away because he is afraid they may stab him when the avalanche hits him.

4. **Scotty is able to act with calm and control in the face of impending disaster.**
(a) What does Scotty do to prevent his being buried by the avalanche?

He leaps as high as he can toward the oncoming mass of snow and twists around so that his back faces it. When it hits him, he flails his arms and legs, clawing his way up the face of the snow.

(b) What does he do to keep from being smothered by the snow and ice?

With his arms around his head, he keeps clearing the snow away from his face. In this way, he makes a hole of air around his head.

(c) Find one other instance where his ability to remain calm saves his life.

He talks himself out of being afraid because he realizes that his frantic panting is using up too much air. Once he calms down, he is able to slow his breathing and conserve air. Also, he realizes that even under such dire circumstances, natural laws still apply. By rotating his body, he judges the relative difference in the pressure of the blood in his head and thereby establishes which way to dig. (When the pressure is greatest he is upside down, according to the law of gravity.)

5. **Why does Scotty try to save Marick's life, even though he does not like him?** (Inferences)

"Scotty (cannot) simply walk away from a man buried alive. Not even a man like Marick."

SETTING (Literature Skill Questions)

1. **When the avalanche buries him, Scotty seems to lose all reaction, all feelings.**
(a) How does the "heavy, black, velvety, cold darkness" eventually force him to feel?

It makes him feel afraid.

(b) What does he do to overcome this feeling?

He starts talking to himself, saying "cut it *out!* *Stop* this!"

2. **(a) Why doesn't Scotty know which way to dig in order to get out of his icy grave?** (Relationships: Cause/Effect)

   He is completely encased in snow. He cannot see any light. He doesn't know whether he is facing the sky or the ground or the side.

   (b) How does he find which way is up?

   He rotates until he feels the blood rushing to his head. Then he knows he is facing down, since gravity is causing the increased pressure of the blood in his skull. "Up" is directly opposite.

3. **When Scotty escapes he thinks, "... all I've got to do now is get out of this mess, find my snowmobile, and chug on home." (a) Why does he change his mind and decide to search for Marick?** (Relationships: Cause/Effect)

   He decides to check the line of red dust because he will feel better if he knows that Marick made it.

   (b) How do the red dust and the aerosol canisters help him to locate Marick? (Relationships: Cause/Effect)

   The broken but distinct line of red dust which ends abruptly shows Scotty that Marick must be buried in the vicinity. As Scotty looks for something to use as a marker, he finds the rack of canisters. This tells him that Marick might be buried close by, on a line between the canisters and the summit. He digs a trench along that line and discovers Marick.

4. **At the beginning of the story, Marick called Scotty a "gutless wonder." Do you think Scotty's saving Marick's life proves his courage? Why or why not?** (Judgments)

   Yes, it does, because Scotty risks prolonged exposure to the cold and delays his journey back to safety until it is almost dark in order to find Marick, thus endangering his own life.

TEACHING INFERENCES (Reading Skill)

Have students read the explanatory material in their books and complete the skill exercises. Check their answers.

INFERENCES (Reading Skill Exercises)

Making Inferences About Future Actions and Events

1. **As you read "Avalanche" you might have inferred that Marick was headed for trouble. Which details below helped you make that inference?**
   a. **He was an excellent skier.**
   b. **He was boastful and vain.**
   c. **He was careless.**
   d. **He made fun of Scotty's warnings.**
   e. **He didn't know much about the danger of avalanches.**
   f. **He wore expensive boots.**
   g. **He wanted glory at any risk.**
      b, c, d, e, g

2. **Which of the following details support the inference that Scotty will escape from his snow prison?**

a. Scotty is familiar with mountains and avalanches.
b. Scotty is a strong man.
c. Scotty did not like Marick.
d. Scotty is eighteen years old.
e. Scotty is intelligent and resourceful.
  a, b, e

TEACHING WORD ATTACK

Have the students read the explanatory material in their books. Then ask them to volunteer any compound words they can think of. Write some or all of the compound words they can think of on the chalkboard and draw a line between the component parts. Then have them complete the skill exercises and check their answers.

WORD ATTACK (Exercises)

Understanding Compound Words

1. **First decide which of the following words are compound words. Then, for each compound word, write the two words that make up the larger word.**

   a. **yelled**

   b. **paperback**
   paper back

   c. **outside**
   out side

   d. **thousands**

   e. **overpower**
   over power

   f. **snowfall**
   snow fall

   g. **catapult**

   h. **candlelight**
   candle light

   i. **bombardment**

   j. **basketball**
   basket ball

2. **For each of the compound words above, write an original sentence.**
   Students' sentences will vary.

3. **A snowmobile is a vehicle used for traveling through snow. Use your dictionary to find out how this word was formed.**
   Snowmobile comes from *snow* and *mobile* (movable).

WORD ATTACK CHECK TEST

▶ Identify all the compound words in the sentences below.
   a. The former star was making his second comeback try.
   b. Practically every schoolroom in the United States has a chalkboard.
   c. The seamstress shortened Ramona's hemline.
   d. "Man overboard!" he shouted, but nobody responded to his distress call.
   e. Every mechanic needs two pairs of coveralls.

ANSWERS TO WORD ATTACK CHECK TEST

▶ a. comeback   b. schoolroom, chalkboard

c. hemline

d. overboard, nobody

e. coveralls

ABOUT THE AUTHOR

Robb White sold his first story to *The American Boy* magazine after resigning his commission in the Navy. He rejoined the Navy a short time later, but still managed to write several novels while at sea. Now a captain in the Naval Reserve, he writes television and film scripts. He has published several books, including the popular novel *Up Periscope*, upon which the motion picture was based.

Crow Call

LOIS LOWRY
pp. 358–367

Summary While crow-hunting, the narrator, decked out in her new over-sized plaid hunting shirt, gets reacquainted with her father, who has just returned from war.

BEFORE READING

Write the word *love* on the chalkboard. Tell students there are many types of love. One type is the love between parent and child. Ask students on what factors they think this type of love is based (e.g., trust, acceptance, familiarity). Then have students read "Crow Call" to find out how the father who has been away at war deepens the bond of love between him and his daughter. (Flexibility: Setting a Purpose)

Glossary Words

*addendum
  (addenda, p. 360, a, 6)
arrogantly (p. 361, b, 8)
disdain (p. 360, a, 1)
disgruntle
  (disgruntled, p. 363, b, 6)
dubiously (p. 360, a, 2)
*encounter
  (encountered, p. 361, b, 5)

etch
  (etched, p. 360, b, 7)
*inclusive (p. 359, a, ℓ. 1)
mute
  (muted, p. 363, b, 1)
resolute (p. 363, b, 6)
ruddy (p. 359, b, ℓ. 2)
*speculatively (p. 363, b, 6)
tentatively (p. 363, b, 3)

TEACHING THE GLOSSARY WORDS

Write the glossary words on the chalkboard. Say each word aloud and have the students repeat each word after you. Have students look up the starred words in the glossary. Then write the following sentences on the chalkboard and have students decide which word best fits in each blank.

"I glanced over quickly to see if he was laughing at me, but his smile was _____; I chuckled too, hugging my shirt around me." (inclusive)

"They screamed with harsh voices and I responded, blowing again and again as they flew from the hillside in circles, dipping and soaring, landing _____, lurching from the limbs in afterthought, and then settling again . . . ." (speculatively)

"The diner's menu, grease-spotted and marred with penciled notations and paper-clipped _____, seemed not to include honey." (addenda)

" 'Guess the cows didn't hear it,' I teased him when we _____ silence." (encountered)

Have the students look up the remaining words for homework and write their meanings in their notebooks. (Word Attack: Dictionary Context)

CHECK TEST

(T) 1. The girl's father puts her in charge of the crow call.
(F) 2. The girl wears her father's old army jacket to go hunting.
(T) 3. The girl's favorite thing to eat is cherry pie.
(F) 4. The father teaches his daughter how to shoot crows.
(T) 5. At the end of the story, the girl takes her father's hand.

AFTER READING

Ask students to discuss why they did or did not enjoy this story.

CLOSE UP (Comprehension Questions)

1. **At the beginning of this story, the girl feels awkward with her father.**
(a) Where has he been for the last few years?
Her father has been away at war.
(b) Why does this make him seem like a stranger to her? (Relationships: Cause/Effect)
He doesn't really know her; he hasn't watched her grow up.
2. **The father takes his daughter hunting so that he can get to know her again.**
(a) What reason does he give for buying her a shirt that is too large for her? (Relationships: Cause/Effect)

He jokes that the shirt is a very practical present, since she will never, *ever* outgrow it.

(b) What is his real reason? (Inferences)

His real reason is that she has lingered in front of the sporting-goods store every chance she has had since the hunting shirts appeared. He buys it to please her and to establish a bond between them.

3. **When her father asks her what is her favorite thing to eat, the girl thinks, "If he hadn't been away for so long, he would have known. It was a family joke in a family that hadn't included him." Why do you think the father orders two pieces of cherry pie for his daughter?** (Inferences)

He is trying to please her and show his love. Also, the waitress has mistaken his daughter for a boy—by ordering two pieces of pie for his "hunting companion," he makes a joke out of the waitress's mistake. (This joke does include him.)

4. **(a) How does the daughter feel when the crows answer her call?**

She is thrilled. (She feels they think that she is a crow and their friend.)

(b) Why does the father decide not to shoot the crows? (Inferences)

He realizes how she feels. He will not do anything that will destroy the quality of the experience for her (which is one of identification with nature).

MOOD (Literature Skill Questions)

1. **When the girl wakes up, it is barely light outside and cold for November. (a) Why does her shirt make her feel surrounded by warmth?**

Her thick wool shirt reaches her knees—it literally surrounds her with warmth. The shirt also represents the warmth of her father's love—once he had realized how much she wanted the shirt, he bought it, even though it was actually a man's shirt.

(b) How do the shirt's colors create a happy feeling? (Imagery)

The shirt is a rainbow plaid: rainbows symbolize joy, optimism, and happy endings.

2. **Find three words or phrases that create a vivid picture of the cold November woods. (For example, notice the *italicized* words and phrases in the following sentence: "Grass, *frozen after its summer softness, crunched* under our feet.")** (Imagery)

Students' answers will vary. The following are examples:

". . . our words seemed *etched* and *breakable* on the *brittle* stillness."
". . . even the occasional leaf that fell within our vision did so in silence, *spiraling* slowly down to *blend in brownly* with the others."
"Our breath was *steam*."

3. **When the girl blows the crow call in the cold woods, she feels surrounded by the warmth of friendship. Why?**

The crows communicate with her. She feels as though they think she is one of them—"Maybe (as) their baby, all grown up!"

4. **Sounds are important in creating the mood of this story. Find three sounds that fill the November morning and help create the mood of happiness (for example, the sound of laughter).** (Imagery)

Students' answers will vary. [For example, the girl blows the crow call and the "muted sound of a sleepy crow (comes) as a surprise to (her)." Her father makes sounds imitating cows, tigers, and bears.]

5. **Reread the last paragraph of the story. (a) Find the sentence that describes the November sky.** (Imagery)

"We stood there, he and I, halfway up the November hillside, and the newly up sun was a pink wash across the Pennsylvania sky."

(b) Do you think this image adds to the mood of the story? Why or why not? (Inferences)

Yes. The father and daughter are "halfway up the . . . hillside." This is a positive image—they seem well on their way to a promising future. This notion is reinforced by nature—the sun has just risen; the sky is bathed in pink, a very cheerful color (as in "seeing the world through rose-colored glasses"). The new day is full of hope and promise—it is as if the world is being reborn at early morning.

ADDITIONAL ACTIVITIES

1. Argue for or against the following proposition: Hunting crows should be outlawed.
2. **Composition.** Write a letter from a son or daughter to a father who is overseas during wartime.

TEACHING INFERENCES (Reading Skill)

Have the students read the explanatory material in their books and complete the skill exercises. Check their answers.

INFERENCES (Reading Skill Exercises)

Identifying Valid Inferences

1. **Which of the inferences below were valid and which were not?**
   a. **The father inferred that his younger daughter would love the hunting shirt, even though it was too large.**
   valid
   b. **The waitress inferred that the father was with his son.**
   not valid
   c. **The waitress inferred that the father meant to order two pieces of pie.**
   not valid
   d. **The father inferred that his daughter did not want him to shoot the crows.**
   valid

2. **At the end of the story, the girl infers that her father will shoot the crows sometime in the future. Do you think her inference is valid? Why or why not?**
   Yes, it is, because the crows "would always be there and they would always eat the crops . . . ."

TEACHING WORD ATTACK

Write the following letters on the chalkboard: *khgp*. Ask the students to pronounce them. Explain that they cannot pronounce them because they do not contain a vowel sound. A syllable is a sound unit containing a vowel sound. Let the students construct groups of letters without vowels and try to pronounce them. Then have them read the explanatory material in their books and complete the skill exercise. Check their answers.

WORD ATTACK (Exercise)

Using a Dictionary to Break Words into Syllables

▶ Find the following words in a dictionary and divide them into syllables.

a. **grateful**
   grate ful

b. **dubious**
   du bi ous

c. **enormous**
   e nor mous

d. **memorize**
   mem o rize

e. **waitress**
   wait ress

f. **Pennsylvania**
   Penn syl va ni a

g. **cereal**
   ce re al

h. **companion**
   com pan ion

i. **imitation**
   im i ta tion

j. **brittle**
   brit tle

k. **adolescent**
   ad ol es cent

l. **operate**
   op er ate

m. **inclusive**
   in clu sive

n. **mannequin**
   man ne quin

o. **linger**
   lin ger

p. **practical**
   prac ti cal

q. **notation**
   no ta tion

r. **addendum**
   ad den dum

s. **condescend**
   con de scend

t. **arrogant**
   ar ro gant

WORD ATTACK CHECK TEST

▶ Which of the following groups of letters could be one syllable?

a. ghtr
b. pem
c. appor
d. bro
e. jsxt

f. pendu
g. ful
h. candi
i. dsrg
j. gar

ANSWERS TO WORD ATTACK CHECK TEST

▶ Items b, d, g, and j

ABOUT THE AUTHOR

Lois Lowry is a freelance journalist and photographer and a novelist. Her books include *Find a Stranger, Say Goodbye* and *Autumn Street*. Her first book, *A Summer to Die*, won the International Reading Association's Children's Book Award for the best book written by a new author.

Crows

DAVID McCORD

Haikai II

SADAKICHI HARTMANN

Cynthia in the Snow

GWENDOLYN BROOKS
p. 369

Summary   Three poems describing nature.

BEFORE READING

Explain that the mood of a poem is the impression it creates and the emotions it arouses. Tell students to look for the mood of these three poems as they read. (Mood; Flexibility: Setting a Purpose)

ABOUT THE AUTHORS

David McCord (1897–   ) was the first recipient of the National Council of Teachers of English Award for Excellence in Poetry for Children, 1977. He wrote and published several volumes of poetry, including *The Crows, Bay Window Ballads,* and *Odds Without Ends*. He collected his earlier poems for children in a volume called *One at a Time*. His most recent book of poetry is *Speak Up,* a collection of forty new poems for children. He is the editor of *The Modern Treasury of Humorous Verse.*

Sadakichi Hartmann (1867–1944), a Japanese American, belonged to the bohemian circles of Greenwich Village and, later, of Hollywood. He was a prolific writer whose books include *Conversations with Walt Whitman* (1895); *A History of American Art* (1902); and *Drifting Flowers of the Sea* (1916), a collection of poetry.

Gwendolyn Brooks (1917–   ) won the Pulitzer Prize in 1950 for *Annie Allen*, a collection of poems about a black girl growing up in Chicago. *A Street in Bronzeville* (a nickname for a black section in Chicago) was her first volume of poetry. She wrote all the time as a child, and still has the writing notebooks she kept when she was eleven years old.

One Alaska Night

BARRETT WILLOUGHBY
pp. 371–383

Summary   Lost in the woods one Alaska night, a young girl wanders into a cabin belonging to "Cub Bear" Butler, a crazy trapper who supposedly killed five prospectors. Her troubles begin when she finds outside twelve skeleton hands, all cut off at the wrist. Later that night, when she hears knocking on the door, she fears a ghostly visit.

BEFORE READING

Have students turn to p. 371. Ask one student to read the title of the story and the headnote aloud. Then have them read the story to find out what happens to a young woman who spends a night in the sinister cabin. (Flexibility: Setting a Purpose)

Glossary Words

alternate
  (alternating, p. 380, a, 6)
*carnivorous (p. 371, b, 3)
*consolingly (p. 377, a, 10)
deflate
  (deflated, p. 377, b, 3)

musky (p. 371, b, 2)
*nonchalant (p. 376, b, 5)
peninsula (p. 371, b, 1)
*premonition (p. 371, b, 2)
*rancid (p. 374, a, 4)

TEACHING THE GLOSSARY WORDS

Write the glossary words on the chalkboard. Say each word aloud and have the students repeat it after you. Then have them look up the meaning of each starred word to determine which word best fits in each sentence below.

She had a _____, or forewarning, of death. (premonition)

The Alaskan brown bear is the largest _____, or meat-eating, animal in the world today. (carnivorous)

"You shouldn't be embarrassed," he said _____, "many people have made the same mistake." (consolingly)

She tried to reply in a _____, or casual, manner. (nonchalant)

The butter was so old it had turned _____. (rancid)

CHECK TEST

(T)   1. The narrator is shocked when she learns she has been following a bear's tracks.
(T)   2. Around the chopping block, the narrator finds the skeletons of hands or feet.
(F)   3. It is known as a fact that Bear Cub Butler killed the prospectors.
(F)   4. After she first hears the knocking, the narrator opens the door and sees three flying squirrels.
(F)   5. The narrator made the marks that she finds on the door.

AFTER READING

Ask students to discuss the plots of other stories they have read that have been scary. What elements do these plots have in common?

CLOSE UP (Comprehension Questions)

1. **The young woman who tells this story sets out on a ten-mile hike to her friend's fox ranch. Why does she leave the trail?** (Relationships: Cause/Effect)
She realizes that she has been following a bear trail.

2. **When the woman first sees the cabin, she feels there is something sinister, or evil, about it. (a) What does she find by the chopping block that further frightens her?** (Relationships: Spatial Order)
She finds twelve skeleton hands, all cut off at the wrist.
(b) Why does this discovery convince her that the cabin belongs to Cub Bear Butler? (Relationships: Cause/Effect)
Five prospectors vanished on that peninsula a few years before, and it is rumored that they met foul play at the hands of Cub Bear Butler. The skeleton hands could belong to them (although there are two more than there should be).

3. **In the middle of the night, she is awakened by a thumping on the door.**
(a) What does the woman find when she looks outside?
She finds nothing at all when she looks outside.
(b) Why does this frighten her? (Relationships: Cause/Effect)
It occurs to her that something nonhuman might be trying to get in—that is, some kind of ghost.

4. **In the morning, Dad accuses her of letting her writer's imagination get away**

from her. (a) How does he explain the skeleton hands and the thumping on the door?

Dad says that the skeleton ''hands'' are the paws of bear cubs. The noise, he explains, is made by flying squirrels landing on the roof and bounding down to the eaves.

(b) Why do the marks on the door suggest a different explanation? (Relationships: Cause/Effect)

The marks on the door suggest that someone was knocking the previous night—there are ''depressions on the weathernap of the wood, such as might have been made by the edge of heavily pounding fists.'' (A heavy gale two days before and ''yesterday's sun'' would have obliterated any marks made on the door before the narrator's arrival.)

5. **The woman says that Dad has ''no very high opinion of a woman's ability to take care of herself in the woods.'' Find three instances in this story where the woman proves her competence, or ability.** (Judgments)

She recognizes that she is on a bear trail from a tuft of fur, the musky scent, and an occasional paw print. She manages to escape from a bear and find shelter in a cabin. She realizes that there must be a trail leading from the cabin, which she can follow in the morning. She has a belt ax with her, which she uses both for protection and for chopping an armload of wood. She conquers her quite justifiable fears several times.

MOOD (Literature Skill Questions)

1. **Find two statements that foreshadow, or hint at, the danger to come. (For example, ''Something queerly crawling touched my cheek. I slapped my hand over it, and, with a chill of premonition, looked at what I'd caught—a long tuft of coarse brown hair dangling from a twig above.'')** (Inferences)

Students' answers will vary. The following are examples:

''I was running toward this refuge with all the speed left in me when something in the look of the place caused me to slow up . . . . There was something distinctly sinister in the very quality of the silence that hung over the cabin—a feeling as if death brooded there.''

''The first thing that popped into my mind was the story of five prospectors who, a few years before, had vanished on this peninsula without leaving a trace. Rumor had it that they had met foul play at the hands of a crazy trapper—'Cub Bear' Butler.''

2. **Make a list of details that add to the mood of terror. (For example, darkness.)** (Imagery)

Students' answers will vary. (For example, sounds: although no one is at the door, the woman hears ''a faint rustling, as of a loose garment brushing against the rough log wall outside.'')

3. **The author uses body signals to indicate terror. (For example, ''I chilled to the pit of my stomach . . . .'') Find three other body signals that indicate terror.** (Inferences)

Students' answers will vary. The following are examples:

"In that instant of realization all my strength seemed to ooze out of me. Then panic came upon me."

"My brain went into a sickening tailspin. I tried to scream, but could make no sound. I tried to run, but my legs seemed turned to water."

"But I was hollow with dread."

"I was startled to find I had spoken aloud."

"Then goose flesh broke out all over me."

4. **Make a list of descriptive words and phrases that help create terror. (For example, the author describes the meadow as "a meadow of the dead.") (Imagery)**

Students' answers will vary. The following are examples:

"The boarded windows . . . stared back at me like eye sockets in a brown and weathered skull."

". . . my groping fingers touched something which made me recoil so violently that all my wood fell to the ground."

". . . the summons was curiously muffled, as if the visitor were rapping not with firm knuckles, but with——I shoved the horrible thought from me."

"It was like the fleshy stub of an arm hammering on wood."

ADDITIONAL ACTIVITIES

1. **Composition.** Write a brief account of a time you were scared half to death.
2. Create a different title for this story.
3. Make a list of items you would want to carry with you if you took a ten-mile hike in the Alaskan wilderness in summer.

TEACHING INFERENCES (Reading Skill)

Have the students read the explanatory material in their books and complete the skill exercises. Check their answers.

INFERENCES (Reading Skill Exercises)

Making Inferences About Past Events

1. **The woman makes several inferences about past events. Find evidence that supports each of these inferences.**
   a. **No one had opened the door of the cabin for many months.**
      The latch thong was curled up into a hard, dry knot.
   b. **The skeleton hands were the hands of the five missing prospectors and one other person.**
      There were twelve skeleton hands that looked human.
   c. **The cabin had belonged to a trapper.**
      It smelled as if raw furs had been dried in it.
   d. **The cabin had been abandoned.**
      The door had not been used for some time.

e. **The meadow was the site of foul murders.**
   There were ax marks and skeletons in the area.

2. **Which two inferences above are not valid; that is, do not turn out to be true? What evidence had the woman overlooked?**
   Inferences b and e are not valid. She overlooked the fact that the skeleton of a bear cub's paw is similar to that of a human hand.

TEACHING WORD ATTACK

Have the students read the explanatory material in their books. Ask them to create a simile. Give them one or both of the following incomplete sentences to work with:

The soup was as cold as _____.

The running fullback was like _____.

Then have them complete the skill exercise and check their answers.

WORD ATTACK (Exercise)

Understanding Similes
▶ **Find the simile in each sentence below. Then tell what two objects are being compared.**
   a. **"All along it, evenly spaced in the damp, brown mold, were deep depressions, round and large as dinner plates."**
   depressions and dinner plates
   b. **"The boarded windows on each side of the closed door stared back at me like eye sockets in a brown and weathered skull."**
   windows and eye sockets
   c. **"I tried to convince myself that the knocking had been born of my overwrought nerves when——*Thump! . . . Thump-thump-thump! Thump! . . . Thump-thump-thump!* It was like the fleshy stub of an arm hammering on wood."**
   thumping and the stub of an arm hammering
   d. **" 'I told you she'd be cool as a cucumber!' "**
   she and a cucumber

WORD ATTACK CHECK TEST

▶ Find the simile in each sentence below. Then tell what two objects are being compared.
   a. The night was as dark as the ocean bottom.
   b. An angry bear can be as persistent as a hornet.
   c. The meadow was like a playground for the mad trapper.
   d. Like guards, the tall trees stood guard around the meadow.
   e. The flying squirrels were like tiny battering rams.

ANSWERS TO WORD ATTACK CHECK TEST

▶ a. The simile is "as dark as the ocean bottom"; a night and the ocean bottom are being compared.
b. The simile is "as persistent as a hornet"; a bear and a hornet are being compared.
c. The simile is "like a playground for the mad trapper"; a meadow and a playground are being compared.
d. The simile is "Like guards"; trees and guards are being compared.
e. The simile is "like tiny battering rams"; flying squirrels and battering rams are being compared.

ABOUT THE AUTHOR

Barrett Willoughby grew up on her father's trading schooner, cruising the Alaskan coastline. She gathered material for her novels from the traders, trappers, explorers, Indians, and scientists who frequented her father's trading post. She was the first native Alaskan to write about her home state.

The Night the Ghost Got In

JAMES THURBER
pp. 384–391

Summary　In this humorous tale, pandemonium breaks loose when a family hears footsteps in the middle of the night and calls in the police. The grandfather, who believes he is still fighting the Civil War, thinks that the policemen are deserters from Meade's army and shoots one of them.

BEFORE READING

Ask the students to describe their favorite humorous television show. Help them to specify the elements in the show that make it humorous. (For example, the appearance of the characters, the gestures, the dialogue, the surprise endings.) Then read the first two paragraphs of the story aloud while they read them silently. Have them finish the story.

Glossary Words

advent (p. 384, a, 1)   beveled (p. 386, b, ℓ. 5)

cadence
(cadenced, p. 384, a, 2)
commendably (p. 386, a, 2)
despondent (p. 384, b, 1)
froth
(frothing, p. 386, a, 1)
hullabaloo (p. 384, a, 1)
incomparable (p. 385, b, 4)

indignant (p. 388, a, ℓ. 6)
interval (p. 384, a, 2)
intervene (p. 387, b, ℓ. 5)
ransack (p. 386, b, 2)
rend
(rending, p. 386, b, ℓ. 6)
wispy (p. 388, a, 1)

TEACHING THE GLOSSARY WORDS

Write the glossary words on the chalkboard. Say each word aloud and have the students repeat it after you. Have the students select one word from the glossary list, look it up, and use the word in an original sentence. Then have the students compare the words they selected and the sentences they wrote. (Word Attack: Dictionary, Context)

CHECK TEST

(F) 1. James finds that the footsteps belong to his grandfather.
(T) 2. Mother throws a shoe through her next-door neighbor's window.
(F) 3. When the police come, they immediately find the burglars.
(T) 4. Grandfather, thinking the police officer is a deserter, takes his gun and shoots him.
(F) 5. The next morning, Grandfather captures the real burglar.

AFTER READING

Tell students that people often create humor by exaggerating. Have them find examples of exaggeration in this story. Then have them bring in jokes that contain exaggeration.

CLOSE UP (Comprehension Questions)

1. **When the narrator first hears the footsteps, he thinks they might belong to his father or brother returning from Indianapolis. What does he finally realize the footsteps are?**
He claims that the footsteps belong to a ghost.

2. **The narrator and his brother Herman do not want to alarm their mother, but she has heard the footsteps also. To whom does she think they belong?**
She thinks they belong to a burglar.

3. **The mother wants to call the police, but the telephone is downstairs. (a) Why is she afraid to go downstairs?**
She fears that the burglar may harm anyone who goes downstairs.
(b) How does she signal her neighbors to call the police? (Relationships: Cause/ Effect)

Instead of telephoning, she whams a shoe through the neighbors' window and shouts "Burglars! Burglars in the house!"

4. **(a) Why does Grandfather think the police are deserters from Meade's army?** (Relationships: Cause/Effect)

Grandfather is going through a phase in which he believes that General Meade's men, under steady hammering by Stonewall Jackson, are beginning to retreat and even desert. (In other words, he is reliving the Civil War.)

(b) How does he manage to expel them from the attic? (Relationships: Cause/Effect)

He smacks one officer alongside his head, sending him sprawling. Then he grabs the policeman's gun from its holster and fires, wounding another officer in the shoulder and filling the attic with smoke. The narrator and the police retreat downstairs and lock the attic door.

5. **The police are reluctant to leave without taking somebody into custody since they do not like the "layout." What things might seem strange to them?** (Inferences)

Several things might seem strange to them. The doors and windows are all locked; in fact, the police have to break into the house in order to enter, since no one will go downstairs to answer the door when they arrive. Also the narrator is wearing only a towel. The police consider his outfit a bit odd. They find it odder still when he dons his mother's blouse (the only thing handy) and identifies the zither as "an old zither our guinea pig used to sleep on."

6. **(a) What does Grandfather ask the narrator and his brother at breakfast?**

Grandfather demandingly asks, "What was the idee of all them cops tarryhootin' round the house last night?"

(b) Why does this surprise them?

"Grandfather was fresh as a daisy and full of jokes at breakfast"—the family assumed he had forgotten all about what had happened. (Not only hasn't he forgotten, he even realizes that the men were policemen—not deserters from Meade's army.)

MOOD (Literature Skill Questions)

1. **In the opening paragraph of the story, Thurber briefly recounts the events of the night the ghost got in his house. What feeling does the opening paragraph help create?** (Imagery)

The opening paragraph creates an immediate feeling of whimsy and humor.

2. **(a) What has Herman always suspected would happen in the night?**

He has "always half suspected that something would 'get him' in the night."

(b) What kind of picture does this give of Herman? (Imagery)

This suggests Herman is somewhat eccentric.

3. **How do the mother's actions, especially in the scene about the shoe, help create the mood of the story?** (Inferences)

The narrator's mother seems to be slightly wacky—in particular, after throwing the shoe, she wants to throw another because the thrill of it has "enormously taken her fancy." Her ludicrous behavior adds to the humor.

4. **Without the strange collection of characters that make this a humorous story, the events would not have happened. How does Grandfather's character help add to the humorous mood?** (Inferences)

In his long flannel nightgown, long woolen underwear, nightcap, and leather jacket, Grandfather is the "last straw" in this embattled family. His delusion that he is in the midst of the Civil War caps the story and creates the most comic moment in the story.

ADDITIONAL ACTIVITIES

1. **Composition.** Write a note to James Thurber telling him why you did or did not enjoy reading his story.
2. If you had the talent and skill to be a professional writer, what kind of material would you like to write? Explain your answer.
3. Make a list of topics you think could be written about with humor—for example, a student's first day in high school.

TEACHING INFERENCES (Reading Skill)

Have the students read the explanatory material in their books. Then ask them to identify a topic they would like to write about if they were professional writers (for example, school, television, sports, politics, the economy, automobile safety, crime). For each topic they select, ask them what tone they would try to achieve (for example, lighthearted, serious, angry, sarcastic). Finally, have them complete the skill exercise and check their answers.

INFERENCES (Reading Skill Exercise)

Making Inferences About Tone

► **Which of the items below set an amused tone for "The Night the Ghost Got In"? Two do not set this tone.**
  a. "Its advent caused my mother to throw a shoe through a window of the house next door and ended up with my grandfather shooting a patrolman."
  b. "... grandfather was in the attic, in the old walnut bed which once fell on my father."
  c. "They were the steps of a man walking rapidly around the dining-room table downstairs."
  d. "... I tiptoed to Herman's room. 'Psst!' I hissed, in the dark, shaking him. 'Awp,' he said, in the low, hopeless tone of a despondent beagle ...."
  e. "I stepped back onto the landing."
  f. "Bodwell was at the window in a minute, shouting, frothing a little, shaking his fist."
  g. "They caught me standing in my towel at the top."
  h. "He bounded out of bed wearing a long flannel nightgown over long woolen underwear, a nightcap, and a leather jacket around his chest."

i. " 'What was the idee of all them cops tarryhooten' round the house last
night?' "
Items a, b, d, f, g, h, and i

TEACHING WORD ATTACK

Read the explanatory material in the students' book aloud while they read it
silently. Then have the students do items 1a and 1b in the skill exercise and
explain their answers. Have them complete the rest of the skill exercise and
check their answers.

WORD ATTACK (Exercise)

Understanding Figurative Expressions

▶ Which of the items below contain figurative expressions and which do not?
  a. " 'Nothing,' he said, gruffly, but he was, in color, a light green."
  b. "Bodwell was at the window in a minute, shouting, frothing a little, shaking
     his fist."
  c. "Bodwell at first thought that she meant there were burglars in his house
     . . . ."
  d. " 'You haven't a stitch on,' she pointed out. 'You'd catch your death.' "
  e. "Their lights played all over the living room and crisscrossed nervously in
     the dining room, stabbed into hallways, shot up the front stairs and finally
     up the back."
  f. " 'All ya windows and doors was locked on the inside tight as a tick.' "
  g. "Police were all over the place . . . ."
  h. "They all nodded, but said nothing, just looked at me."
  i. "They began to poke into things again."
  j. "He gazed at me a long time as if I were a slot machine into which he had,
     without results, dropped a nickel."
  Items a, b, d, e, f, g, i, and j contain figurative expressions; items c and h
  do not.

WORD ATTACK CHECK TEST

▶ Identify the figurative expressions in the sentences below.
  a. Jose's sister was as beautiful as a bouquet of freshly picked flowers as she
     stood at the top of the steps.
  b. The waves pounded out a message on the beach that said, "Be careful if you
     try to swim in the ocean today."
  c. The truck, fully loaded, thundered down the highway and across county line
     after county line.
  d. Every line of the letter was dripping with sugar.
  e. The Green Bay Packers were soundly spanked by the Dallas Cowboys.

ANSWERS TO WORD ATTACK CHECK TEST

▶ a. as beautiful as a bouquet of freshly picked flowers

b. pounded out a message
c. thundered down
d. dripping with sugar
e. were spanked

ABOUT THE AUTHOR

Over a thirty-year period, James Thurber, long considered one of the finest American humorists, created hundreds of short stories, essays, and articles for *The New Yorker* magazine. In addition to his talent for writing, Thurber also was a gifted cartoonist. His drawings and stories, collected in the books *My World and Welcome to It, The Middle-Aged Man on the Flying Trapeze,* and *The Beast in Me and Other Animals,* are populated with people attempting to cope with one another and the world at large. Thurber also wrote several children's books, including *The White Deer* and *The Thirteen Clocks.* Both are considered classics.

REVIEW QUIZ

ON THE SELECTIONS

p. 392

1. **In "Beware of the Dog," why does the nurse hide her nationality from Peter?** (Inferences)
   It is essential that Peter believe he is in England if the Germans are to extract useful information from him.

2. **Why is Peter confused when the nurse complains about the hardness of the water?** (Relationships: Cause/Effect)
   He recalls that the water in Brighton is soft.

3. **In "Otero's Visitor," why doesn't Otero tell the three armed men about his visitor?** (Inferences)
   He is "a Spanish gentleman—a caballero!"—he honors the wish of his visitor to "hide (the box) carefully and tell no one!"

4. **At the beginning of "Back There," Corrigan is described as a skeptic. How has he changed by the end of the play?** (Relationships: Comparison/Contrast)
   He believes that if you go back into the past you can change some things. (" . . . the threads of history are woven tightly and the skein of events cannot be undone; but, on the other hand, there are small fragments of tapestry that *can* be altered.")

5. **When does Corrigan learn Wellington's true identity?** (Relationships: Time Order)

He notices the initials J.W.B. on Wellington's handkerchief and realizes that Wellington is really John Wilkes Booth.

6. **In "Crime on Mars," why is Rawlings returning to Earth?** (Inferences)
He says the chief reason is because there is little crime on Mars. ("If I stayed here much longer, I'd get completely out of practice.") His real reason is that he's hoping to arrest Mr. Maccar, the art dealer.

7. **In "Avalanche," who is more cautious—Scotty or Marick?** (Relationships: Comparison/Contrast)
Scotty is more cautious. (He wants to turn back as soon as he sees the sunballs—sure signs of an avalanche.)

8. **In "Crow Call," why does the father put the girl "in charge of the crow call"?** (Inferences)
He says it's an art and he's sure she can do it. (She has never gone hunting before and doesn't know what to do. He makes her feel useful and important by putting her in charge of the crow call.)

9. **At the beginning of "One Alaska Night," the woman feels "a chill of premonition." This premonition—or look into the future—warns her of what creature?**
It warns her of an Alaskan brown bear—"the largest carnivorous animal that walks the world today." (She has been following a bear trail.)

10. **In "The Night the Ghost Got In," what event begins the confusion?** (Relationships: Time Order)
The narrator hears footsteps in the night.

ON INFERENCES

p. 393

1. **(a) In "Beware of the Dog," how do you think the nurse feels when Peter says he heard a Junkers 88 overhead?**
She probably is apprehensive.
(b) Why would she feel this way?
Peter might realize that he is in enemy territory (France). The Germans might not gain any information from him.

2. **Find three details in "Otero's Visitor" that tell you the family is prosperous.**
Students' answers will vary. (Examples: the Oteros were a noble family— "Many sons there were with much gold claimed from conquest . . . ." The hacienda is beautifully furnished with possessions the family had brought from Spain. They have lace curtains at the windows and "the highest of luxuries, an organ," in the long living room. They have two servants. Don Otero's jacket is trimmed in black satin. He is a caballero, or Spanish gentleman.)

3. **Find three details in "Crime on Mars" that tell you this story takes place in the future.**
Students' answers will vary. (Examples: the theft occurs on Mars. Interplanetary travel is common. Mars is covered with a force field that makes it habitable. The thief uses a *microsaw* driven by an ultrasonic powerpack to cut through the base of the cabinet.)

4. In "Avalanche," when Scotty is buried alive, how does he infer which way is up?

He rotates his body until the blood pressure in his head is the greatest—he then knows that, according to the law of gravity, his feet point toward the surface.

5. In "One Alaska Night," what inference does the woman make when she wakes and hears a pounding on the door?

She infers that someone is knocking to get in. (Also, she infers that the caller is a ghost: "I knew that anyone knocking at this hour of the night would identify himself—unless he were a——")

ON LITERATURE SKILLS

p. 393

▶ Decide whether the following statements are true or false.

a. The setting of "Beware of the Dog" is Brighton during World War II.
   false

b. All the events in "Otero's Visitor" take place during one day.
   false

c. The setting of a story can affect its plot.
   true

d. The mood of a story is the impression it creates and the emotions it arouses in the reader.
   true

e. "Back There" creates a mood of humor.
   false

BEFORE GOING ON

p. 395

How People Flew Before Airplanes Were Invented

ROBERT MILLER
pp. 397–401

Summary   This fascinating article describes forerunners of the airplane.

BEFORE READING

Ask for one or more volunteers to sketch a hot-air balloon on the chalkboard.

Ask also for someone to tell how hot-air balloons function or how they would guess they function. Tell them to read this selection to learn more about balloons. (Flexibility: Setting a Purpose)

Glossary Words

*diplomat (p. 397, a, 2)   *gondola (p. 398, b, 1)

TEACHING THE GLOSSARY WORDS

Write the words *diplomat* and *gondola* on the chalkboard. Have the students look up their meanings and tell how they think the words might be used together in the selection.

TEACHING FLEXIBILITY (Reading Skill)

Read the explanatory material in the book aloud while the students read it silently. Urge students to ask questions and request clarification if they are having trouble following the concepts that are presented. Then have them complete the skill exercise and check their answers.

FLEXIBILITY (Reading Skill Exercise)

Outlining

▶ After you finish reading "How People Flew Before Airplanes Were Invented," copy the outline below on a separate piece of paper. Then fill in the missing subtopics and specific information about these subtopics.

I. The history of balloons
   A. Hot-air balloons
      1. Made by Étienne and Joseph Montgolfier
      2. Worked on principle that hot air rises
   B. Hydrogen balloons
      1. Contained gas that is lighter than air
      2. Could lift more weight than hot-air baloons of the same size
II. The history of zeppelins
   A. The first zeppelins
      1. Had two gondolas below the cylinder
      2. Had engines located at the rear
   B. The Graf Zeppelin
      1. Established regular service between Europe and the Americas
      2. Carried scientific expedition into the Arctic
   C. Reasons why zeppelins lost popularity
      1. Crashes of *Hindenburg* and other dirigibles
      2. Fear of using hydrogen
III. The uses of balloons today

A. In outer-space research
B. In weather research
C. In transportation
Accept any similar answers.

Reading Skills Unit Test (Vistas)

1. **What is the best inference you can make from each of the following passages?**
   a. "A root tripped me and threw me flat in the trail that led through the blueberry thicket. For a moment I was too tired to stir. I lay there, face on my arms, feeling that I'd been foolhardy to start out alone on a ten-mile hike across an unfamiliar peninsula."
      (1) The narrator will meet a friend.
      (2) The narrator may be headed for trouble.
      (3) The narrator has a broken leg from the fall.
         (2)
   b. "Suddenly, nose to the ground, I became aware of a rank, musky odor that brought my head up with a jerk. Something queerly crawling touched my cheek. I slapped my hand over it, and, with a chill of premonition, looked at what I'd caught—a long tuft of coarse brown hair dangling from a twig above."
      (1) A brown bear is in the area.
      (2) It is illegal to hunt bears in the area.
      (3) There are many different kinds of wild animals in the area.
         (1)
   c. "And then I paused to stare at a murky clump which I hoped was only bushes. The clump, big as a truck horse, started toward me. It kept coming, slowly, heavily, swinging a great, low head. Brush rattled under its shambling tread. I smelled the rank, musty odor of bear."
      (1) The murky clump is a truck horse.
      (2) The murky clump is a huge bush.
      (3) The murky clump is a bear.
         (3)
2. **Which of the following inferences can you make from the passage below?**
      "It was morning, early, barely light, cold for November. I was nine and the war was over. At home, in the bed next to mine, my older sister still slept, adolescent, her blond hair streaming over the edge of the sheet. I sat shyly in the front seat of the car next to the stranger who was my father, my blue-jeaned legs pulled up under the too-large wool shirt I was wearing, making a bosom of my knees.
      'Daddy,' I said, the title coming uncertainly, 'I've never gone hunting before. What if I don't know what to do?' "
   a. The girl's sister is not going hunting.
   b. The girl's father has recently returned from the war.
   c. The girl's father is wounded.

d. The girl's father has not been home long.

e. The girl's sister is sick.

f. The girl's father is going hunting.

g. The girl is not used to calling this man "Daddy."

h. Early morning is the best time for hunting whatever they are hunting.

a, b, d, f, g, and h

3. Make an inference about how the character described in each passage below feels.

a. "In that instant of realization all my strength seemed to ooze out of me."
   (1) weak
   (2) angry
   (3) amused
      (1)

b. "There was something distinctly sinister in the very quality of the silence that hung over the cabin—a feeling as if death brooded there."
   (1) angry
   (2) uneasy
   (3) unhappy
      (2)

c. " 'Just you watch me, lady,' I answered in a deep, I thought boyish, voice, pulling my face into stern, serious lines. We laughed again, driving out into the gray-green hills of the early morning."
   (1) afraid
   (2) nervous
   (3) happy
      (3)

d. "I tried not to laugh, wanting to do rabbits next, but couldn't keep from it. He looked so funny with his neck pulled away from his shirt collar and a condescending, poised, giraffe look on his face."
   (1) fearful
   (2) amused
   (3) suspicious
      (2)

e. "I blew the crow call once more, to say good morning and goodbye and everything that goes in between. Then I put it into the pocket of my shirt and reached over out of my enormous cuffs and took my father's hand. We stood there, he and I, halfway up the November hillside, and the newly up sun was a pink wash across the Pennsylvania sky. The brown grass and curled leaves were thick around our feet, and above our heads the air was filled with the answering sound of the circling crows."
   (1) miserable
   (2) contented
   (3) amused
      (2)

4. Which of the passages below contain fantastic details?

a. "The man hesitated, as if weighing on his mind whether to inform Reyes of the purpose of his visit."

b. "He sat stooped over in his chair toward the fire, in a disconsolate manner."

c. "The (ghost's) footsteps had walked over to the organ, and stopped."

d. "As Reyes stood (alone) in the room and looked about him, his eyes saw a small panel in the leg of the organ slide softly shut."

e. "The wind from the entrance blew the door open leading to the patio, and the curtains parted as if someone walked through them and closed them gently."

c, d, and e

5. Which of the following sentences allow you to infer that the character described is going to have trouble in the near future?

a. "The truth came with a shock—I had been following a bear trail! It was already getting dark, and I was unarmed."

b. "Almost at once the bushes thinned out, and I was able to make good time through stretches of short ferns . . . ."

c. "Oddly, it was only now, when I was safely away from the bear trail, that it dawned on me that I had no idea which way to go."

d. "The sensible thing to do now was build a fire and then eat a sandwich."

e. "I don't know what awakened me; but suddenly I found myself sitting bolt upright, heart pounding, ears straining."

a, c, and e

6. Below each of the following passages are three inferences. Identify the one that is valid.

a. "To get his picture on TV and his name, in small print, in a paperback book of records, this man was climbing straight into an avalanche."

   (1) The man loves glory.
   (2) The man will die.
   (3) The man is a TV star.
      (1)

b. "Scotty, whose entire life had been influenced by the daily—even hourly—moods and changes, the violence and tranquility of this mountain, was appalled by this outsider's lack of understanding of the warning the mountain was giving them."

   (1) The man with Scotty has never climbed a mountain before.
   (2) Scotty knows more about this mountain than the man does.
   (3) Scotty knows more about this mountain than anyone else does.
      (2)

c. "And, slowly, the terrifying sound of it faded away: that sound replaced by a profound, heavy silence."

   (1) The avalanche is over.
   (2) Scotty will never be caught in another avalanche.
   (3) This is the only avalanche Scotty was ever caught in.
      (1)

d. " . . . the darkness was absolute. There was no light of any kind; just a heavy, black, velvety, cold darkness."

   (1) The sun is shining on the mountaintop.

(2) Scotty is completely buried in the snow.

(3) Scotty will freeze to death.

  (2)

e. "His mind, affected by the growing poison of the air he was breathing, began to drift . . . ."

(1) Scotty is not very intelligent.

(2) Scotty should shout for help.

(3) The shortage of clean air is affecting Scotty's thinking.

  (3)

7. Which of the following passages allow you to make inferences about past events?

a. "My fingers, absently exploring the stump's broad top, felt a crosshatch of ax marks."

b. "I slapped my hand over it, and, with a chill of premonition, looked at what I'd caught—a long tuft of coarse brown hair dangling from a twig above."

c. "I looked closely at the path leading forward under the leafy tunnel in which I lay."

d. "Beyond those electronic shields is the utterly hostile emptiness of the Martian Outback, where a man will die in seconds without protection."

e. " 'Yes, young man. Which army *were* you in?' "

 a, b, d, and e

8. Match each passage below with the tone in which it is written.

a. "The ghost that got into our house on the night of November 17, 1915, raised such a hullabaloo of misunderstandings that I am sorry I didn't just let it keep on walking, and go to bed."

b. "Then panic came upon me. I had a senseless, almost uncontrollable impulse to dash madly through the trees . . . ."

c. " 'What about the people who put Danny up to it? There must have been a lot of money behind him. Did you get them?' "

d. "But there was something a little uneasy about her eyes. They were never still. They never looked at anything for more than a moment, and they moved too quickly from one place to another in the room."

e. "Don't get lost back in time now, Corrigan."

(1) suspicious

(2) humorous

(3) sarcastic

(4) excited

(5) mysterious

a. (2)

b. (4)

c. (5)

d. (1)

e. (3)

9. Fill in the missing words in the incomplete sentences below.

a. When you outline, you organize the important information. To do this you

_____ and then _____ the information.

divide   subdivide

b. **A topic is not a complete _____.**

sentence

c. **A major topic is indicated by _____.**

a roman numeral

d. **A subtopic is indicated by _____.**

a capital letter

e. **Specific information about each subtopic is indicated by _____.**

an Arabic numeral

MOSAIC

SELECTION	TYPE	LITERATURE SKILL	READING SKILL	WORD ATTACK SKILL
On the Edge by Robert Russell pp. 404–411	fiction	Theme. Understanding what a character learns as a key to theme	Main Idea. Finding topic sentences	Context. Understanding words used as nouns and verbs
My First Life Line by Maya Angelou pp. 413–421	non-fiction	Theme. Understanding significant statements as a key to theme	Main Idea. Distinguishing between the topic and the main idea	Imagery. Understanding vivid compound words
Portrait of a Neighbor by Edna St. Vincent Millay *Who Am I?* Miguel Leon-Portilla (An Aztec Poem) pp. 422–423	poetry	Poetry. Understanding tone		
Mike and the Grass by Erma Bombeck pp. 424–427	fiction	Reading an anecdote		
The Little Lizard's Sorrow by Mai Vo-Dinh pp. 428–435	fiction	Theme. Understanding symbols as a key to theme	Main Idea. Finding supporting details	Meaning. Finding synonyms
The Baroque Marble by E. A. Proulx pp. 437–449	fiction	Theme. Understanding symbols as keys to theme	Main Idea. Finding implied main ideas	Figurative Language. Understanding comparisons

SELECTION	TYPE	LITERATURE SKILL	READING SKILL	WORD ATTACK SKILL
Where the Sidewalk Ends by Shel Silverstein pp. 450–451	poetry	Poetry. Understanding imagery		
Review Quiz pp. 452–453				
Composition. Exposition p. 454				
Before Going On p. 454			Flexibility and Main Idea. Skimming for main ideas	
Further Reading *Gifts of the Indians* by C. Fayne Porter pp. 456–461	non-fiction			

On the Edge

ROBERT RUSSELL
pp. 404–411

Summary Frank Summers goes mountain climbing alone and falls onto a ledge. Using his shoe as a weight and cut-up strips from his jeans as rope, he manages to wedge the shoe into a crack in the mountain and climb to safety.

BEFORE READING

George Bernard Shaw once wrote, "Independence? that's blasphemy. We are all dependent on one another, every soul of us on earth." Ask students if they agree or disagree with this statement. Why? Then have students read "On the Edge" to find out what Frank learns about depending on others. (Main Idea; Flexibility: Setting a Purpose)

Glossary Word

*pendulum (p. 404, b, 1)

TEACHING THE GLOSSARY WORD

Write the glossary word on the chalkboard. Say this word aloud and have the students repeat it after you. Have the students look up the meaning of the glossary word. Then have them write an original sentence for it, and read their sentence aloud. (Word Attack: Dictionary, Context)

CHECK TEST

(F) 1. Frank falls over thirty feet down to a ledge.
(T) 2. Frank wishes he had a partner with a rope.
(T) 3. Frank cuts his pants into strips in order to use them as a rope.
(F) 4. Frank is unable to jam his shoe in the rock.
(F) 5. At the end of this story, Frank is rescued by Mr. Johnson.

AFTER READING

At the end of this story, Frank is filled with a new sense of how beautiful life is, and how dangerous. Ask students if they think danger heightens the experience of living. Why or why not? (Judgments)

CLOSE UP (Comprehension Questions)

1. What does Frank want to prove to himself by going into the mountains alone?

He thinks he'll prove that he is a man. [He feels that "sometimes a man (needs) to be alone."]

2. **(a) Why is Frank afraid to look down from the ledge?** (Relationships: Cause/Effect)

   The ledge is only eighteen inches wide. If Frank looks down he might get dizzy or panicked and fall.

   (b) What does he plan to do first? (Relationships: Time Order)

   He plans to inch his way to a wider part of the ledge where he can sit down, calm himself, and work out a plan of action.

3. **After Frank overcomes his first fears, he understands why Mr. Johnson had said that no one should go into the mountains alone. How would having a partner have helped Frank?**

   With a partner, Frank easily could have ascended the twelve feet. (A partner would have a rope. He could secure one end of the rope and pass the other end to Frank.)

4. **(a) Since Frank is without a rope or any of his gear, what does he use to save himself?**

   Frank uses his knife to cut his jeans into long, even strips. He knots the strips together, ties a shoe to one end of his new "line," and throws the shoe up the face of the cliff and wedges it into a crack. Then he climbs to safety.

   (b) What does this show about Frank's ability to think under pressure? (Inferences)

   It shows that Frank can think clearly under pressure. (Instead of giving in to his initial panic, Frank cooly evaluates the situation and finds a logical solution to his problem.)

THEME (Literature Skill Questions)

1. **Frank feels he has to prove he is a man. When he disregards Mr. Johnson's advice, do you think his behavior is more like a boy's than a man's? Why?** (Judgments)

   Students' answers will vary. Most should see that Frank is acting like a boy—an adult would take an expert's advice.

2. **After Frank falls from the cliff, why does he wish another person were with him?** (Relationships: Cause/Effect)

   A partner would have a rope and could help him climb the twelve feet to the top with little or no problem.

3. **Frank is filled with mixed emotions as he lies gasping on the edge of the slope. (a) Why does he feel shame?** (Relationships: Cause/Effect)

   He cried when he first reached the slope. He feels shame because he considers crying a weakness—especially in himself, Frank Summers, the school push-up champion. (Also, he now understands how foolish he was to ignore Mr. Johnson's advice about going into the mountains alone.)

   (b) What does this experience teach him about needing people?

   It dispels his notion that "sometimes a man (needs) to be alone." It teaches him that needing others is a strength, not a weakness, in a man.

4. **Which of the following statements best expresses the theme of this story?**
   a. **Needing other people can be a strength, rather than a weakness.**
   b. **People have to learn how to get along without help from anyone else.**
   c. **Climbing mountains can be dangerous.**
   Statement a best expresses the theme.

ADDITIONAL ACTIVITY

▶ Create a different title for this story.

TEACHING MAIN IDEA (Reading Skill)

Have the students read the explanatory material in their books and complete the skill exercise. Check their answers.

MAIN IDEA (Reading Skill Exercises)

Finding Topic Sentences

1. **Find the topic sentence in each of the paragraphs below.** (Note to teachers: Topic sentence is underlined.)
   a. "Slowly turning his head, he examined the ledge. It was about eighteen inches wide. He dared not look down. Three feet to his right it widened a little. If he could creep over there—if he could hang on somehow, shuffle sideways—there would be room to sit down to get himself together."
   b. "He shouted: 'Help! Help! Help!' His call soared over the empty valley, which threw back three faint cries, mocking his weakness. *Weak? Frank Summers!* What about all those push-ups? Why, nobody in school could come close to him. But, then, he wasn't in school now. He was in the mountains, and mountains didn't care if he could do a thousand push-ups or even ten thousand."
   c. "The big knot was going to be a problem. He wouldn't have enough line for a knot that he could be sure would jam in the crack. It would have to be heavy enough, too, or he wouldn't be able to throw it accurately. He hunted about the ledge for a loose stone or a dead branch, but there was nothing except his shoes. *Why not?* Picking up his right shoe, he flexed the heavy leather. *Perfect!*"

2. **Write a paragraph for each of the topic sentences below.**
   a. **Frank was foolish to go into the mountains alone.**
   b. **People shouldn't be ashamed to admit they need other people.**
   c. **Admitting your weaknesses can be a sign of strength.**
   d. **Mountain climbers need to rely on their wits as well as their physical prowess.**
   Check that students' paragraphs develop or support the topics.

TEACHING WORD ATTACK

Read the explanatory material in the book aloud while the students read it

silently. Ask them to volunteer other words that can be used as both nouns and verbs. Have them use the words they volunteer in sentences. Then have them complete the skill exercise and check their answers.

WORD ATTACK (Exercise)

Understanding Words Used as Nouns and as Verbs

▶ Read each of the *italicized* words in the sentence pairs below. Then decide whether the word is used as a noun or a verb. Find the dictionary definition that fits how that word is used in the sentence.

   a. The trees *sloped* sharply to the river.
      verb
      Frank slipped down the steep *slope*.
      noun
   b. **Frank tried to *thread* his gaze through the cracks in the rock.**
      verb
      The river looked like a silver *thread*.
      noun
   c. **If he had his belt, he would *buckle* it to his shoe.**
      verb
      He could have used the *buckle* on his belt.
      noun
   d. **He pulled himself off his *perch*.**
      noun
      He *perched* on the narrow ledge.
      verb
   e. **He tried to *edge* his way along the side.**
      verb
      The shoe hit the *edge* and fell back down.
      noun
      Accept any definitions that fit the sentences.

WORD ATTACK CHECK TEST

▶ Decide whether each *italicized* word below is used as a verb or a noun.
   a. The *walk* down the mountain trail was slippery and dangerous.
   b. *Walk* with me until we reach the fork in the trail.
   c. The *rescue* would probably have been a success.
   d. Would they have to *rescue* him from the ledge?
   e. He *eyed* the cracks in the rocks.
   f. His *eye* fell upon a spot he could reach with his rope.
   g. He cut his jeans into narrow *pieces*.
   h. The parts of his plan were *pieced* together in his mind.
   i. Easy, Frank. Now! *Climb* for your life.
   j. He knew that this *climb* was for his life.

ANSWERS TO WORD ATTACK CHECK TEST

▶ a. noun   f. noun
   b. verb   g. noun
   c. noun   h. verb
   d. verb   i. verb
   e. verb   j. noun

My First Lifeline

MAYA ANGELOU
pp. 413–421

Summary In this moving true story, Mrs. Flowers teaches Marguerite (Maya Angelou) to value herself. She gives Marguerite her first "lessons in living"—to be "intolerant of ignorance but understanding of illiteracy" and to appreciate "mother wit."

BEFORE READING

Ask the students to tell about one person who has had a positive influence on their lives. Then tell them to read about Bertha Flowers to find out what kind of person she was and how she influenced the life of a young girl. (Flexibility: Setting a Purpose)

Glossary Words

*aura (p. 418, a, 5)
*benign (p. 413, b, ℓ. 6)
*cascade
  (cascading, p. 417, b, 4)
*equivalent (p. 414, b, 4)
*ignorance (p. 417, b, 2)
*illiteracy (p. 417, b, 2)
*incessantly (p. 414, a, 3)

*inclusively (p. 413, b, ℓ. 5)
*inedible (p. 413, a, 1)
*infuse (p. 415, b, 5)
*intolerant (p. 417, b, 2)
*sacrilegious (p. 414, b, 4)
*sophistication (p. 418, a, 5)
*taut (p. 413, a, 2)

TEACHING THE GLOSSARY WORDS

Write the glossary words on the chalkboard. Say each word aloud and have the students repeat it after you. Then have students look up these words in the glossary in order to complete the following puzzle.

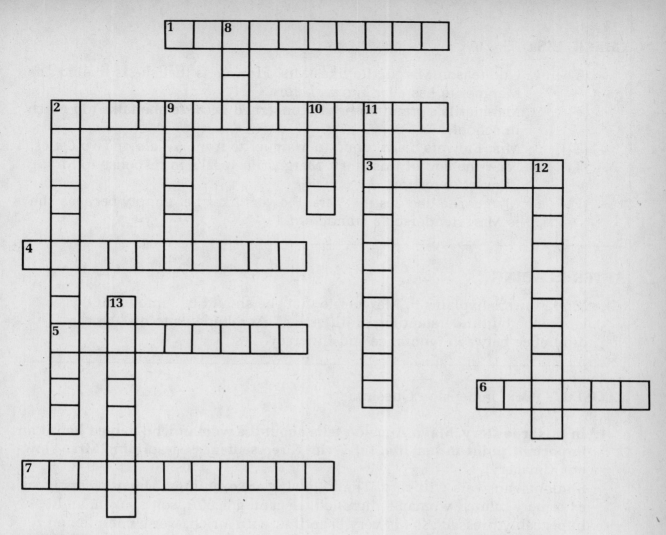

ACROSS

1. not understanding of
2. an understanding and knowledge of the ways of the world
3. to fall
4. the inability to read or write
5. lack of knowledge
6. gentle
7. in a manner that takes everything into account

DOWN

2. sinful, irreverent
8. stretched tight
9. instill
10. glow
11. continuously
12. equal
13. not fit to eat

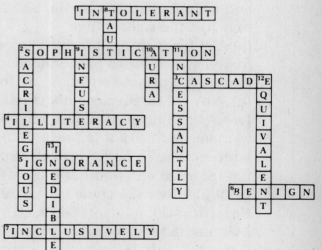

CHECK TEST

AFTER READING

Mrs. Flowers explains to Marguerite that she should be "intolerant of ignorance but understanding of illiteracy." Ask students to discuss the difference between ignorance and illiteracy.

CLOSE UP (Comprehension Questions)

1. **In this true story, Maya Angelou tells about the woman who helped her at an important point in her life. (a) Write three sentences describing Mrs. Flowers.** (Imagery)
Students' answers will vary. The following are examples: Mrs. Flowers is an extremely refined woman—dignified, elegant, graceful, soft-spoken, and impeccably dressed. She is very beautiful, with a rich, warm complexion and a slow, effortless smile. She is intuitively understanding and always says just the right thing.
(b) List three things Marguerite admires about her.
Marguerite admires her refinement, her beauty, her voice, her "careful diction," and her consideration for Marguerite as an individual.

2. **(a) Why is Marguerite embarrassed when her mother calls Mrs. Flowers "Sister"?** (Relationships: Cause/Effect)
Marguerite thinks it is presumptuous of her mother to use this form of address. She feels that worlds separate the two women, and that "Sister" is too informal and familiar a term.
(b) What does she come to realize about her mother and Mrs. Flowers? (Relationships: Comparison/Contrast)
Marguerite realizes many years later that they are "as alike as sisters, separated only by formal education."

3. **Marguerite considers herself unimportant and she refuses to speak. What simple things does Mrs. Flowers do to show that she values Marguerite?**
She asks that Marguerite accompany her home and clearly states that she wishes to talk to her; she shares her life views with Marguerite and encourages her to do as much as she can with her own life; she is extremely hospitable to Marguerite—she serves her tea cookies and lemonade and

reads to her; she lends her books; she tries to help Marguerite to overcome shyness—she asks her to be prepared to recite a poem from memory the next time she comes to tea.

4. **Mrs. Flowers tells Marguerite, "Words mean more than what is set on paper. It takes the human voice to infuse (fill) them with the shades of deeper meaning." What do you think this statement means?** (Sentence Meaning)

Mrs. Flowers is suggesting that the spoken word is more powerful than the written word. She is making a case for oral communication, in the hopes of encouraging Marguerite to speak out. Her point is that oral communication is a more effective tool for expressing and sharing points of view than are written words—since the feelings and emotions invoked are what give words their power. Mrs. Flowers is suggesting also that each speaker makes an individual decision about what is most important in a sentence or group of sentences and then emphasizes with his or her voice the meaning behind the words. (In acting, this skill is called *pointing*.) She also alludes to this idea (that a speaker decides what to emphasize) when she suggests that Marguerite practice trying "to make a sentence sound in as many different ways as possible."

5. **(a) Why do you think Mrs. Flowers reads aloud to Marguerite?**

She is trying to prove her point that "language is man's way of communicating with his fellow man and it is language alone which separates him from the lower animals." She is trying to encourage Angelou to talk.

(b) How does Marguerite show that she is grateful?

She allows Mrs. Flowers' interest in her to change her life: she takes the lifeline. Also, she responds "yes, ma'am" when Mrs. Flowers asks how she liked the reading from *A Tale of Two Cities*. ["It was the least (she) could do, but it was the most, also."]

THEME (Literature Skill Questions)

1. **Marguerite's problem is her self-concept, the way she feels about herself. Find two things Marguerite does that show she feels inferior and unimportant.**

She mopes around "like an old biscuit, dirty and inedible." She doesn't talk in class when she is called on.

2. **Marguerite feels inferior because she is poor and her family has not had much schooling. (a) Go back to the story and find what Mrs. Flowers tells Marguerite about ignorance and mother wit.**

"She said that I must always be intolerant of ignorance but understanding of illiteracy. That some people, unable to go to school, were more educated and even more intelligent than college professors. She encouraged me to listen carefully to what country people called mother wit. That in these homely sayings was couched the collective wisdom of generations."

(b) Paraphrase these words; that is, put them into your own words.

Students' answers will vary.

3. **Write a statement that you think expresses the theme of this selection.**

The theme of this story is how Marguerite developed a sense of self-worth. (Accept any similar answers.)

ADDITIONAL ACTIVITIES

1. Find out what happened to Marguerite as she grew older. Share your findings with your classmates.
2. Write a note from Marguerite to Mrs. Flowers after their visit.
3. In your own words, tell what you think Mrs. Flowers was trying to do for Marguerite. Why did she pick Marguerite?

TEACHING MAIN IDEA (Reading Skill)

Read the explanatory material aloud while the students read it silently. Ask one student to supply a topic, and ask a different student to supply a topic sentence for that topic. If the students are unable to supply a topic, suggest one or more of the following for them: School, Television, Living in the United States. Have them write topic sentences for the topics supplied. Then have them complete the skill exercise and check their answers.

MAIN IDEA (Reading Skill Exercises)

Distinguishing Between the Topic and the Main Idea

1. **State the topic of each paragraph below. Then, in your own words, state the main idea—what the paragraph says about the topic.**
   a. **"Mrs. Bertha Flowers was the aristocrat of Black Stamps. She had the grace of control to appear warm in the coldest weather, and on the Arkansas summer days it seemed she had a private breeze which swirled around, cooling her. She was thin without the taut look of wiry people, and her printed voile dresses and flowered hats were as right for her as denim overalls for a farmer."**
   The topic is "Mrs. Bertha Flowers." The main idea is that she was "the aristocrat of Black Stamps" (a dignified, elegant woman).
   b. **"The chifforobe was a maze. What on earth did one put on to go to Mrs. Flowers' house? I knew I shouldn't put on a Sunday dress. It might be sacrilegious. Certainly not a house dress, since I was already wearing a fresh one. I chose a school dress, naturally. It was formal without suggesting that going to Mrs. Flowers' house was equivalent to attending church."**
   The topic is "choosing the right dress." The main idea is that Marguerite chooses a school dress.
   c. **"As I ate she began the first of what we later called 'my lessons in living.' She said that I must always be intolerant of ignorance but understanding of illiteracy. That some people, unable to go to school, were more educated and even more intelligent than college professors. She encouraged me to listen carefully to what country people called mother wit. That in those homely sayings was couched the collective wisdom of generations."**

The topic is "lessons in living." The main idea is that Mrs. Flowers taught Marguerite the difference between ignorance and illiteracy. Accept any similar answers.

2. **For the topic of your paragraph, choose a part-time job. (a) Write a paragraph expressing the following main idea: _____ is the best way to earn extra money. (b) Keep the same topic, but write a paragraph expressing the opposite main idea: _____ is the worst way to earn extra money.**
Check that students provide details that support the main idea.

TEACHING WORD ATTACK

Have the students read the explanatory material in their books. Then have them complete the skill exercise. Check their answers.

WORD ATTACK (Exercise)

Understanding Vivid Compound Words

▶ **Find the meaning of the compound word** *italicized* **in each sentence below.**
  a. **"But they talked, and from the side of the building where I waited for the ground to open up and swallow me, I heard the** *soft-voiced* **Mrs. Flowers and the textured voice of my grandmother merging and melting."**
     having a gentle voice
  b. **"Women who walked over the 'heath' and read** *morocco-bound* **books and had two last names divided by a hyphen."**
     bound in expensive leather
  c. **"One summer afternoon,** *sweet-milk* **fresh in my memory, she stopped at the Store to buy provisions."**
     like fresh milk in which the cream has not separated
  d. **"They gave each other** *age-group* **looks."**
     understood by people of the same age
  e. **" '***Store-bought*** clothes ain't hardly worth the thread it take to stitch them.' "**
     bought in a store

WORD ATTACK CHECK TEST

▶ Match each of the hyphenated words with its definition.
  a. Mrs. Flowers wasn't slippery-tongued like some intelligent folks.
  b. Mrs. Flowers was always dressed fashion-right.
  c. Mrs. Flowers was a people-person above all.
  d. Marguerite was peacock-proud to be noticed by Mrs. Flowers.
  (1) in an up-to-date and proper fashion
  (2) fast talking; lying
  (3) according to the book; correctly
  (4) someone who likes and respects others

ANSWERS TO WORD ATTACK CHECK TEST

▶ a. (2) fast-talking; lying
  b. (1) in an up-to-date and proper fashion
  c. (4) someone who likes and respects others
  d. (5) happy with oneself; feeling good about oneself
  e. (3) according to the book; correctly

ABOUT THE AUTHOR

Maya Angelou (1928–   ) was the Northern Coordinator for the Southern Christian Leadership Conference at the request of Martin Luther King, Jr. She has written two poetry books, *Just Give Me a Cool Drink of Water . . . 'Fore I Diiie* and *Oh Pray My Wings Are Gonna Fit Me Well*. She also has published three autobiographical volumes: *I Know Why the Caged Bird Sings, Gather Together in My Name,* and *Singin' and Swingin' and Gettin' Merry Like Christmas*.

Portrait by a Neighbor

EDNA ST. VINCENT MILLAY

Who Am I?

MIGUEL LEON-PORTILLA
pp. 422–423

Summaries   In "Portrait by a Neighbor," the poet fondly remembers her neighbor. In "Who Am I?" the poet expresses the joy of composing songs.

BEFORE READING

Explain that tone in poetry is the poet's attitude toward what he or she has written about and the impression the poem creates. Ask students to look for the tone of each of these poems.

CLOSE UP (Comprehension Question)

▶ **List the reasons the poet enjoys having the woman in the first poem as a neighbor.** (Relationships: Cause/Effect)
The woman is unconventional. For example, she sunbathes before attacking

her household chores; she comes home late and gets up late; she uses a shovel and spoon as her gardening tools; she weeds by the light of the moon; she rarely mows the lawn and when she does, she leaves the clover standing; she daydreams and is forgetful. The poet also appreciates her neighbor's love of life.

ABOUT THE AUTHOR

Edna St. Vincent Millay (1892–1950) wrote "Renascence," a long poem about the joys of nature, when she was nineteen. *The Harp-Weaver and Other Poems* won the Pulitzer Prize in 1923, making her the first woman to win a Pulitzer.

Mike and the Grass

ERMA BOMBECK
pp. 424–427

Summary The lawn holds many memories for Mike's father. When the grass finally grows in, Mike has grown up.

Glossary Words

BEFORE READING

Have students look for the reason that Mike's father changes his mind about the grass. (Flexibility: Setting a Purpose)

CLOSE UP (Comprehension Questions)

1. **At the beginning of this selection, Mike's father seems very concerned about the grass. What does Mike's mother mean when she says, "It'll come back"?** (Sentence Meaning)
She is convinced that nothing can keep the grass from growing in again. (Her statement also implies that Mike's happiness is more important to her than is the condition of the lawn.)
2. **At the end of the story, what does the father say that shows he cares much more about Mike than about the grass?** (Inferences)
He says, "He will come back, won't he?" Now that the grass has grown in,

Mike's father can't really enjoy it—he misses Mike too much. (He doesn't care if the grass comes back or not—he just wants Mike to return.)

ABOUT THE AUTHOR

Erma Bombeck (1927–   ) was born in Dayton, Ohio. She is the author of the best-selling books *At Wit's End, Just Wait Till You Have Children of Your Own, I Lost Everything in the Post-Natal Depression, If Life Is a Bowl of Cherries—What Am I Doing in the Pits?* and *Aunt Erma's Cope Book.* Bombeck writes a syndicated newspaper column, and she has appeared regularly on the television series *Good Morning, America.* She has a husband and three children and lives in Paradise Valley, Arizona.

The Little Lizard's Sorrow

MAI VO–DINH
pp. 428–435

Summary This Vietnamese fable explains the origin of a certain type of lizard. (A stranger wins a bet, takes possession of a rich man's estate, and distributes the wealth among the poor and needy. The rich man dies and returns as a lizard.)

BEFORE READING

Ask students what they think real wealth is; then have them read "The Little Lizard's Sorrow" to find out what this Vietnamese folktale says about wealth. (Flexibility: Setting a Purpose)

Glossary Words

*gaunt (p. 428, b, ℓ. 10)
*harass
  (harassed, p. 432, b, 2)

*intrigue
  (intrigued, p. 428, b, ℓ. 16)
*malice (p. 430, a, 6)

TEACHING THE GLOSSARY WORDS

Write the glossary words on the chalkboard. Say each word aloud and have the students repeat it after you. Then have the students look up each word and write sentences using them. (Word Attack: Dictionary, Context)

CHECK TEST

AFTER READING

Ask the students to discuss why the rich man agrees to the stranger's conditions. (Inferences)

CLOSE UP (Comprehension Questions)

1. **(a) In the rich man's game, what does one player have to do when the other player announces one of his rare possessions?**
He must "counter the challenge by saying that he, too—if he really (does)—(owns) such a treasure." Then it would be his turn to announce a rare possession.
(b) When does a player lose?
A player loses if he cannot honestly counter the other player's challenge—in other words, when he does not possess what the other player names.

2. **Why is the rich man curious about the wanderer?** (Relationships: Cause/Effect)
The wanderer is a pauper. The rich man is curious as to why this pauper thinks he can match the possessions of a rich man.

3. **(a) The wanderer requests two conditions before they play. What are they?**
The conditions are that they play on a winner-take-all basis and that he, the wanderer, be allowed to ask the first question.
(b) By asking the first question, what does the wanderer force the rich man to do? (Relationships: Cause/Effect)
He forces the rich man to lose. (If the rich man had asked the first question, the wanderer would not have been able to match the possession and he would have lost.)

4. **Why does the rich man lose?** (Inferences)
On one level, the rich man loses because he does not possess a chipped coconut-shell drinking cup. He has no need of such an implement since he can afford to buy brand-new cups. On another level, the rich man loses because of his pride.

THEME (Literature Skill Questions)

1. **The rich man cares so much about his possessions that he loses sight of other things. (a) What does he think symbolizes, or stands for, wealth?**
To the rich man, material things (possessions) symbolize wealth.

(b) What does the wanderer think is more important than possessions?
Freedom is more important than possessions to the wanderer. (Wealth, to him, is spiritual, not material.)

2. **(a) Why is the chipped coconut shell more valuable to the wanderer than all the rich man's fine china?** (Relationships: Cause/Effect)
It is practical—something he can use (he needs it to drink from)—and it is his sole possession.
(b) What do you think determines the value of something? (Judgments)
Answers will vary, but students should see that the true value of something is rarely, if ever, determined by its cost.

3. **Why does the wanderer give away all of the rich man's possessions?** (Relationships: Cause/Effect)
He doesn't want them. He uses them to help the poor and needy. (He places no value on material possessions in and of themselves—their worth, to him, is measured by the amount of suffering they can alleviate. In other words, he values material goods only when they can be used in a spiritual way.)

4. **What do you think is the theme of this story? (Think about what it says about wealth and freedom. Which should people value more?)**
People should value freedom over wealth. The theme of this story is that spiritual wealth is more important than material wealth.

ADDITIONAL ACTIVITIES

1. Create a different title for this story.
2. Discuss the advantages and disadvantages of having more money than you really need.
3. Which of the men in this story had more courage? Explain your answer.

TEACHING MAIN IDEA (Reading Skill)

Have the students read the explanatory material in their books and complete the skill exercise. Check their answers.

MAIN IDEA (Reading Skill Exercises)

Finding Supporting Details

1. **The following are main ideas from paragraphs in "The Little Lizard's Sorrow." Under these main ideas are supporting details from the story. Identify the details that support each main idea.**

Main Ideas
a. **The visitor was obviously a poor man.**
   (1), (3)
b. **The visitor was not impressed by the rich man's wealth.**
   (2), (5), (6)
c. **The rich man did not have a chipped coconut-shell drinking cup in his house.**
   (4), (7)

Supporting Details

(1) The visitor was dressed in mended clothes.

(2) The visitor gave the rich surroundings only a passing, casual look.

(3) The visitor looked as if he had not had a meal in days.

(4) Even the servants in the rich man's house would not drink from a chipped cup.

(5) The visitor answered the rich man in a proud, self-assured voice.

(6) The visitor was perfectly at ease sipping tea from a rare porcelain cup.

(7) The servants searched the entire house for a chipped, coconut-shell cup.

2. Find three supporting details to back up each of the following main ideas.

(a) **The very rich man was vain.**

One of his greatest pleasures is "beating other rich men at the game he himself had invented." He surrounds himself with only the best treasures. It never occurs to him that the stranger might beat him.

(b) **The rich man did not believe the stranger would win the game.**

The rich man only agrees to see the stranger out of curiosity and surprise—he can't imagine why a pauper would think he could beat a rich man at the game of possessions. He agrees to the winner-take-all condition. He willingly lets the pauper go first. He genuinely is shocked when he loses. ("But, why you don't mean that I do not have a thing like this?")

(c) **The stranger valued his freedom above worldly possessions.**

He tells the rich man that he considers himself "one of the most fortunate men alive." His sole possession is of a practical nature—the coconut-shell drinking cup. After he wins the game, he gives away the rich man's possessions to the poor and needy.

TEACHING WORD ATTACK

Have the students read the explanatory material in their books and complete the skill exercise. Check their answers.

WORD ATTACK (Exercise)

Finding Synonyms

▶ Match each word in Column A with its synonym in Column B.

A	B
a. immense (4)	(1) cherish
b. wealth (6)	(2) home
c. owner (5)	(3) sadness
d. treasure (1)	(4) huge
e. pauper (8)	(5) possessor
f. usher (7)	(6) riches
g. residence (2)	(7) guide

    h. inquire (9)   **(8) beggar**
    i. sorrow (3)   **(9) ask**

WORD ATTACK CHECK TEST

► Which of the sentences below have the same or almost the same meaning?
  a. The man was poverty-stricken.
  b. He had enormous wealth.
  c. He was clearly a pauper.
  d. His intelligence was well known.
  e. He was almost completely without worldly possessions.
  f. He was no more than a beggar.

ANSWERS TO WORD ATTACK CHECK TEST

► Sentences a, c, e, f

ABOUT THE AUTHOR

Mai Vo-Dinh (1933–   ), an artist and author, was born in Hue, Vietnam, and educated in France. He became a naturalized U.S. citizen in 1976. He wrote and illustrated *The Toad Is the Emperor's Uncle* (a collection of animal folktales from Vietnam) and *The Jade Song*.

The Baroque Marble

E. A. PROULX
pp. 437–449

Summary   Until Sister Opal can buy the baroque pearl from Sonnier's, her antique marble collection just won't be complete.

BEFORE READING

Have students turn to p. 437. Ask one student to read the title of the story and the author's name aloud. Then have students study the illustration. Ask them to list as many details as they can. Read the first two paragraphs of the story aloud. On the basis of the title, the illustration, and the information in the first two paragraphs, ask students to predict what this story will be about. Then have them read the story to see if their predictions are correct. (Inferences; Flexibility: Setting a Purpose)

Glossary Words

*baroque (title)
*enthrall
   (enthralled, p. 439, a, 1)
*ephemeral (p. 446, b, ℓ. 5)
*exotic (p. 445, a, 2)
*fathom
   (fathomed, p. 443, a, 1)
*inarticulate (p. 442, b, ℓ. 10)

*incredulous (p. 442, a, ℓ. 1)
*judiciously (p. 445, b, ℓ. 2)
*lucent (p. 440, a, 3)
*scurvy (p. 438, b, ℓ. 7)
*sensuous (p. 446, a, ℓ. 10)
*sinister (p. 438, a, ℓ. 3)
*transmute
   (transmuted, p. 438, b, 2)

TEACHING THE GLOSSARY WORDS

Write the glossary words on the chalkboard. Say each word aloud and have the students repeat it after you. Then have students find each word in the story. Have them copy in their notebooks the sentences in which they find each word. Then have them write the word's definition under each sentence. (Word Attack: Dictionary, Context)

CHECK TEST

(F)   1. Opal Foote treasures her marbles mainly because she considers them a good investment.
(T)   2. At first, Opal thinks that the baroque pearl is a marble.
(F)   3. R. Sonnier's behavior toward Opal shows that he thinks she is a person of value.
(F)   4. Opal's father gives her the money to buy the pearl.
(T)   5. R. Sonnier sells the baroque pearl to someone else.

AFTER READING

Ask students to discuss Opal Foote's character. What traits of hers will help her to succeed in life? (Judgments)

CLOSE UP (Comprehension Questions)

1. **(a) Why does Opal start thinking about collecting beautiful things?** (Relationships: Cause/Effect)
Sister Opal is inspired by a film shown in her art class "about ordinary people who started art collections with inexpensive things that became rare and valuable as time went by."

The Baroque Marble 201

(b) How does she picture herself someday?

Sister Opal imagines herself "in her own apartment with rare items of art in glass cases and white walls hung with glowing works of great artists" which she "picked up years before for just a song."

2. **(a) Why does Mr. R. Sonnier dismiss Opal as a person of no importance?** (Inferences)

What he sees is only a poor girl in wet shoes who is wearing a cotton dress in late October. He doubts she has the money to be a serious customer.

(b) How does his dismissal make her feel and what does it make her do? (Relationships: Cause/Effect)

His sarcasm causes her to feel "a horrible combination of shame, embarrassment, anger, pride, and sadness," and "in a burst of pride and fantasy" she tells him to save the pearl for her until she comes to buy it.

3. **(a) What steps does Opal take to obtain the pearl?**

Sister Opal discusses the situation with her family, and finally gets permission to get a job and save half her earnings for college and half for the baroque pearl. She gets a job in a drugstore after school and on Saturdays.

(b) How do the members of her family help her work toward her goal? (Relationships: Cause/Effect)

Her brother Andrew volunteers to get home a little earlier and take over her job of starting supper. Her brother Roy packs his own dinner pail. Her mother shows extra tenderness in little ways as a form of emotional support.

4. **How does Opal's father show that he approves of Opal's desire to buy the pearl?** (Inferences)

Saying "I always did like Picasso," her father scotch-tapes a reproduction of *The Three Musicians* over the kitchen calendar. [This shows that he has revised his previous opinion about the value of collecting art.]

5. **Opal's father tells her that Mr. Sonnier wasn't being mean or malicious when he sold the pearl, just "businesslike." Do you agree with this statement? Why or why not?** (Judgments)

The antique dealer had little reason to believe that Opal would ever return. She left no deposit. She did not appear to be a serious customer (she seemed to be poor and antiques are expensive). He probably simply forgot about her as soon as she left. He says, " . . . how was I to know you were serious? We get people in here every day saying they like something and they'll be back the next day or next week. They never show up, never! . . . I'd go out of business if I believed everything people tell me." Opal's father tells Opal, "you should have checked back with that R. Sonnier every week or so, so that he'd know that you were really serious about buying it."

6. **At the end of the story, Opal pretends that the lopsided marble is the baroque pearl. Do you think this story ends on a hopeful note or a sad note? Why?** (Inferences)

Answers probably will vary, since the ending is ambiguous. Some students may feel that it is healthy and natural for Opal to comfort herself as best she can. They may feel that she is making the best of a bad situation. (They may feel that in this way she manages to hold on to her dream.) Others may feel that the story ends on a sad note—there have been hints throughout the story that Opal has a tendency to dissociate herself from reality, so this last pretense may be seen as a regrettable form of backsliding.

THEME (Literature Skill Questions)

1. **(a) Why does Opal think of her jar of marbles as a kind of wealth?**
   Opal feels this way because the eight hundred forty-three marbles represent the most that she owns, and she takes a kind of "miser's satisfaction in pouring them out onto the bed" and examining them.
   (b) Why does she especially value the deformed white marble?
   The deformed white marble is a "lopsided freak," and it is special to Opal because it is different. In the jar, it sits "with more space around it than the other marbles, as if they (avoid) getting too close to it." Perhaps Opal identifies with this marble because she too feels different, or like a social misfit.

2. **Why doesn't Opal like to look at her marbles under a magnifying glass?**
   Opal loves the "classic Greek perfection" of her marbles' roundness— "Under (her) father's magnifying glass, the perfect marbles (disclose) blemishes, pits, and scratches."

3. **What does the baroque marble represent to Opal?** (Figurative Language)
   It represents hope—with it, she can look forward to a future of collecting valuable things. It also stands for her dream of "someday (being) in her own apartment with rare items of art in glass cases and white walls hung with glowing works of great artists which she, Sister Opal, had picked up years before for just a song." It also represents a lifeline—Opal seems to feel that the marble will be the beginning of something that will transport her to much more exotic times and places, such as China, ancient Peru, ancient Rome, France, Istanbul, Alexandria (all the places she has dreamed about). It represents the one bright spot in her drab existence—owning it will make her feel important, like an artist.

4. **Think about what the baroque marble means to Opal. Then write a statement that you think best expresses the theme of this story.**
   The theme is about the roles dreams or fantasies play in a person's life. (Accept any similar answers.)

ADDITIONAL ACTIVITIES

1. Select one of Sister Opal's father's "lectures" and read it orally as you think he would have said it.
2. Do you blame Mr. R. Sonnier for selling the pearl? Explain why or why not.
3. **Composition.** Write a character sketch of Sister Opal's father.

TEACHING MAIN IDEA (Reading Skill)

Have the students read the explanatory material and complete the skill exercise. Check their answers.

MAIN IDEA (Reading Skill Exercise)

More Practice in Finding Main Ideas

▶ In your own words, state the main idea of each of the following paragraphs.

a. " 'Well, Sister, I think for a family in the kind of situation we got, where we all work to keep some kind of decency in our lives, and where we are trying to work toward an education for all you kids, an education of some kind, that any ideas about collecting art are just plain *crazy*. We are poor people and it's no use you pretending otherwise. Maybe someday your children, or more likely, grandchildren can collect art, but right now, girl, we can't gather enough money together to collect milk bottles! Wait!' "

Our family is too poor to be thinking about collecting art.

b. "Sister Opal's brother Andrew stood up. 'I am sick and tired of hearing about Roy's dinner pail. I expect the sun isn't going to come up and set anymore—no, it's going to be Roy's dinner pail! I say that if Sister Opal sees more in life than groceries and trying to get along, she should at least have the chance to try. I can get home a little earlier and start supper myself, and Roy can pack up his own dinner pail. You've told us yourself, Papa, that if a person wants something bad enough, and works hard enough *for* it, he'll get it. I'm willing to see Opal get that baroque pearl. I wouldn't mind seeing a few nice things around here myself.' "

Sister Opal deserves a few nice things if she is willing to work for them.

c. "The jar of marbles was a kind of wealth. It was the most Sister Opal owned. Eight hundred and forty-three marbles. She took a miser's satisfaction in pouring them out onto the bed, watching them roll into the valleys, gathering up their heavy, glassy weight, cold but soon warming in her hand. Each marble was individually beautiful. A kind of classic Greek perfection shone in their roundness. Under Sister Opal's father's magnifying glass, the perfect marbles disclosed blemishes, pits, and scratches. Sister Opal liked them unmagnified; in their smallness she found their greatest value."

Sister Opal's marble collection was like a fortune to her.

Accept any similar answers.

TEACHING WORD ATTACK

Have the students read the explanatory material and complete the skill exercise. Check their answers.

WORD ATTACK (Exercise)

Understanding Comparisons

▶ Tell what is being compared to what in each passage below.

a. "The bureau loomed, a skyscraper in dull, dark varnish."

a bureau to a skyscraper

b. "The chair arms seemed to have clenched hands at their ends, like brown old men sitting anxiously in the doctor's office waiting to hear the bad news."

chair arms to brown old men

c. "Sister Opal thought of homework as yellow leaves dropping softly down, like the yellow blank pages she had dropped into the wastepaper basket last night."

homework to leaves

d. "On a piece of blue velvet, quite like Sister Opal's best dress, there lay a large, glowing, misshapen marble."

velvet to a dress

e. "At the table that night Sister Opal's father looked on her with disfavor. His cheerful supper face was cloudy, and Sister Opal knew the storm would break before she poured out his coffee."

a face to the sky

WORD ATTACK CHECK TEST

▶ Tell what is being compared to what in each sentence below.
   a. Sister Opal's marble collection was her own private carnival, circus, and amusement park in one jar.
   b. Sister Opal had a purpose—she was like a hound dog on the trail of a rabbit.
   c. The baroque marble was the moon in Sister Opal's sky.
   d. The family grew brighter, more cheerful, like a group of fireflies in a once-dark sky.
   e. Mr. R. Sonnier was the biggest rain cloud Sister Opal ever had in her short life.

ANSWERS TO WORD ATTACK CHECK TEST

▶ a. a marble collection to a carnival, a circus, and an amusement park
   b. Sister Opal to a hound dog
   c. a baroque pearl to the moon
   d. a family to a group of fireflies
   e. Mr. R. Sonnier to a rain cloud

ABOUT THE AUTHOR

E. A. Proulx grew up in Brookfield, Vermont. He writes stories and articles for *Country Journal* and *Seventeen*. "Goin' Downhill Fast" is one of his nonfiction stories.

Where the Sidewalk Ends

SHEL SILVERSTEIN
pp. 450–451

Summary A short poem describing a magical place.

BEFORE READING

Tell students to look for words and phrases that create a vivid image of this magical place. (Imagery; Flexibility: Setting a Purpose)

CLOSE UP (Comprehension Questions)

1. **Why does the poet want to leave this place?** (Relationships: Cause/Effect)
   It is full of black smoke; the street is dark, winding, and bending; everything seems to be made of concrete ("Past the pits where the asphalt flowers grow . . ."). The poet is seeking a more natural setting.
2. **What makes the place where the poet wants to go magical?** (Imagery)
   There the grass is soft and white, the sun is crimson, and a "moon-bird" cools itself in a "peppermint wind."

ABOUT THE AUTHOR

Shel Silverstein has published many prose and poetry books, including *Where the Sidewalk Ends* (a collection of his poems and drawings).

REVIEW QUIZ

ON THE SELECTIONS

p. 452

1. **In "On the Edge," what event first makes Frank feel fear?**
   Frank falls onto the ledge.
2. **How does Frank use his shoe to save himself?** (Relationships)
   He ties it to cut-up strips from his jeans, wedges it into a crack in the mountain, and climbs to safety.
3. **In "My First Life Line," why does Mama ask Marguerite to take off her dress?** (Relationships: Cause/Effect)
   She wants to show the needlework on the inside of the dress (especially the French-seams around the armholes) to Mrs. Flowers.
4. **Find two things Mrs. Flowers does in order to make Marguerite feel special.**
   She has her to tea and serves her home-baked cookies and lemonade. She reads to her from her favorite books and poems. She lends her books.

5. **In "Mike and the Grass," why does the father object to his son's having a sandbox?** (Relationships: Cause/Effect)

He thinks it will ruin the yard—Mike will bring other kids home to play in it and "they'll throw sand into the flowerbeds and cats will make a mess in it and it'll kill the grass for sure."

6. **In which country does "The Little Lizard's Sorrow" take place?** (Relationships: Spatial Order)

7. **Why does the rich man agree to see the stranger who appears at his door?**

He is curious to find out why a pauper thinks he can possibly beat a rich man at the game of possessions.

8. **In "The Baroque Marble," why does Opal favor the white marble in her collection?** (Relationships: Cause/Effect)

She likes it because it is "different" from the others.

9. **At first, why does Opal's father object to her getting a job after school to pay for the baroque marble?** (Relationships: Cause/Effect)

He feels that if she can get a job, she should use all her salary to put herself through college.

10. **In Shel Silverstein's poem, what is special about the place where the sidewalk ends?** (Imagery)

Grass grows "soft and white" there; the sun burns "crimson bright"; moonbirds rest from flight by cooling themselves in a "peppermint wind." (Also, it is a place that children "know": suggesting imagination.)

ON MAIN IDEA

p. 453

1. **What is the topic of the paragraph below?**

   Mountain climbers should follow three important rules. First, they should never go into the mountains alone. This way, if one person gets into trouble, someone else is there to help. Second, they should carry necessary equipment. A rope, a compass, and a knife can help climbers get out of tight spots. Third, they should learn to read the mountains. Spotting a safe foothold or handhold can save a life.

   Safety rules for mountain climbers (Accept all similar answers.)

2. **What is the topic sentence in the paragraph above?**

   "Mountain climbers should follow three important rules."

3. **Write a topic sentence for a paragraph that would include the following details.**

   (a) He was wearing broken straw sandals.

   (b) His clothes looked as if they had been mended hundreds of times.

   (c) He looked as though he had not eaten in days.

   The man had fallen on hard times. (Accept any reasonable answers.)

4. **List three points supporting the following main idea: Language separates human beings from the lower animals.**

   Through language human beings communicate ideas. Communication of ideas results in interaction: that is, in human beings working together to achieve a common goal. Lower life forms lack that capability.

ON THEME

p. 453

▶ **Decide whether the following statements are true or false.**
   a. The theme of a story is its central insight into, or generalization about, life.
   true
   b. In "My First Life Line," Mama makes a very important statement about sewing that points to the theme.
   false
   c. A symbol is never a real object.
   false
   d. A symbol can help you discover the theme of a story.
   true.

BEFORE GOING ON

p. 454

Gifts of the Indian

C. FAYNE PORTER
pp. 456–461

Summary This article explores modern customs and products that originated with the American Indians.

BEFORE READING

Give the students one minute to list all the objects they can think of that originated with American Indians. Have them compare their lists. (Relationships: Simple Listing)

Glossary Words

conception (p. 460, a, 1)
constitute
   (constituted, p. 460, a, 1)

domesticate
(domesticated, p. 458, b, ℓ. 1;
   p. 459 a, 1)

emulate
  (emulating, p. 460, b, 1)
inaccessible (p. 460, a, 3)
incomprehensible (p. 460, b, 1)
indelibly (p. 461, b, ℓ. 2)
misnomer (p. 456, a, 1)
occidental (p. 460, b, 1)

opulent (p. 460, b, ℓ. 11)
propagation
  (self-propagation, p. 458, b, ℓ. 2)
scrupulously (p. 460, a, 1)
sonorous (p. 461, b, ℓ. 1)

TEACHING THE GLOSSARY WORDS

Write the glossary words on the chalkboard. Say each word aloud and have the students repeat it after you. Have them find each word in the story and copy in their notebook the sentence in which they find each word. Then have them look up each glossary word and write the meaning of each word under the appropriate sentence. (Word Attack: Dictionary, Context)

TEACHING FLEXIBILITY AND MAIN IDEA (Reading Skill)

Have the students read the explanatory material. Then have them complete the skill exercises and check their answers.

FLEXIBILITY AND MAIN IDEA (Reading Skill Exercises)

Skimming for Main Ideas

1. **Read paragraphs 1–5 of "Gifts of the Indians."**
   a. **Which statement expresses the main idea of paragraph 1?**
   (2) Ever since Columbus, there have been many misconceptions about the first Americans.
   b. **Which statement expresses the main idea of paragraph 2?**
   (1) Most students know little about the first Americans.
   c. **Which statement expresses the main idea of paragraph 3?**
   (2) The reason many people know so little about the first Americans may be that they incorrectly assume "everything in the twentieth-century Americas came from Europe."
   d. **Which statement expresses the main idea of paragraph 4?**
   (2) The first Americans developed the products that account for more than half of America's cash farm crop.
   e. **Which statement expresses the main idea of paragraph 5?**
   (1) The first Americans developed corn, which is the most valuable crop grown in the United States.
2. **Read paragraphs 6–10. If the statement below expresses the main idea of the paragraph, label it true. (Statement a is for paragraph 6, b for 7, etc.) If it does not, write a sentence stating the main idea.**
   a. **Sweet potatoes and some types of yams are of American origin.**
   true

b. **A large number of valuable crops are of American origin.**
   true
c. **South-American Indians often made rubber toys for their children.**
   Rubber is of American origin.
d. **The scientific study of biology and medicine is indebted to the medicinal knowledge of American Indians.**
   true
e. **Sixteenth-century Europeans did not bathe often.**
   The Indians had a better conception of hygiene than did the Europeans.

3. **Read paragraphs 11–15. For each paragraph, write a statement expressing the main idea.**
   a. The Indians invented the hammock. (paragraph 11)
   b. Cigarettes, chewing gum, and chocolate are of American origin. (paragraph 12)
   c. Popcorn and peanuts are of American origin. (paragraph 13)
   d. Europeans ("with centuries of supposedly superior occidental learning behind them") were able to survive in the New World only by emulating the Indians. (paragraph 14)
   e. There are many Indian place names in the United States. (paragraph 15)

4. **Write a statement expressing the main idea of the entire essay.**
   Many of our modern customs and products originated with the American Indians. (Accept any similar answers.)

READING SKILLS UNIT TEST (Mosaic)

1. **Identify the topic sentence in each of the paragraphs below.**
   a. "They took, too, the Indian's names for the rich and varied land upon which he lived. Probably in every country in the United States today (exclusive of Hawaii) there is an Indian place name—of a stream or a mountain or a city—whispering of the time when another people lived and worked and played here. The sonorous roll of the old Indian names is indelibly stamped into the fabric of the land—Mississippi and Mononga-hela, Narragansett and Natchez, Savannah and Seattle, Tishomingo and Taos, Winnemucca and Wichita—and half of our fifty states bear names which stem from Indian words."

      They took, too, the Indian's names for the rich and varied land upon which he lived.

   b. "In fact, the Indians whom the first settlers found had a far better conception of what constituted good health and how to maintain it than did the settlers themselves. They were a scrupulously clean people, unlike the Europeans who first came to their shores. Columbus took back the news of how often the Indians bathed, and one of the first dictates set down by Queen Isabella of Spain was to the point, if misdirected: 'They are not to bathe as frequently as hitherto.'"

      In fact, the Indians whom the first settlers found had a far better conception of what constituted good health and how to maintain it than did the settlers themselves.

2. State the topic of each paragraph below.

   a. "Mrs. Bertha Flowers was the aristocrat of Black Stamps. She had the grace of control to appear warm in the coldest weather, and on the Arkansas summer days it seemed she had a private breeze which swirled around, cooling her. She was thin without the taut look of wiry people, and her printed voile dresses and flowered hats were as right for her as denim overalls for a farmer."

   Marguerite's impression of Mrs. Flowers (Accept any similar answers.)

   b. "One day, a stranger came to the rich man's house. Judging from his appearance, the gatekeeper did not doubt that the visitor was a madman. He wanted, he said, to play the famous game with the mansion's master. Yet, dressed in clothes that looked as if they had been mended hundreds of times and wearing broken straw sandals, the stranger appeared to be anything but a wealthy man. Moreover, his face was gaunt and pale as if he had not had a good meal in days . . . ."

   First impressions of the stranger (Accept any similar answers.)

3. Select the main idea of the following paragraph.

   " 'Young lady," said R. Sonnier, highly amused, 'that is *not* a marble. That is a baroque pearl, an antique baroque pearl, and even though I am letting it go at an unbelievably low price, I doubt you could afford it.' He looked her up and down, seeing the wet shoes, the cotton dress in late October, the brown skin and thinness that was Sister Opal. 'It is for sale for four hundred and fifty dollars. A bargain for those who can afford such things. Marbles, I believe, you'll find at Woolworth's.' "

   (1) Mr. Sonnier was amused because Sister Opal had thought a pearl was a marble.

   (2) Mr. Sonnier was sure Sister Opal could not afford the pearl.

   (3) The pearl was a bargain.

   (1)

4. The following are main ideas of paragraphs in "Gifts of the Indian." Decide which supporting details belong with each main idea.

   a. The Indians have made many contributions to American agriculture.
      (1), (6), (7), (10)

   b. The Indians have made many contributions to the rubber industry.
      (8)

   c. The Indians have contributed to the development of confections.
      (4), (5), (9)

   d. The Indians have contributed to medical science.
      (2), (3)

   Supporting Details

   (1) The Indians developed corn.

   (2) The guinea pig was domesticated by the South American aborigines.

   (3) Quinine, cascara, and ipecac were understood and used by the Indians.

   (4) Chocolate was of Indian origin.

(5) The Indians put maple syrup on popcorn to make caramelcorn.

(6) Tobacco was grown by the Indians.

(7) Yams and sweet potatoes were grown and eaten by the Indians.

(8) Indians made rubber playthings from the "tears" of "the weeping tree."

(9) We owe our chewing gum to the Indians.

(10) Tomatoes are the leading crop canned in the United States today, and they were grown by the Indians.

THE HOBBIT

SELECTION	TYPE	LITERATURE SKILL	READING SKILL	WORD ATTACK SKILL
The Hobbit by J. R. R. Tolkien Dramatized by Patricia Gray pp. 463–507	drama	Drama. Reading a two-act play	Reading a longer selection	
Act One pp. 464–490		Understanding plot development Understanding characterization	Relationships. Listing Relationships. Understanding cause/effect Inferences	
Act Two pp. 491–507		Understanding plot development Understanding characterization	Relationships. Understanding time order Inferences	

The Hobbit

J. R. R. TOLKIEN
Dramatized by Patricia Gray
pp. 463–507

Summary In this play, Gandalf, a great wizard, convinces the hobbit Bilbo Baggins to help a band of dwarves slay an evil dragon.

BEFORE READING

Ask students to discuss the elements of a good adventure. Would it contain danger? Would it contain mystery? Would it contain unusual characters? Then ask them what type of person chooses to go on an adventure. Have them read *The Hobbit* to find out why Bilbo chooses to go on an adventure and how his adventure turns out. (Flexibility: Setting a Purpose)

Glossary Words

*accursed (p. 491, a, 2)
*agape (p. 481, a, 2)
*brandish
    (brandishing, p. 482, a, 5)
*brolly (p. 474, a, 6)
*bulbous (p. 484, b, 2)
*calamity (p. 505, b, 3)
*conspirator (p. 470, b, 5)
*despondency (p. 494, a, 6)
*despondent
    (despondently, p. 496, a, 5)
*doff
    (doffing, p. 467, b, 5)
*drone
    (droning, p. 501, a, 9)
*duress (p. 495, b, 2)
*emanate (p. 503, b, 11)

*esteem
    (esteemed, p. 501, b, 3)
*expansively (p. 466, b, 4)
*flourish (p. 476, a, 6)
*formidable (p. 505, b, 7)
*imperiously (p. 492, b, 9)
*indigestible (p. 487, a, 9)
*parley (p. 502, a, 8)
*placate
    (placatingly, p. 491, a, 9)
*rune (p. 482, b, ℓ. 2)
*saturation (p. 499, b, 1)
*scandalize
    (scandalized, p. 467, b, ℓ. 1)
*smite (p. 495, a, 7)
*unobtrusive (p. 485, a, 1)
*vanquish (p. 503, a, 7)

TEACHING THE GLOSSARY WORDS

Write the glossary words on the chalkboard. Say each word aloud and have the students repeat it after you. Then tell the students to find the words in the following puzzle. The words may read from left to right, from right to left, from top to bottom, from bottom to top, or diagonally. After they find each word, have them look it up in the glossary and write its meaning in their notebooks.

A C C U R S E D D E A P W I E T I M S A T
N G E T A N A M E N E A I N E P A C T S E
B R A N D I S H S S R R O A X R I A C C O
R U A P D I D C P T T L R Y P I A N G A M
O R L A E Y D R O N E E J R A R T I E N H
L O Y B L K C T N S C Y E G N A R L E D A
L B T O O J R C D S O I E M S F G H S A S
Y K I A M U D E E U M F I A I G H Q T O P
F A M L O K S N N D R Q R F V C U U D E H
P Q A N B W B U C E R E F B E F T G I H S
F P L A C A T E Y O P U S F L O U R I S H
F K A E X M C V R V Y H N S Y R J K M I A
O L C O N S P I R A T O R E L M O P P U F
D E S P O N D E N T D S A K F I K E E Q C
S C A N D A L I Z E M U M S S D E A R N A
A J M A E E C N O I T A R U T A S T I A N
F M P C H P I N D I G E S T I B L E O V U
A I A A S E R I N O T A C O D L E F U H M
F U N O B T R U S I V E B G N E S I S V R
M A F L N I M P E R I E X P A N V E L A B
O U R C O N S P I R A V A N Q U I P Y N O

A C C U R S E D D E A P W I E T I M S A T
N G E T A N A M E N E A I N E P A C T S E
B R A N D I S H S S R R O A X R I A C C O
R U A P D I D C P T T L R Y P I A N G A M
O R L A E Y D R O N E E J R A R T I E N H
L O Y B L K C T N S C Y E G N A R L E D A
L B T O O J R C D S O I E M S F G H S A S
Y K I A M U D E E U M F I A I G H Q T O P
F A M L O K S N N D R Q R F V C U U D E H
P Q A N B W B U C E R E F B E F T G I H S
F P L A C A T E Y O P U S F L O U R I S H
F K A E X M C V R V Y H N S Y R J K M I A
O L C O N S P I R A T O R E L M O P P U F
D E S P O N D E N T D S A K F I K E E Q C
S C A N D A L I Z E M U M S S D E A R N A
A J M A E E C N O I T A R U T A S T I A N
F M P C H P I N D I G E S T I B L E O V U
A I A A S E R I N O T A C O D L E F U H M
F U N O B T R U S I V E B G N E S I S V R
M A F L N I M P E R I E X P A N V E L A B
O U R C O N S P I R A V A N Q U I P Y N O

CHECK TEST

Act One

(F)   1. Hobbits are famous for their love of adventure.

(F)   2. Bilbo hangs a sign on his door asking for work as a burglar.

(T)   3. Gandalf has a key to the mountain's secret entrance.

(F)   4. When Bilbo tries to steal food from the trolls, they turn him into stone.

(T)   5. Bilbo plays a game of riddles with Gollum and wins his magic ring.

Act Two

(T)   1. Gandalf warns the dwarves and Bilbo not to leave the path.

(F)   2. The elves capture Bilbo and throw him into the dungeon, but the dwarves manage to escape.

(T)   3. Bilbo steals the keys from the guards.

(T)   4. The prisoners escape by hiding in empty barrels.

(T)   5. The elves and the dwarves decide to work together to slay Smaug and to share his treasure.

AFTER READING

Use the composition assignment on p. 507 as the basis of a discussion. Then ask students if they think Gandalf made a wise choice. Why or why not? (Judgments)

CLOSE UP (Comprehension Questions)

Act One

1. **Make a list of facts you learn about hobbits at the beginning of this play. (For example, hobbits do not like adventure.)** (Relationships: Listing)
   Hobbits are hearty eaters; they are hospitable; they are curious about one another's affairs; they love stories; they love the comforts of home; and they don't normally mix with dwarves.

2. **(a) As the dwarves arrive, why does Bilbo invite each one in to tea?** (Relationships: Cause/Effect)
   Bilbo is habitually polite to anyone who comes to his door. Since he is a hobbit, he is noted for his hospitality.
   (b) Why does Bilbo decide to join the dwarves on their adventure? (Relationships: Cause/Effect)
   Gandalf tricks him into joining by implying that he isn't a true descendant of the famous Took family. Bilbo impetuously decides to go along to uphold the honor of the Took family.

3. **Gandalf says of Bilbo, "There's more to him than you guess or he has any idea of himself." (a) How does Bilbo prove his bravery when the dwarves lose their supplies?** (Inferences)
   Bilbo sneaks up on the trolls and attempts to steal their mutton.

(b) How does Gandalf help him escape being cooked? (Relationships: Cause/ Effect)

Gandalf mimicks the trolls' voices and says provoking things, thereby setting them to quarreling with one another. Preoccupied, they don't realize that dawn is imminent (the first shaft of light turns them to stone).

4. **After the battle with the goblins, Bilbo is lost in a dark cave. (a) Find two ways in which Bilbo's cleverness helps him escape.** (Inferences)

He successfully matches wits with Gollum, riddle for riddle. Also, he realizes the nature of the ring's power, and secretly follows Gollum to an exit (Gollum thinks that he is following Bilbo).

(b) How does the ring he finds aid him? (Relationships: Cause/Effect)

The ring makes him invisible. He is able to come and go among enemies as he pleases.

CLOSE UP (Comprehension Questions)

Act Two

1. **(a) What happens to the dwarves when they stray from the path through Mirkwood Forest?** (Relationships: Time Order)

The dwarves are captured by the Elven-Queen and her guards, and are sent to her dungeons because they remain silent when she asks them why they are in Mirkwood Forest.

(b) Why doesn't this happen to Bilbo? (Relationships: Cause/Effect)

When the guards come, Thorin whispers to Bilbo that he should put on his invisible ring. Since he isn't seen, he isn't imprisoned.

2. **(a) How does Bilbo show he is a good burglar when the dwarves are locked in the dungeon?** (Inferences)

Bilbo stealthily manages to get the keys to the cell off the guard's key ring. When she feels for them, he places them so that she can touch them so she doesn't realize that they are off the ring.

(b) What does his plan for escaping from the dungeon show about Bilbo? (For example, it shows that he is daring.) (Inferences)

Bilbo's scheme shows that he is ingenious and can make long-range plans. He is also observant and knowledgeable: he knows the elves' habits and the river's destination. He is a hobbit with real leadership qualities.

3. **How does the dragon's vanity help Bilbo to defeat it?** (Inferences)

Bilbo says he hears that the diamonds in the dragon's waistcoat are only fakes. The dragon's vanity gets the better of him—he tells Bilbo to see for himself and displays the waistcoat, revealing the black spot over the heart that is bare of diamonds. Thorin then stabs him there with the Elven-Queen's sword.

4. **Composition. Why do you think Gandalf chose a hobbit, rather than a dwarf, to go on this adventure? Write a paragraph explaining your answer.**

Hobbits are cunning and resourceful. (Dwarves seem to lack these qualities.) Bilbo's cunning and resourcefulness make the adventure a success. (Accept any similar answers.)

ABOUT THE AUTHORS

J. R. R. Tolkien (1892–   ) received the *New York Herald Tribune* Children's Spring Book Festival Award in 1938 for *The Hobbit*. He also received the International Fantasy Award in 1957 for *The Lord of the Rings*. In these books and in *The Silmarillion*, Tolkien, a Middle English scholar, not only invented languages, but a whole world called Middle-Earth. Some of his other books are *Sir Gawain and the Green Knight; Beowulf: The Monsters and the Critics; The Road Goes Ever On: A Song Cycle;* and *Smith of Wooton Major*.

Patricia Gray breeds and shows horses in California. She has contributed over thirty-five short stories to various magazines. Her novels include *The Horse Trap, Show Ring Rogue,* and *Show and Tell*.

TEACHING WRITING

Cascade is structured so that writing is an integral part of the textbook. It is taught with the literature, at the end of units, and in the writing handbook that begins on page 508. With the exception of some prewriting and revision activities in the handbook, all writing activities are in response to the literature.

In addition, extra writing activities are provided in the *Teacher's Manual* for almost all selections. These activities may be used as enrichment for those students who have mastered the skills taught with the particular selection.

Teaching the Writing Activities with the Selections

Cascade provides an abundance of writing activities with the selections. These activities are a natural outgrowth of what the students have learned about the selection itself. Since reading and writing are treated as related skills in *Cascade*, in many cases, the before reading and after reading discussion of the selection will set the stage for writing.

We recommend that before assigning any writing activity, you remind your students that writing is a process. Putting words down on paper is only part of their job. Equally important are getting ideas for writing and developing these ideas and, once their paragraphs or compositions are written, revising and proofreading them.

PREWRITING

Many activities in the textbook concentrate on prewriting. They involve listing, discussing, sketching, additional reading, researching, dramatizing, and questioning. These activities help students get their creative juices flowing without actually asking them to write formally. They can be found on the following pages: 27 (Activity 2), 33 (Activity 1), 41 (Activity 2), 79 (Activity 1), 91 (Activity 1), 119 (Activity 1), 173 (Activity 2), 151 (Activities 1 and 2), 167 (Activity 2), 193 (Activity 2), 237 (Activity 2), 295 (Activity 2), 305 (Activity 1), 325 (Activity 2), 337 (Activity 1), 355 (Activity 1), 389 (Activities 1 and 2), 409 (Activity 2), 419 (Activity 2), 447 (Activities 1 and 2).

The *Teacher's Manual* contains additional activities that concentrate on prewriting. These activities can be found on the following pages: 6 (Activities 1 and 2), 11 (Activities 1, 2, 3, and 4), 28, 45 (Activity 2), 62 (Activities 1 and 2), 76 (Activities 1 and 2), 93 (Activity 3), 99-100 (Activities 1, 2, and 3), 105 (Activity 2), 110, 130 (Activities 1, 2 and 3), 143 (Activities 1 and 2), 149 (Activities 1 and 2), 160 (Activity 1), 166 (Activities 2 and 3), 171 (Activities 2 and 3), 186, 192 (Activities 1 and 3), 198 (Activities 1, 2, and 3), 203 (Activities 1 and 2).

Tips for Teaching the Prewriting Activities

We suggest that you make speaking and listening an important part of prewriting. Students often feel more comfortable talking about their ideas than putting their ideas down on paper. Have students share their ideas with their classmates. Ask them to read aloud their lists and react to the lists of others. Have them brainstorm in small groups. Ask them to share their illustrations and talk about them. When an activity calls for dramatization, encourage students to discuss the roles they will play and the method they will use to put on the play.

Create an environment that encourages the free exchange of ideas. Have students prepare charts of additional reading they do in connection with the selection, and ask them to share their reading with their classmates. You might set up a book day. On this day, students could discuss their additional reading and make recommendations.

All of these activities set the stage for writing. They help the student who can never think of anything to write about realize that he or she actually has a great many things to say.

WRITING

Many activities in *Cascade* concentrate on writing. They have students write paragraphs, compositions, notes, letters, reviews, and advertisements. In the textbook, these writing activities can be found on the following pages: 15 (Activities 1 and 2), 27 (Activity 1), 33 (Activity 2), 41 (Activity 1), 79 (Activity 2), 91 (Activity 2), 101 (Activities 1 and 2), 119 (Activity 2), 137 (Activity 1), 141, 167 (Activities 1 and 3), 193 (Activity 1), 215 (Activities 1 and 2), 227 (Activities 1 and 2), 231, 237 (Activity 1), 281, 295 (Activity 1), 305 (Activity 2), 325 (Activity 1), 337 (Activity 2), 355 (Activity 2), 365, 369, 381, 409 (Activity 1), 419 (Activity 1), 433 (Activities 1 and 2), 507.

The *Teacher's Manual* contains additional activities that concentrate on writing. These activities can be found on the following pages: 45 (Activity 1), 70 (Activities 1, 2, 3, and 4), 93 (Activities 1 and 2), 105 (Activity 1), 137 (Activities 1 and 2), 143 (Activity 3), 160 (Activity 2), 166 (Activity 1), 171 (Activity 1), 192 (Activity 2), 203 (Activity 3).

In addition, the After Reading questions on the following pages in the *Teacher's Manual* may be turned into writing assignment for your better students: 5, 9, 14, 18, 24, 39, 44, 49, 56, 68, 74, 87, 92, 98, 104, 109, 121, 129, 136, 141, 148, 153, 158, 164, 184, 190, 197, 201.

Tips for Teaching the Writing Activities

Before students write a composition, review prewriting techniques with them. (You can have them refer to pages 508-516 in the textbook.) If an activity requires students to find a topic for writing, remind them to examine their personal interests, their personal experiences, and their journals.

Once students have a topic for writing, have them employ techniques for developing ideas about their topic. Alternate these methods. On some days, have the students work independently, making lists of ideas and then sharing these ideas with their classmates. On the other days, have them brainstorm in groups or as a full-class activity.

In addition, have them ask and answer questions about the topic. This technique will probably involve some library work. Students can work together to find the answers and to make up even more questions.

For longer assignments for which all the students are writing on the same topic, have them use clustering. Students can work together as a class to develop as many ideas as possible about the topic and then organize these ideas in clusters.

Some activities require students to step into a character's shoes. For these activities, have the students discuss what the character is like before they start to write. Have them determine how their character feels about other characters in the story. Have them establish their character's likes and dislikes. Require the students to be quite specific.

Some selections ask students to write to a specific audience. For those that don't, have your students select an audience for their writing. Some possibile audiences are their fellow classmates, younger children, senior citizens, recent immigrants, pen pals in other countries, and characters in the stories they have read. Discuss with your students what they can expect their audience to know and how they can adapt their writing to their audience.

Also establish a purpose for writing. Discuss each activity with your students and have them decide if their primary purpose for writing is to inform, to persuade, to amuse or entertain, to request something, to describe, or to narrate.

Remind students of the need to limit their topic before they write. For short assignments, they need develop only a rough outline. For longer assignments, they should develop a topic outline or a sentence outline. (See pages 518–519 in the textbook.)

REVISION

Unfortunately, most students do not spend enough time at this stage of the writing process. They think that their first draft is their final draft. They turn in writing that would receive a much higher grade if they had simply taken a little time to read it over and improve it.

Tips for Teaching Revision

Emphasize the need for revision. Refer your students to the guidelines for revision on pages 508-16 in the textbook. Ask your students to keep these guidelines in mind when they reread their written assignment. Then, on the basis of these guidelines, have them revise their assignment. Once it is revised to their satisfaction, have them proofread it to correct errors in spelling, punctuation, and capitalization. Finally have them copy their assignment on a clean piece of paper and again reread it before turning it in.

PROCEDURES FOR EVALUATING THE WRITING ASSIGNMENTS

Discuss your standards for evaluation with your students before they turn in any writing assignments. The assignments can be evaluated on three levels: holistic, primary purpose, and usage and mechanics. Holistic evaluation looks at the overall accomplishments of the writing. It is concerned with such questions as: Is the writing well organized? Is it unified? Is it well developed? Does it display coherence? Are the ideas in it original and well developed?

Primary-purpose evaluation looks at the effect of the writing. It is concerned with whether or not the writing accomplishes its purpose. For example, if an assignment calls for a student to compare and contrast two characters, primary purpose evaluation would be concerned with whether or not the writing fulfills this obligation and whether it does so in an original or insightful way.

Usage and mechanics evaluation looks at the correctness of the writing. It focuses on the sentence level of writing and is concerned with grammatical errors and errors in spelling, punctuation, and capitalization.

Obviously, all three forms of evaluation are important. Which one you emphasize depends on the nature of the assignment and the ability of your students. For groups that feel threatened by writing, you might start the year by emphasizing primary-purpose concerns. As the year goes on and the students begin to feel less intimidated, you could place equal stress on usage and mechanics concerns. Some teachers choose to give more than one grade: 85/80. The first grade is a holistic or a primary-purpose evaluation; the second a usage and mechanics one.

Peer Editing

Students can learn from the mistakes of their peers. Set up editing partners. These partners will exchange assignments. Then they will revise and evaluate each other's work. As they work, have them keep in mind the revision guidelines on pages 525-26 in the textbook.

In addition, have each editor write a two-paragraph evaluation of the partner's work. In the first paragraph, the editor should explain the changes he or she made and the reasons for these changes. In the second paragraph, the editor should give advice to the writer and tell what is good about the work.

For short assignments, you might want to use a less formal form of peer editing. Simply have the students read their work aloud and listen to and respond to reactions from the class. However, do not let a student who is commenting merely say, "That was good" or "That was bad." Pin down the student. Ask questions such as the following: What made it good? What made it bad? What in particular did you like about it? In what spot did you think it was particularly weak?

Teaching the Writing Exercises at the End of Units

Each unit ends with a short lesson on writing. The first two lessons concentrate on improving sentences through combining. The next three lessons concentrate on recognizing and writing narration, description, and exposition.

TIPS FOR TEACHING SENTENCE COMBINING

The lesson on page 66 in the textbook comes at the end of a unit that has focused on sentence meaning. It is a fitting conclusion to the material students have covered about sentences. Write the following sentences on the chalk board:

> Lee peeled the potatoes.
> Lee chopped the onions.
> Lee grated the cheese.

Ask the students to identify the core parts in each sentence. Help them see that each sentence has the same subject. Explain that the student can combine three short choppy sentences with the same subject into one sentence.

> Lee peeled the potatoes, chopped the onions, and grated the cheese.

Write the next three sentences on the chalk board:

> Janet removed the tire from the rim.
> Janet cleaned the area around the puncture.
> Janet patched the hole.

Once again, have the students identify the core parts in each sentence. Help them to see that the subject of each sentence is the same. Then have them combine these three sentences into one:

> Janet removed the tire from the rim, cleaned the area around the puncture, and patched the hole.

Finally, have the students complete the exercise on page 66 in the textbook. Select four students. Assign an item to each student. Have these students write their answers on the chalk board. Have the class correct the answers.

The lesson on page 172 comes at the end of a unit that has focused on relationships. It gives students practice in writing sentences by using words that signal relationships. Write the following sentences on the chalk board:

> Marv worked out every day. He wanted to qualify for the wrestling team.

Ask students to identify how the ideas in these two sentences are related. Help them to see the cause and effect relationship. Then ask them to name some of the words that signal a cause and effect relationship. Explain that they can use a signal word to combine these two sentences.

Marv worked out every day because he wanted to qualify for the wrestling team.

Now write the next sentence on the chalkboard:

Anita started to dance. She heard the music.

Ask students to identify how the ideas in these two sentences are related. Help them to see the time-order relationship. Then ask them to name some of the words that signal a time-order relationship. Explain that they can use a signal word to combine these two sentences.

Anita started to dance when she heard the music.

Finally, have students complete the exercise on page 172 in the textbook. Select four students. Assign an item to each student. Have these students write their answers on the chalkboard. Have the class correct the answers.

TIPS FOR TEACHING NARRATION

The lesson on page 242 in the textbook comes at the end of a unit that has focused on point of view. It serves as a fitting conclusion to a unit that has emphasized the story teller. Explain that a narrative narrates, or tells, a story. Have students read paragraph 1, column a on page 234 in the textbook. Explain that this is a narrative paragraph. Have students find other narrative paragraphs in the textbook.

Then have students discuss the writing assignments on page 242 in the textbook. Ask them to brainstorm together to develop ideas for each of the assignments. Also have them decide on an audience and a purpose for each assignment. Then have each student choose an assignment.

Remind students of the importance of planning and of revision. Once they are satisfied with their paragraphs, have the students break into groups. All the students who completed assignment a will be in one group, all those who completed b in another, all those who completed c in a third, and all those who completed d in a fourth. Have the students circulate their paragraphs to all members of their group. Then have each group discuss the paragraphs and choose the best one. Have this one read to the class.

TIPS FOR TEACHING DESCRIPTION

The lesson on page 394 in the textbook comes at the end of a unit that has focused on setting. It serves as a nice conclusion to what the students have learned about the details that establish setting. Explain that description describes, or creates a clear picture of something. Have students read paragraph 8, column b on page 360 in the textbook. Explain that this is a descriptive paragraph. Have students find other descriptive paragraphs in this textbook.

Then have students discuss the writing assignments on page 394 in the textbook. Ask each student to select an assignment. Then tell the students to make lists in order to develop ideas for their topics. Also have them decide on an audience and a purpose for their assignment.

Remind students of the importance of planning and of revision. Once they are satisfied with their paragraphs, have the students break into groups. All the students who completed assignment a will be in one group, all those who completed b in another, all those who completed c in a third, and all those who completed d in a fourth. Have the students circulate their paragraphs to all members of their group. Then have each group discuss the paragraphs and choose the best one. Have this one read to the class.

TIPS FOR TEACHING EXPOSITION

The lesson on page 454 in the textbook comes at the end of a unit that has focused on main idea. It gives students the opportunity to put into practice the information they have mastered on main idea, topic sentence, and support. Tell students that exposition is writing that explains or gives information. Have students read paragraph 1, column b on page 397. Explain that this is an expository paragraph. Have students find other expository paragraphs in this textbook.

Then have students discuss the writing assignments on page 454 in the textbook. Ask each student to select an assignment. Then tell the students to ask and find the answers to questions in order to develop ideas for their topics. Also have them decide on an audience and a purpose for their assignment.

Remind students of the importance of planning and of revision. Once the students are satisfied with their paragraphs, have them select an editing partner. Tell them to keep the guidelines for revision in mind as they edit their partner's work. Have them discuss with their partner the changes they made and the changes their partner made.

Teaching the Writing Process Handbook

Cascade provides a writing handbook at the back of the book. This handbook focuses on the writing process. It leads students through the stages of prewriting, writing, and revision and proofreading.

Quotations about writing by writers are placed throughout this handbook. These quotations serve two functions. First, they help students see that the writing process reflects the way professional writers write. Second, show the students that even professional writers have to work at writing. Therefore, the fact that they, the students, have difficulty writing should not discourage them. With some thought and some work, they can master this vital skill.

TIPS FOR TEACHING PREWRITING

The prewriting section provides strategies for making choices, getting ideas for writing, and developing ideas. We suggest you take a block of time at the beginning of the year to teach this section, since students will be able to apply what they learn in this section to all their writing assignments.

Making Choices. Make sure students understand the terms *audience* and *purpose*. Have them list various audiences and various purposes they might have for writing.

Choosing a topic. Ask students to discuss whether they prefer to be assigned a topic for writing or to select a topic on their own. Ask them what methods they use to come up with ideas for writing. Then explain that three strategies for choosing a topic are to write about personal interests or about personal experiences and to keep a journal.

Developing Ideas About the Topic. Encourage students to talk about the way they write. Ask them to discuss what they do after they have a topic. Most likely, many students will tell you that they simply start writing. Explain that they may find writing easier if they take some time to warm up their minds. Four strategies they can use to do this are making lists, asking questions, brainstorming, and clustering.

Evaluating the Prewriting Activities

It is important during the prewriting stage to create an environment in which students feel free to write without fear of criticism. Therefore, we suggest that you keep evaluation of prewriting activities very informal. You might have the class work together to evaluate these assignments. Have them judge the activities on the basis of whether or not they achieve their primary purpose, in other words, whether or not they meet the demands of the exercise (see primary-purpose evaluation on page 222).

Answers to Prewriting Activities

Students' answers to these activities will vary.

TIPS FOR TEACHING WRITING

The writing section of the handbook provides strategies for planning and for writing the first draft. We suggest you reserve one day a week for teaching this section.

Planning. Ask students which would be a better choice for a topic for a composition: the history of a war or a day in the life of the mayor of the town. Ask them to explain the reason for their choice. Help them to see the importance of whittling down a topic to a manageable size.

Then explain that a topic sentence tells the main idea about the topic. Ask them to explain the difference between a main idea and a topic. Then have them look through current magazines to find paragraphs with effective topic sentences.

Emphasize the importance of outlining. Explain that they probably make rough outlines all the time. A topic outline and a sentence outline are simply more formal and more complete than a rough outline.

The First Draft. Explain to students that during this stage their concern is to put their thoughts down on paper following their organization pattern – their outline. However, what they write during this stage must be considered and rewritten.

This section provides instruction in writing on three levels: sentences, paragraphs, and compositions. Explain to students that two key features of effective sentences are variety and emphasis. Variety refers to the variations in the way sentences are begun and in their length. Emphasis refers to the stress given to a certain element of the sentence.

Explain that three key features of paragraphs are topic sentence, support, and arrangement. Have students find examples of paragraphs with the topic sentence placed at the beginning, near the middle, and at the end. Have them discuss the effect of the placement of the topic sentence.

Then have them examine the support for the topic sentence. Have them tell which of their sample paragraphs are developed by examples, which by reasons, and which by facts or statistics.

Finally have them look at their paragraphs to determine their method of arrangement. Have them tell which are arranged through time order, through spatial order, through climatic order, through cause and effect, and through comparison and contrast.

Ask students to discuss the difference between a paragraph and a composition. Explain that a paragraph has three distinct parts: the introduction, the body, and the conclusion.

Evaluating the Writing Activities

Refer to the information on evaluation on page 222. Before the students start an activity, make sure they understand your method of evaluating it.

Answers to Writing Activities

Students' answers for the following activities will vary: 14, 15, 16, 17, 18, 19, 20, 23, 24, 25, 26.

Activity 21.   Rewrite each of the sentences below by following the directions at the end of it.

(The word or phrase the students use will vary. Here are some suggested answers.)

1. **The speaker spoke for two hours.** (Begin with an adverb)
   Unexpectedly, the speaker spoke for two hours.
2. **The picture fell from the wall.** (Begin with a prepositional phrase)
   In the middle of the night, the picture fell from the wall.
3. **The new teacher walked into the room.** (Begin with an adjective)
   Unafraid, the new teacher walked into the room.
4. **You have to answer ninety percent of the questions correctly.** (Start with an infinitive phrase)
   To get an *A*, you have to answer ninety percent of the questions correctly.
5. **She saw that it was going to rain.** (Begin with a participial phrase)
   Looking out the window, she saw that it was going to rain.

Activity 22.   Each of the sentences below is written in the passive voice. Rewrite each sentence in the active voice.

1. **The pies were baked by the members of the home-economics class.**
   The members of the home-economics class baked the pies.
2. **The food was donated by the club.**
   The club donated the food.
3. **Transportation was provided by the students.**
   The students provided transportation.
4. **The solo was sung by Marie.**
   Marie sang the solo.
5. **Harry was rewarded by the principal.**
   The principal rewarded Harry.

TIPS FOR TEACHING REVISION AND PROOFREADING

This section contains guidelines for revision and rules for capitalization, punctuation, and spelling. It also provides practice in correcting two common sentence errors: fragments and run-ons. In addition, it focuses on two special language problems: appropriate word choice and clarity. We suggest you block out a week of time to teach the material on sentence fragments, run-ons, appropriate word choice, and clarity.

At the beginning of the year, make sure students understand that there are guidelines and rules in this section of the book. Have them refer to this material whenever they write an assignment.

Evaluating the Writing Activities

Refer to the information on evaluation on page 222. Before the students start an activity, make sure they understand your method of evaluating it.

Most of the activities in this section are exercises requiring students to make specific corrections. Evaluate these activities on the basis of their correctness.

Answers to Revising and Proofreading Activities

Students' responses to the following activities will vary: 30, 31, 32, 34.

Activity 27.   Each item below is a fragment. On a separate piece of paper, correct each fragment by rewriting it as a complete sentence or by connecting it to a complete sentence that you provide.

(Students' answers will vary. Here are some suggested answers.)

1. **Because they defy gravity.**
   She likes to watch the aerialists because they defy gravity.
2. **Sherlock Holmes always outwitting the criminal.**
   Sherlock Holmes always outwits the criminal.
3. **For example, trolls, goblins, and dwarves.**
   The forest was populated by monsters, for example, trolls, goblins, and dwarves.
4. **That are interested in training dolphins.**
   These are several groups that are interested in training dolphins.
5. **On the first page of this book.**
   He wrote his signature on the first page of this book.
6. **Returning only to discover that the town had changed.**
   He returned only to discover that the town had changed.
7. **Forgot my books at the movie theater.**
   I forgot my books at the movie theater.
8. **A moan from the patient in the bed.**
   A moan came from the patient in the bed.
9. **The woman jogging in the park.**
   The woman jogs in the park.
10. **Since he wanted to become a medicine man.**
    He wanted to become a medicine man.

Activity 28. On a separate piece of paper, correct each of the following run-on sentences.

(Students' answers will vary. Here are some suggested answers.)

1. **Tommy tried to be a good florist, Teruo wanted to be a good florist, too.**
   Tommy tried to be a good florist; Teruo wanted to be a good florist, too.

2. **Thapthim came whenever he was called Madame Phloi considered this uncatly behavior.**
   Thapthim came whenever he was called. Madame Phloi considered this uncatly behavior.

3. **At first, Corrigan doesn't believe in time travel, by the end of the story, he has learned better.**
   At first, Corrigan doesn't believe in time travel, but by the end of the story, he has learned better.

4. **Frank turned his head slowly to examine the ledge he saw it was about eighteen inches wide.**
   When Frank turned his head slowly to examine the ledge, he saw it was about eighteen inches wide.

5. **In the Shire the air is filled with comfort, in the woods it is filled with danger.**
   In the Shire the air is filled with comfort; in the woods it is filled with danger.

6. **An adventure is not the thing for Bilbo he would rather stay where he is comfortable.**
   An adventure is not the thing for Bilbo. He would rather stay where is is comfortable.

7. **The bushmaster is the deadliest snake in the world, what a terrible creature to be loose aboard ship!**
   The bushmaster is the deadliest snake in the world. What a terrible creature to be loose aboard a ship!

8. **Basil had found gold in the Transvaal now he was rich.**
   Basil had found gold in the Transvaal, and now he was rich.

9. **Holmes claimed that he had contracted a rare disease from Sumatra, can he be dying?**
   Holmes claimed that he had contracted a rare disease from Sumatra. Can he be dying?

10. **The morning was gray and threatening it promised to storm before noon.**
    The morning was gray and threatening. It promised to storm before noon.

Activity 29. Rewrite each sentence below in standard English. Replace each example of slang, dialect, or jargon, printed in italics, with an appropriate word or group of words.

(Students' answers will vary. Here are some suggested answers.)

1. **Watson felt *in the pits* as he looked at his dying friend.**
   Watson felt depressed as he looked at his dying friend.

2. **The way he could play the trumpet was *simply awesome*.**
   The way he could play the trumpet was impressive.

3. **The speaker made a *massive goof* in the middle of his talk.**
   The speaker made a serious mistake in the middle of his talk.

4. **The novelist's first book was a *flop*.**
   The novelist's first book was a failure.
5. ***T'aint nobody's business* what you *done*.**
   What you did is no one else's concern.
6. **The Current-Events Club meets every Wednesday at 3:15 *to shoot the breeze*.**
   The Current-Events Club meets every Wednesday at 3:15 to discuss matters.
7. **Club members must *shell out* five dollars to attend the annual party.**
   Club members must pay five dollars to attend the annual party.
8. **The candidate's remarks *made a big splash* in the newspapers.**
   The candidates's remarks were featured prominently in the newspapers.
9. **Students should learn *to utilize their resources* to *the maximum degree*.**
   Students should learn to make the fullest use of their resources.
10. **Everything is *A-OK*.**
    Everything is fine.

Activity 33. Correct the capitalization problems in each sentence below. Write your answers on a separate piece of paper.

1. **we vacationed at yellowstone national park.**
   We vacationed at Yellowstone National Park.
2. **ronald reagan, the president of the united states, will address the nation at six o'clock this evening.**
   Ronald Reagan, the President of the United States, will address the nation at six o'clock this evening.
3. **mr. and mrs. sampson announced the engagement of their daughter, may louise, a lawyer at the firm of verderber and lewis.**
   Mr. and Mrs. Sampson announced the engagement of the daughter, May Louise, a lawyer at the firm of Verderber and Lewis.
4. **who is the current prime minister of india?**
   Who is the current Prime Minister of India?
5. **the pershing school high school explorer's club took a trip to washington, d.c.**
   The Pershing High School Explorer's Club took a trip to Washington, D.C.

Activity 35. Correct the punctuation problems in each sentence below. Write your answers on a separate piece of paper.

1. **Janet asked, "Bill did you borrow my book last week.**
   Janet asked, "Bill, did you borrow my book last week?"
2. **Wow thats a great idea.**
   Wow, that's a great idea!
3. **Nancys family came to America in preRevolutionary times.**
   Nancy's family came to America in pre-Revolutionary times.
4. **Because he didnt know the answer Ron tried to avoid the teachers eye.**
   Because he didn't know the answer, Ron tried to avoid the teacher's eye.
5. **Jane asked, do you know who said "No man is an island?"**
   Jane asked, "Do you know who said, 'No man is an island'?"

6. **The three squads were made up of the following members, James, Harry and Jean, Marilyn, Maura and Sidney, George, Herman and Susan**
   The three squads were made up of the following members: James, Harry and Jean; Marilyn, Maura and Sidney; George, Herman and Susan.

7. **Carol couldnt find her homework assignment, therefore, she called Annette to find out which poem in the book An American Anthology of Poetry to read.**
   Carol couldn't find her homework assignment; therefore, she called Annette to find out which poem in the book *An American Anthology of Poetry* to read.

9. **Poe 1809-1849 died mysteriously in Baltimore, Maryland**
   Poe (1809-1849) died mysteriously in Baltimore, Maryland.

10. **Although some might disagree many critics consider Poe the most important American poet before Walt Whitman.**
   Although some might disagree, many critics consider Poe the most important American poet before Walt Whitman.

Teaching the Additional Writing Assignments

The additional writing assignments provide practice in writing paragraphs and compositions. They ask students to write using a variety of organizational patterns and in a variety of modes.

TIPS FOR TEACHING THE WRITING ASSIGNMENT

Make sure the students follow the steps of the writing process to complete these assignments. Let them determine the method they will use to develop ideas.

Evaluating the Additional Writing Assignments

To successfully complete these assignments, students must apply all the skills they have learned in the handbook. Therefore, we suggest that you evaluate the assignments in terms of both holistic concerns and usage and mechanics concerns. (See page 222.)

Answers to Additional Writing Assignments

Students' answers will vary.

Teaching the Reading Handbook

The *Reading Handbook* contains skills that will help students become more effective at studying. These skills will help them in all of their subject areas.

TEACHING THE READING HANDBOOK

We suggest you teach these skills after you have taught the flexibility skills at the end of units. We have placed these skills in a separate handbook, since they do not relate to the selections.

You might decide to individualize your instruction. You could assign these skills only to students who need extra help with reading. While these students work on study skills, your better students could complete some of the additional reading assignments.

Answers to the Reading Exercises

EXERCISE 1.

QUESTIONS. Number your paper from 1 to 10. If the direction below is accurate based on the recipe, write *True* on your paper. If the direction is inaccurate, write *False*.

1. **Add enough water to cover the chicken.**
   True
2. **Bring the water to a boil before you add the club soda.**
   False
3. **Add the carrots and onions to the water before it boils.**
   False
4. **Cut the carrots and onions into cubes.**
   True
5. **Use either 2 small onions or 4 large onions.**
   False
6. **Cut celery into cubes.**
   False
7. **Add 1 tablespoon of salt.**
   False
8. **Add 1 teaspoon of pepper.**
   True
9. **Cook until the meat falls off the bone.**
   True
10. **Do not add any extra water.**
    False

EXERCISE 2.

Follow the directions below. then write your answers on a separate piece of paper.

1. **Turn to the title page of this book. It is a two-page spread appearing before page iv. Since this book is part of a series, it has a series title, which appears on the left-hand page. What is the series title?**
   Journeys: A Reading and Literature Program
2. **The book title appears on the right-hand page. What is it?**
   Cascade

3. **Two professors helped to prepare this book and are listed under Curriculum and Writing. What are their names?**
   Richard J. Smith and Max F. Schulz

4. **Who is the publisher of the book?**
   Harcourt Brace Jovanovich

5. **Now turn to page iv, the copyright page. In what year was this book copyrighted?**
   1986

6. **The acknowledgments give credit for the selections used from other publications. How many pages of acknowledgments are there?**
   3

7. **Now turn to page vii. This page gives thanks to people who helped to evaluate, or judge, the material in this book. How many people are listed?**
   6

8. **Now turn to page viii, the start of the table of contents. How many selections are in the chapter *Woodnotes*?**
   8

9. **In the table of contents, find the selection "I Love All Gravity Defiers" by Lillian Morrison. On what page does this selection begin?**
   page 207

10. **Pages xiv-xvii provide an outline of skills for this book. On what page will you find the inference skill *making inferences about past events*?**
    page 382

EXERCISE 3.

Follow the directions below. Then write your answers on a separate piece of paper.

1. **Turn to page 545. The glossary in this book begins with a chart. What is this chart?**
   the Pronunciation Key

2. **The glossary is arranged alphabetically. On what page do you find such an entry for the word *inertia*?**
   page 550

3. **On what page do you find an entry for the word *boutique*?**
   page 547

4. **This book contains two types of indexes. Turn to page 556. What index is provided here?**
   an Index of Contents by Type

5. **How many types, or categories, of selections does this index list?**
   four

6. **How many selections do you find under *Poetry*?**
   19

7. **Look under *Drama*. On what page would you find the selection "The Dying Detective"?**
   page 122

8. **On what page would you find the selection "Crime on Mars"?**
   330

9. **What index do you find on page 557?**
   Index of Authors and Titles

10. **According to this index, on what page in the body of the book would you find a selection by Langston Hughes? On what pages would you find selections by Gwendolyn Brooks?**
    page 105; pages 45, 369

EXERCISE 4.

Use reference books to answer each of the questions below. Write your answers on a separate piece of paper. Indicate the type of reference book you used for each type of question.

1. **From what language did the word *patio* come into English?**
   Spanish/dictionary

2. **What is the capital of Colorado?**
   Denver/almanac

3. **When were mirrors first invented?**
   about 2500 B.C. in Egypt/encyclopedia

4. **What country borders Poland on the east?**
   the U.S.S.R./atlas

5. **According to the latest census, how many people live in the United States?**
   226,545,805/almanac

6. **What is the postal abbreviation for Texas?**
   TX/almanac

7. **The French and Indian War was part of a larger world conflict. What conflict was this?**
   The Seven Years' War/encyclopedia

8. **What body of water borders Florida to the west?**
   the Gulf of Mexico

9. **How is the word *sincerity* divided into syllables?**
   sin-cer-i-ty/dictionary

10. **When did Gerald Ford become President of the United States?**
    August 9, 1974 /almanac

EXERCISE 5.

QUESTIONS

1. **How many types of primary teeth do we have?**
   five

2. **How many types of adult teeth do we have?**
   eight

3. **Look at the category *primary teeth*. At what age do the first molars appear?**
   14 to 17 months

4. **At what age do the lateral incisors appear?**
   9 to 11 months

5. **What is the first type of primary teeth to appear?**
central incisors
6. **Look at the category *adult teeth.* What is the last type of adult teeth to appear?**
third molars
7. **What is the second type to appear?**
central incisors
8. **At what age do the premolars appear?**
10-12 years
9. **At what age do the central incisors appear?**
7 to 8 years
10. **At what age do the second premolars appear?**
10 to 12 years

EXERCISE 6.

QUESTIONS

1. **The three graphs below show the reasons why the Japan National Railways is in trouble. These reasons are soaring losses, mounting debt burden, and static ridership. Study the graph labelled *Soaring Losses.* In which year did Japan National Railways experience the greatest losses?**
1983
2. **What was the net loss for the railways in 1981?**
4.5 billion dollars
3. **In what year did the railways experience a net loss of 3.4 billion dollars?**
1979
4. **Study the graph labelled *Mounting Debt Burden.* What was the debt for the railways in 1982?**
74.0 billion dollars
5. **In what year did the railways have the lowest debt?**
1979
6. **In what year did the railways have the greatest debt?**
1983
7. **Study the chart listed *Static Ridership.* How many passengers rode the railways in 1980?**
6.8 billion people
8. **How many rode in 1981?**
6.8 billion people
9. **How many rode in 1982?**
6.7 billion people
10. **Why is *Static Ridership* a good title for this graph?**
During this five-year period, the number of people riding the railways has remained relatively the same.

ANSWER KEY

Cat-About-Town
A. 1 b 2 d 3 b 4 c 5 d
B. 6 c 7 d 8 a 9 c 10 b
C. 11 Jim 12 Jim 13 Tristan 14 Jim
15 Tristan
D. 16 e 17 b 18 a 19 c 20 d

Last Cover
A. 1 b 2 b 3 a 4 d 5 c
B. 6 a 7 b 8 d 9 a 10 b
C. 11 they? 12 talent, 13 met,
14 hard. 15 foothills?
D. 16 c 17 c 18 a 19 b 20 b

Meadow Mouse
A. 1 d 2 c 3 c 4 b 5 b
B. 6 c 7 a 8 d 9 b 10 e
C. 11 him, 12 him? 13 tremble.
14 palm? 15 hapless,
D. 16 mĕd′o 17 bē nēth′ l 18 strŭg′l
19 bĕl′i 20 trĕm′bəl

Unforgettable Grizzly Bears
A. 1 b 2 d 3 b 4 c 5 a
B. 6 b 7 c 8 d 9 c 10 a
C. 11 shot - grazed - bear
12 wrangler - met - Old Two Toes
13 ranchers - consider - grizzlies
14 bear - roamed - country
15 Ratcliff - discovered - Old Mose
D. 16 c 17 a 18 c 19 d 20 b

A Shipment of Mute Fate
A. 1 b 2 b 3 c 4 d 5 a
B. 6 a 7 d 8 c 9 d 10 d
C. 11 It will 12 That is 13 There is
14 Do 15 There are
D. 16 it has 17 might have 18 board is
19 How will 20 we would

You Can't Take It With You
A. 1 d 2 a 3 a 4 d 5 b
B. 6 d 7 b 8 c 9 d 10 c
C. 11 d 12 a 13 b 14 e 15 c
D. 16 d 17 a 18 b 19 c 20 e

The Promised Visit
A. 1 b 2 d 3 d 4 d 5 a
B. 6 b 7 b 8 c 9 d 10 c
C. 11 consequently 12 so 13 Since
14 therefore 15 Because
D. 16 talked 17 gone 18 built
19 hid 20 driving

Say It with Flowers
A. 1 d 2 c 3 c 4 b 5 a
B. 6 c 7 a 8 c 9 b 10 d
C. 11 so 12 consequently 13 Because
14 therefore 15 Since
D. 16 right 17 not 18 their
19 No 20 would

A Running Brook of Horror
A. 1 b 2 c 3 b 4 b 5 c
B. 6 b 7 c 8 d 9 c 10 c
C. 11 c 12 b 13 b 14 b 15 c
D. 16 b 17 c 18 d 19 a 20 b

The Dying Detective
A. 1 b 2 c 3 c 4 d 5 d
B. 6 b 7 a 8 d 9 b 10 b
C. 11 but 12 Although 13 by contrast
14 but 15 In spite of
D. 16 a 17 b 18 d 19 c 20 d

Big Red
A. 1 d 2 a 3 d 4 b 5 a
B. 6 d 7 c 8 d 9 a 10 d
C. 11 a 12 b 13 c 14 a 15 a
D. 16 title: named
17 win: triumphing or succeeding
18 press: to put down
19 disturb: calm
20 perceptible: not noticeable

The Wall
A. 1 a 2 c 3 b 4 c 5 b
B. 6 b 7 c 8 d 9 a 10 b
C. 11 d 12 c 13 a 14 d 15 b
D. 16 c 17 d 18 a 19 b 20 e

Alone on a Hilltop
A. 1 d 2 c 3 a 4 c 5 b
B. 6 d 7 c 8 b 9 b 10 a
C. 11 a 12 b 13 b 14 b 15 a
D. 16 a 17 a 18 b 19 a 20 b

Contest
A. 1 c 2 c 3 a 4 a 5 d
B. 6 b 7 a 8 c 9 d 10 b
C. 11 opinion 12 opinion
13 fact 14 opinion 15 fact
D. 16 play 17 ate greedily 18 all
(or most) 19 quiet, stealthy
20 imitate

Night Rider
A. 1 d   2 b   3 a   4 c   5 b
B. 6 d   7 c   8 d   9 c   10 b
C. 11 c   12 a   13 b   14 a   15 c
D. 16 b   17 d   18 b   19 b   20 d

The Sin of Madame Phloi
A. 1 c   2 d   3 c   4 d   5 b
B. 6 b   7 c   8 d   9 a   10 c
C. 11 a   12 a   13 a   14 b   15 a
D. 16 ignore   17 expect   18 after
19 defend   20 involved

How the Leopard Got Its Spots
A. 1 b   2 a   3 a   4 d   5 a
B. 6 b   7 c   8 d   9 a   10 c
C. 11 egotistical   12 foolhardy   13 lazy
14 cowardly   15 miserly
D. 16 a   17 d   18 c   19 b   20 d

Winter Thunder
A. 1 a   2 b   3 b   4 b   5 d
B. 6 a   7 d   8 c   9 c   10 a

Beware of the Dog
A. 1 c   2 d   3 b   4 d   5 c
B. 6 d   7 a   8 b   9 d   10 c
C. 11 b   12 c   13 c   14 b   15 a
D. 16 verb   17 verb   18 noun
19 noun   20 verb

Otero's Vistor
A. 1 d   2 b   3 a   4 b   5 d
B. 6 d   7 d   8 b   9 c   10 d
C. 11 b   12 c   13 b   14 d   15 c
D. 16 b   17 c   18 a   19 e   20 d

Back Then
A. 1 b   2 b   3 c   4 a   5 d
B. 6 c   7 d   8 a   9 d   10 d
C. 11 c   12 a   13 b   14 a   15 a
D. 16 angrily   17 slowly   18 promptly
19 carefully   20 contentedly

Crime on Mars
A. 1 d   2 a   3 c   4 c   5 d
B. 6 d   7 c   8 c   9 a   10 c
C. 11 b   12 b   13 a   14 a   15 c
D. 16 b   17 d   18 d   19 a   20 b

Avalanche
A. 1 b   2 d   3 a   4 d   5 c
B. 6 c   7 a   8 b   9 c   10 c
C. 11 a   12 a   13 b   14 a   15 c
D. 16 overrun   17 anywhere   18 downhill
19 something   20 oncoming

Crow Call
A. 1 b   2 b   3 d   4 d   5 a
B. 6 b   7 c   8 a   9 d   10 b
C. 11 c   12 b   13 c   14 d   15 b
D. 16 sur•round•ed   17 oc•ca•sion•al
18 ac•knowl•edged   19 aft•er•thought
20 spec•u•la•tive•ly

One Alaska Night
A. 1 a   2 c   3 c   4 c   5 b
B. 6 a   7 b   8 d   9 b   10 a
C. 11 b   12 b   13 a   14 b   15 d
D. 16 c   17 d   18 c   19 a   20 b

The Night the Ghost Got In
A. 1 b   2 c   3 c   4 c   5 c
B. 6 c   7 b   8 a   9 d   10 c
C. 11 b   12 a   13 a   14 b   15 a
D. 16 b   17 b   18 a   19 a   20 a

On the Edge
A. 1 b   2 c   3 d   4 c   5 d
B. 6 b   7 a   8 d   9 a   10 c
C. 11 b   12 b   13 c   14 a   15 b
D. 16 V-N   17 N-V   18 V-N   19 V-N
20 V-N

My First Life Line
A. 1 b   2 a   3 d   4 c   5 c
B. 6 d   7 c   8 b   9 a   10 d
C. 11 c   12 b   13 a   14 d   15 c
D. 16 having clouds around the top
17 no exit at the end
18 afraid of guns
19 lowered halfway down the mast
20 not full-time

The Little Lizzard's Sorrow
A. 1 c   2 a   3 c   4 c   5 a
B. 6 b   7 a   8 b   9 d   10 c
C. 11 b   12 a   13 c   14 a   15 c
D. 16 b   17 c   18 b   19 d   20 d

The Baroque Marble
A. 1 c   2 b   3 b   4 a   5 d
B. 6 b   7 c   8 d   9 d   10 b
C. 11 b   12 c   13 d   14 a   15 b
D. 16 b   17 c   18 a   19 d   20 c

The Hobbit
A. 1 c   2 b   3 d   4 b   5 c
B. 6 b   7 d   8 d   9 b   10 c

Sentence Combining

1. Harry wrapped the package, put a label on it, and placed it under the tree.

2. Denise turned on some music, sat down in the easy chair, and closed her eyes.

3. Lois hit the ball, ran like the wind, and slid into first base.

4. Gus washed the lettuce, sliced the tomatoes, and diced the celery.

5. Joyce selected the color, bought the paint, and carried the can home.

Sentence Combining

1. I studied hard because I didn't want to fail.

2. Carrie decided to audition for the lead in the play when she found out her best friend already had a part.

3. Pat didn't like to go to parties, even though he usually had a good time once he got there.

4. Jane wanted to go bowling; however, her parents wanted her to do some chores.

5. The workers decided to strike, since their demands had not been met.

Narration, Description, Exposition

Answers will vary.

TEST BOOKLET
Cascade

JOURNEYS

A Reading and Literature Program
Revised Edition with Writing Supplement

TEST BOOKLET

Cascade

JOURNEYS

A Reading and Literature Program
Revised Edition with Writing Supplement

Orville Palmer

formerly with Educational Testing Service
Princeton, New Jersey

HARCOURT BRACE JOVANOVICH, PUBLISHERS

Orlando   New York   Chicago   San Diego   Atlanta   Dallas

Acknowledgments

For permission to reprint copyrighted material, grateful acknowledgement is made to the following sources:

Dorothy Boles and Triangle Communications Inc.: From "The Contest" by Paul Darcy Boles in *Seventeen®* Magazine. Copyright © 1975 by Triangle Communications Inc. All rights reserved.

The Caxton Printers, Ltd., Caldwell, ID: From "Say It With Flowers" in *Yokohama, California* by Toshio Mori.

CBS Radio, a division of CBS Inc.: From "A Shipment of Mute Fate" by Les Crutchfield. Copyright © 1953 by Columbia Broadcasting System, Inc. All rights reserved.

Manuela Williams Crosno: From "Otero's Visitor" in *New Mexico Quarterly*, Vol. 7, No. 4, November 1937. All rights reserved.

Doubleday & Company, Inc.: From "The Meadow Mouse" in *The Collected Poems of Theodore Roethke.* Copyright © 1963 by Beatrice Roethke as Administratrix of the Estate of Theodore Roethke.

Blanche C. Gregory, Inc. and Lilian Jackson Braun: From "The Sin of Madame Phloi" by Lilian Jackson Braun. Copyright © 1962 by Davis Publications.

Harcourt Brace Jovanovich, Inc.: Slightly adapted and abridged from "The Promised Visit" by Grey Cohoe in *Design For Good Reading* by Schumacher, et al. Copyright © 1969 by Harcourt Brace Jovanovich, Inc.

Lawrence Hill & Co., Westport, CT: From "Last Cover" in *The Best Nature Stories of Paul Annixter.* Copyright © 1974 by Jane and Paul Annixter.

Holiday House, Inc.: From "Trophy for Red" (Retitled: "Big Red") in *Big Red* by Jim Kjelgaard. Copyright 1945 by Jim Kjelgaard; renewed © 1973 by Edna Kjelgaard.

International Creative Management, Inc.: From "Back There" by Rod Serling. Copyright © 1960 by Kayuga Productions, Inc.

George Laycock: From "Unforgettable Grizzly Bears" by George Laycock in *Boys' Life*, January 1977.

Lois Lowry, author of A SUMMER TO DIE and AUTUMN STREET: From "Crow Call" by Lois Lowry. Originally appeared in *Redbook* Magazine, December 1975.

Harold Matson Company, Inc.: From "A Running Brook of Horror" in *All Creatures Great and Small* by Daniel Mannix. Copyright © 1963 by Daniel Mannix.

Scott Meredith Literary Agency, Inc., 845 Third AV, New York, NY 10022 and Arthur C. Clarke: From "Crime on Mars" by Arthur C. Clarke.

Scott Meredith Literary Agency, Inc., 845 Third AV, New York, NY 10022 and E. A. Proulx: From "The Baroque Marble" by E. A. Proulx. Originally appeared in *Seventeen* Magazine, 1970.

Noël Murchie: From "The Wall" by Noël Murchie. Copyright © 1975 by Noël Murchie. Originally appeared in *Redbook* Magazine, May 1975.

John Murray (Publishers) Ltd.: From "The Dying Detective" in *The Game's Afoot* by Michael and Mollie Hardwick.

Random House, Inc.: From "My First Life Line," adapted from *I Know Why the Caged Bird Sings* by Maya Angelou. Copyright © 1969 by Maya Angelou.

Paul R. Reynolds, Inc., 12 East 41st ST, New York, NY 10017: From "One Alaska Night" by Barrett Willoughy. Copyright 1936 by Barrett Willoughby.

Robert Russell, author of TO CATCH AN ANGEL: From "On the Edge" by Robert Russell in *Boys' Life*, August 1976.

A Note to the Teacher

The *Test Booklet* consists of tests for each major selection in *Cascade*. Each test is divided into four parts. The first part consists of five questions that test the student's basic comprehension of the selection. The second part contains five vocabulary questions. The third part tests the student's mastery of the reading skill taught with the selection. The fourth part tests the student's mastery of the word attack skill taught with the selection.

There are also two tests covering the two long selections in *Cascade*. These tests are divided into two parts. The first part tests the student's basic comprehension and the second part tests mastery of vocabulary from the selection.

If your students have reading problems, we suggest that you read the test aloud to them before you have them complete the test on their own.

The answer key to the *Test Booklet* appears in the *Teacher's Manual* for *Cascade*.

CONTENTS

VISTAS

MOSAIC

COMPOSITION

WOODNOTES

Cat-About-Town   *James Herriot*   (Text page 3)

A. Reading Comprehension. In the space at the right, fill in the letter of the best answer to each question. *(5 points each)*

1. At the beginning of the story, Jim thinks that Oscar
  a. will recover   **c.** can be treated with drugs
  b. should be put to sleep **d.** can easily be operated on   1. _____

2. After his recovery, Oscar begins to
  a. fight with other cats   **c.** scratch people
  b. go off for weeks at a time **d.** pay social calls   2. _____

3. Gibbons and his sons
  a. accuse Jim of stealing their cat
  b. say that Oscar belongs to them
  c. offer to sell Oscar
  d. offer to share the cat with the Herriots   3. _____

4. After Oscar is returned to his original owners, he
  a. becomes sad and shy   **c.** continues his social visits
  b. becomes ill   **d.** becomes a famous fighter   4. _____

5. At the end of the story, the Herriots
  a. take Oscar back   **c.** buy a cat to replace Oscar
  b. forget about Oscar   **d.** visit Oscar at the Gibbons' cottage   5. _____

B. Vocabulary. Write the letter of the word or group of words closest in meaning to each *italicized* word. *(5 points each)*

6. "The girl shook her head. 'No, he looks like a *stray* to me.'"
  a. friendly animal   **c.** wandering, or lost pet
  b. adopted pet   **d.** injured animal   6. _____

7. ". . . she stretched out a hand and touched the *emaciated* animal . . ."
  a. fat   **b.** uncombed   **c.** wild   **d.** very thin   7. _____

8. "Those guts are *perforated* in several places."
  a. punctured   **b.** swollen   **c.** bruised   **d.** soiled   8. _____

9. ". . . here I was glad to Tristan's *nimble* fingers."
  a. willing   **c.** quick and skillful
  b. clean   **d.** short and stubby   9. _____

10. "I snatched Oscar and tucked him under my arm. 'My wife is *distraught* . . .'"
  a. happy   **b.** upset   **c.** alert   **d.** absent-minded   10. _____

C. Sentence Meaning (*Reading Skill*). Read the passage below. Tristan is talking to Jim. Then answer the questions that follow the passage. (*5 points each*)

> "I don't fancy this much, Jim. Can't we do something?"
> "You mean, put that lot back?"
> "Yes."
> "But the bowels are damaged—they're like a sieve in parts."
> "We could stitch them, couldn't we?"
> I lifted the blanket and looked again. "Honestly, Triss, I wouldn't know where to start. And the whole thing is filthy."

11. Who says, "You mean, put that lot back?"   11. _____

12. Who says, "But the bowels are damaged"?   12. _____

13. Who says, "Can't we do something?"   13. _____

14. Who says, "And the whole thing is filthy?"   14. _____

15. Who says, "We could stitch them, couldn't we?"   15. _____

D. Word Attack. From the following list of words, choose the correct word to complete each sentence below. Then write the letter of the word in the space at the right. Use a dictionary if you need help. (*5 points each*)

a. consolation	**d.** ensue
b. distraught	**e.** abdomen
c. saunter	

16. During the last stage of the operation on Oscar, Jim had to sew up the
_____ of the cat.   16. _____

17. When Oscar disappeared, Helen became _____.   17. _____

18. The Herriots hated to give up Oscar, but it was a _____ to know he
was with people who loved him.   18. _____

19. When Oscar came home after a night out visiting, he would
_____ through the door as if nothing had happened.   19. _____

20. Even after the operation, Jim was afraid that complications would
_____, and that the cat would probably not survive.   20. _____

Last Cover   *Paul Annixter*   *(Text page 18)*

A. Reading Comprehension. In the space at the right, fill in the letter of the best answer to each question. *(5 points each)*

1. Although the story tells us about Bandit's life as a kit, the story actually begins when
   a. Bandit kills a chicken   **c.** Colin draws a picture of him
   b. Bandit runs away   **d.** Bandit finds a mate

   1. _____

2. Who is chiefly responsible for feeding and caring for Bandit?
   a. Stan   **c.** Father
   b. Colin   **d.** Mom

   2. _____

3. After Bandit leaves, the two boys search for him because they want to
   a. keep their bond with him   **c.** bring him food
   b. protect him from hunters   **d.** test their skill in tracking

   3. _____

4. How does the great hunt for Bandit end?
   a. The dogs run him down and kill him.
   b. Two foxes are killed, but not Bandit or his mate.
   c. Bandit's mate is killed, but Colin saves Bandit.
   d. Bandit escapes the hunters but is later killed by a lucky hunter.

   4. _____

5. What brings Colin and his father together at the end of the story?
   a. Bandit's death   **c.** Colin's drawing of Bandit
   b. Colin's long illness   **d.** love of all wildlife

   5. _____

B. Vocabulary. Write the letter of the word or group of words closest in meaning to each *italicized* word. *(5 points each)*

6. "... not even a *rumor* had been heard of him since."
   a. unproven story   **c.** funny story
   b. complete account   **d.** guess

   6. _____

7. "Maybe then he'd make a drawing for the frame and be able to forget his *misery*."
   a. great poverty   **c.** physical pain
   b. great sadness   **d.** deep fear

   7. _____

8. "... I've had an *invalid* for help around the place."
   a. lazy individual   **c.** temporary helper
   b. active person   **d.** sick person

   8. _____

9. "... they'd found Colin *crouched* nearby holding her cub in his arms."
   a. bent low   **c.** standing upright
   b. hiding   **d.** lying flat

   9. _____

10. "... his movements so quiet and *casual* he seemed to be standing still."
    a. tense   **b.** unconcerned   **c.** accidental   **d.** confident

    10. _____

C. Sentence Meaning (*Reading Skill*). Each of the following sentences needs a punctuation mark added to make its meaning clear. The punctuation mark is provided in parentheses after each sentence. In the space at the right, write the word that the punctuation mark should follow. *(5 points each)*

11. "What sleepers are they" I asked. (Add ?)

    11. _____

12. Because of his talent Colin was special. (Add ,)

    12. _____

13. After they met Colin changed his mind. (Add ,)

    13. _____

14. "I had never seen him work so hard I seemed to sense in the air the feeling he was putting into it, how he was *believing* his picture into being." (Add .)

    14. _____

15. "'Did you go up in the foothills' Mom asked." (Add ?)

    15. _____

D. Word Attack. Each of the following items contains an *italicized* word. Choose the definition of the *italicized* word that best fits the context, and write its letter in the space at the right. *(5 points each)*

16. "It goes back to a winter afternoon after I'd hunted the woods all day for a *sign* of our lost pet."
    a. symbol   **b.** gesture   **c.** trace

    16. _____

17. "Why, all the animals that have got *sense* enough to hole up and stay hid in weather like this."
    a. bodily sensation   **b.** meaning   **c.** good judgment

    17. _____

18. ". . . Colin threatened to break the family tradition with his *leaning* toward art . . ."
    a. inclination, or interest in
    b. being off balance
    c. being propped against

    18. _____

19. "There was something *rare* and secret like the spirit of the woods about him . . ."
    a. thinly scattered   **b.** uncommon, or unusual   **c.** undercooked

    19. _____

20. "She *melted* from sight like a shadow."
    a. became kind-hearted   **b.** disappeared   **c.** softened

    20. _____

The Meadow Mouse   *Theodore Roethke*   *(Text page 31)*

A. Reading Comprehension. In the space at the right, fill in the letter of the best answer to each question. *(5 points each)*

   1. All of the following words EXCEPT one describe the baby mouse when it was found. Which is the exception?
      a. frightened   **c.** hungry
      b. alone   **d.** well cared-for   1. _____

   2. When the poet caught the mouse, it
      a. came with him willingly   **c.** tried to get away
      b. followed him home   **d.** bit him   2. _____

   3. Once in the house, the little mouse did a number of things. Which of the following is NOT one of them?
      a. It ate.   **c.** It hid.
      b. It slept.   **d.** It drank.   3. _____

   4. The poet kept the mouse in a
      a. jar   **c.** basket
      b. shoe box   **d.** tool box   4. _____

   5. At the end of the poem, the little mouse
      a. dies   **c.** grows up
      b. disappears   **d.** gets eaten   5. _____

B. Vocabulary. Write the letter of the word or group of words closest in meaning to each of the following numbered words taken from the selection. *(5 points each)*

   6. absurd   **a.** very small   6. _____

   7. miniscule   **b.** breathing with difficulty   7. _____

   8. twitching   **c.** ridiculous, unbelievable   8. _____

   9. gasping   **d.** making jerking movements   9. _____

   10. stunned   **e.** shocked, or astonished   10. _____

C. Sentence Meaning (*Reading Skill*). Each of the following excerpts from the poem needs a punctuation mark added to make its meaning clear. The punctuation mark is provided in parentheses after each excerpt. In the space at the right, write the word that the punctuation mark should follow. *(5 points each)*

   11. "His tail curled under him his belly big as his head . . ."
       (Add ,)   11. _____

Test Booklet   Cascade   5

12. "Do I imagine he no longer trembles when I come close to him" (Add   ?)

12. _____

13. "He seems no longer to tremble" (Add   .)

13. _____

14. "Where has he gone, my meadow mouse, / My thumb of a child that muzzled in my palm" (Add   ?)

14. _____

15. "All things innocent, hapless forsaken." (Add   ,)

15. _____

D. Word Attack. Look up each of the following words in the dictionary and write the diacritical marks for it in the space provided. *(5 points each)*

Example: stocking

_____ stŏk'ĭng

16. meadow

16. _____

17. beneath

17. _____

18. struggle

18. _____

19. belly

19. _____

20. tremble

20. _____

Unforgettable Grizzly Bears   *George Laycock*   (Text page 36)

A. Reading Comprehension. In the space at the right, fill in the letter of the best answer to each question. *(5 points each)*

1. All of the outlaw bears in this essay
   a. were females protecting their young
   b. had been injured by a bullet or a trap
   c. lived in Alaska
   d. were born with a hatred of humans

   1. _____

2. The article gives us a number of important facts about grizzlies. Which of the following is NOT one of them?
   a. They are meat-eating animals.
   b. They have become extinct in much of the United States.
   c. They are very powerful and can be dangerous.
   d. They are very slow, and can be easily outrun.

   2. _____

3. Old Two Toes, Bloody Paws, and Old Mose were all finally destroyed by
   a. being trapped   **c.** falling from a cliff
   b. being shot   **d.** old age

   3. _____

4. The author advises people traveling through grizzly country to
   a. wear a bright red shirt   **c.** make lots of noise
   b. carry both a pistol and a **d.** ride on horseback.
   rifle

   4. _____

5. The author believes that grizzlies should
   a. be allowed to live in their own territory
   b. be kept in zoos
   c. be confined to one or two "grizzly parks"
   d. all be destroyed

   5. _____

B. Vocabulary. Write the letter of the word or group of words closest in meaning to each *italicized* word. *(5 points each)*

6. "Every time a cowboy rode the trails of western Montana around 1902, he *scanned* the ground for the tracks of a very special grizzly bear."
   a. avoided   **b.** looked over   **c.** feared   **d.** anticipated

   6. _____

7. "This bear was said to have *dispatched* more than 500 sheep, including fifty-two in a single night."
   a. eaten   **c.** killed
   b. chased   **d.** frightened

   7. _____

8. "But chasing the big bear was a *risky* business."
   a. slow   **b.** simple   **c.** pleasant   **d.** difficult and dangerous

   8. _____

9. "It is possible that the pain of old wounds helped cause their *cranky* dispositions."
   a. pleasant   **c.** easily angered
   b. sad   **d.** calm

   9. _____

10. "Even if the grizzlies *vanish,* stories about them will live on."
    a. disappear **b.** succeed **c.** escape **d.** multiply   10. _____

C. Sentence Meaning (*Reading Skill*). Find the three core parts of each sentence below, and write them in the space provided. *(5 points each)*

11. The shot grazed the bear.   11. _____

12. One day, the wrangler met Old Two Toes on the
    mountain.   12. _____

13. Many ranchers consider grizzlies a nuisance.   13. _____

14. The renegade bear roamed the mountain cattle country.   14. _____

15. Ratcliff finally discovered Old Mose in a clump of trees.   15. _____

D. Word Attack. Answer the following questions about guide words. *(5 points each)*

16. Imagine that the guide words at the top of a glossary page are *crop* and
    crowd. Which one of the following words would NOT fall on this page?
    a. croquet **b.** crow **c.** coward **d.** croup   16. _____

17. Imagine that the guide words at the top of the page are *date* and
    deacon. Which one of the following words would NOT fall on this
    page?
    a. determine **b.** davit **c.** dawn **d.** dazzle   17. _____

18. Imagine that the guide words at the top of the page are *participate* and
    pass. Which one of the following words would NOT fall on this page?
    a. party **b.** partisan **c.** partial **d.** particular   18. _____

19. Imagine that the guide words at the top of the page are *shave* and *shine.*
    Which one of the following words would NOT fall on this page?
    a. shelter **b.** sheriff **c.** shelf **d.** sharp   19. _____

20. Imagine that the guide words are *top* and *torture.* Which one of the
    following words would NOT fall on this page?
    a. torch **b.** toss **c.** torment **d.** torpedo   20. _____

A Shipment of Mute Fate   *Les Crutchfield*   (Text page 46)

A. Reading Comprehension. In the space at the right, fill in the letter of the best answer to each question. *(5 points each)*

1. Why is Captain Wood against taking the bushmaster on the voyage?
   a. there is no room
   b. he thinks it's too dangerous
   c. he is allergic to snakes
   d. his pet cat is frightened of snakes   1. _____

2. After the snake escapes from its box, the ship's crew and Chris immediately
   a. warn the passengers
   b. search the ship
   c. agree to abandon ship
   d. decide to wait and see if the snake will show up   2. _____

3. Chris finally finds the bushmaster
   a. in his own cabin
   b. back in his damaged box
   c. in the steward's galley
   d. in a dark passageway   3. _____

4. Chris seems to believe that the bushmaster has been
   a. looking for milk
   b. sleeping quietly
   c. searching for mice
   d. waiting for Chris to appear   4. _____

5. The cat fights and kills the bushmaster in order to
   a. protect her kittens
   b. save Chris
   c. save her own life
   d. protect her owner   5. _____

B. Vocabulary. Write the letter of the word or group of words closest in meaning to each *italicized* word. *(5 points each)*

6. ". . . I couldn't forget that a certain pair of *beady* eyes was watching every move I made."
   a. small and shining
   b. angry
   c. frightened
   d. friendly   6. _____

7. ". . . coiled loosely in an *undulant* loop, ready to strike violently at the least movement."
   a. tight
   b. very small
   c. perfectly round
   d. slowly moving   7. _____

8. "It's got to have a stronger box. That crate's too *flimsy*."
   a. large
   b. difficult to open
   c. delicate and easily damaged
   d. awkward to handle   8. _____

9. "I was becoming possessed with an ominous *anxiety*."
   a. hatred
   b. indifference
   c. affection
   d. fear and worry   9. _____

10. "But with proper *precautions*!"
   a. manners
   b. employees
   c. equipment
   d. safety arrangements   10. _____

C. Sentence Meaning (*Word Attack*). Read the following sentences from the play and add the word or words that will make each a complete sentence. *(5 points each)*

      Example: "Got a cable from the head office this morning."   _____ I got _____

11. "Be dark in a little while."   **11.** _____

12. "Fair enough."   **12.** _____

13. "Not another wave that size in sight."   **13.** _____

14. "You agree to that?"   **14.** _____

15. "A thousand places for it to hide."   **15.** _____

D. Word Attack. Each of the following items contains an *italicized* contraction. In the space provided, write the words that have been combined to form each contraction. *(5 points each)*

16. "So *it's* happened!"   **16.** _____

17. "It *might've* crawled overboard."   **17.** _____

18. ". . . everybody on *board's* in the same danger . . ."   **18.** _____

19. "*How'll* we do it, Captain?"   **19.** _____

20. "One pistol shot, and *we'd* have a riot on our hands."   **20.** _____

PROFILES

You Can't Take It With You *Eva-Lis Wuorio* (Text page 75)

A. Reading Comprehension. In the space at the right, fill in the letter of the best answer to each question. *(5 points each)*

1. All of the following words EXCEPT one describe most of Uncle Basil's relatives. Which is the exception?
   a. greedy **b.** wasteful **c.** hopeful **d.** contented

   1. _____

2. How did Uncle Basil first make his money?
   a. He found a gold mine. **c.** He was a salesman.
   b. He inherited it. **d.** He saved wisely.

   2. _____

3. Uncle Basil's favorite relative is
   a. Verner **c.** Aunt Clotilda
   b. Percival **d.** Maud

   3. _____

4. When Uncle Basil dies, he leaves some money to
   a. his sister and Percival **c.** his lawyer
   b. all of the relatives **d.** his housekeeper and Verner

   4. _____

5. What happened to the rest of Uncle Basil's money?
   a. It was buried in the back yard. **c.** It was invested.
   b. It was burned up with the coffin. **d.** It had been given to charity.

   5. _____

B. Vocabulary. Write the letter of the word or group of words closest in meaning to each *italicized* word. *(5 points each)*

6. "The family were *unanimous* about that."
   a. stubborn **b.** hopeful **c.** very angry **d.** all agreed

   6. _____

7. "What *galled* him was the often repeated warning, 'You can't take it with you.'"
   a. worried **b.** irritated **c.** bored **d.** interested

   7. _____

8. ". . . in an unfashionable *suburb*."
   a. apartment house **c.** town close to a large city
   b. business district **d.** center of a large city

   8. _____

9. ". . . got used to his somewhat *unorthodox* business methods."
   a. old-fashioned **c.** clear and simple
   b. farsighted **d.** unusual, or unconventional

   9. _____

10. "Rich men have always been allowed their *foibles*."
    a. secrets **c.** harmless failings
    b. special pleasures **d.** moments of anger

    10. _____

C. Relationships (*Reading Skill*). Arrange the following events in their proper time order. *(5 points each)*

    a. Verner went to work for Uncle Basil.
    b. Uncle Basil was cremated.
    c. Verner told how he lined Uncle Basil's coffin.
    d. Uncle Basil went to South Africa.
    e. Uncle Basil's final statement was read.

11. Which event happened first?   **11.** _____

12. Which event happened second?   **12.** _____

13. Which event happened third?   **13.** _____

14. Which event happened next-to-last?   **14.** _____

15. Which event happened last?   **15.** _____

D. Word Attack. From the list below, choose the word or group of words that is a synonym for each numbered word, and write its letter in the space at the right. Use a dictionary if you need help. *(5 points each)*

    a. danger signal   **d.** mood
    b. pain, or unhappiness   **e.** nonsense
    c. actions

16. temper   **16.** _____

17. warning   **17.** _____

18. misery   **18.** _____

19. proceedings   **19.** _____

20. drivel   **20.** _____

The Promised Visit   *Grey Cohoe*   (Text page 82)

A. Reading Comprehension. In the space at the right, fill in the letter of the best answer to each question. *(5 points each)*

1. At the beginning of the story, the narrator is returning from
   a. a shopping trip   **c.** a visit to relatives
   b. a scholarship examination   **d.** a party   1. _____

2. This selection contains elements of all the following, with one exception. Which is the exception?
   a. a love story   **c.** a spy story
   b. a ghost story   **d.** a modern Indian legend   2. _____

3. Susan Billy can be described in several ways. Which of the following is NOT an accurate description?
   a. mysterious   **b.** shy   **c.** lovely and fascinating   **d.** rude   3. _____

4. Where does the narrator find his sweater?
   a. lying by the side of the road
   b. on the seat of his truck
   c. in his room
   d. hanging on the hogan where Susan is buried   4. _____

5. Susan did all of the following, with one exception. Which is the exception?
   a. She tried to kill the narrator.
   b. She became fond of the narrator.
   c. She promised to visit the narrator.
   d. She killed a number of people.   5. _____

B. Vocabulary. Write the letter of the word or group of words closest in meaning to each *italicized* word. *(5 points each)*

6. "The *aroma* of the flying wet dirt . . ."
   a. clammy touch   **c.** danger
   b. smell   **d.** sight   6. _____

7. "Immediately the chill awakened my *reflexes*."
   a. memories   **c.** five senses
   b. automatic responses   **d.** fears   7. _____

8. "The storm calmed and turned into a *genial* shower."
   a. brief   **b.** fierce   **c.** gentle and cheering   **d.** long-awaited   8. _____

9. "The round moon cast its light on the *soggy* ground . . ."
   a. level   **c.** hilly
   b. dark   **d.** wet   9. _____

10. ". . . I continued to *hasten* on, looking for the lights at Littlewater . . ."
   a. drive slowly   **c.** hurry
   b. struggle   **d.** observe carefully   10. _____

C. Relationships (_Reading Skill_). Each of the following sentences describes a cause-and-effect relationship. In the space at the right, write the word that signals the cause-and-effect relationship. *(5 points each)*

11. He had slept little the night previously; consequently he felt sleepy.

11. _____

12. She seemed to be shivering with cold, so he offered her his sweater.

12. _____

13. Since he could not get her out of his thoughts, he worked slowly.

13. _____

14. He had not wished to be superstitious; therefore, the news came as a great shock.

14. _____

15. Because the old hogan looked long abandoned, he did not believe Susan could be living there.

15. _____

D. Word Attack. Each of the following sentences contains an *italicized* verb. In the space at the right, write the form of the italicized verb indicated in parentheses. Use your dictionary if you need help. *(5 points each)*

16. Although apparently very shy, she *talk* (past tense) with him.

16. _____

17. He had *go* (past participle) to Window Rock for an interview.

17. _____

18. The thunderheads had *build* (past participle) up rapidly.

18. _____

19. The overcast *hide* (past tense) his view of the empty land.

19. _____

20. He was *drive* (present participle) as carefully as he could.

20. _____

Say It With Flowers   *Toshio Mori*   (Text page 95)

A. Reading Comprehension. In the space at the right, fill in the letter of the best answer to each question. *(5 points each)*

1. Which one of the following gets Teruo into trouble with Mr. Sasaki?
 a. a good memory   **c.** a pleasing personality
 b. willingness to learn   **d.** a sense of honesty   1. _____

2. The difference between the flowers in the front of the shop and the flowers in the rear is that the flowers in the front are
 a. fresher   **c.** older
 b. prettier   **d.** more popular   2. _____

3. Mr. Sasaki feels that he must
 a. sell only the freshest flowers
 b. sell only to the wealthiest people
 c. sell all his flowers
 d. please all his customers   3. _____

4. On his last day of work for Mr. Sasaki, Teruo
 a. gets in a fight with Tommy
 b. tries to make all his customers happy
 c. quarrels with several customers
 d. refuses to work at all   4. _____

5. Teruo leaves Mr. Sasaki's shop because of his
 a. honesty and integrity   **c.** youth
 b. inexperience   **d.** ambition   5. _____

B. Vocabulary. Write the letter of the word or group of words closest in meaning to each *italicized* word. *(5 points each)*

6. ". . . his smile *disarmed* a person."
 a. misled   **c.** removed suspicion or unfriendliness
 b. angered   **d.** surprised   6. _____

7. "He was . . . a *glutton* for work."
 a. person with a great capacity   **c.** lazy individual
 b. foolish individual   **d.** slow, thorough person   7. _____

8. ". . . I can say it *convincingly* . . ."
 a. quietly   **c.** persuasively, or with conviction
 b. loudly   **d.** steadily, with complete calm   8. _____

9. "Then one morning the *inevitable* happened."
 a. unexpected event   **c.** surprising event
 b. unavoidable event   **d.** most pleasant event   9. _____

10. ". . . we stood around like his *stooges*."
 a. admirers   **c.** envious friends
 b. superiors   **d.** simple-minded helpers   10. _____

C. Relationships (*Reading Skill*). Each of the following sentences describes a cause-and-effect relationship. In the space at the right, write the word that signals the cause-and-effect relationship. *(5 points each)*

11. The flowers were newly delivered, so they were placed in the back of the store.

11. _____

12. Tommy was an experienced florist; consequently he managed the shop in Mr. Sasaki's absence.

12. _____

13. Because Teruo liked people, he always smiled at them.

13. _____

14. Teruo needed a job; therefore, he tried to become a good florist.

14. _____

15. Since he had learned through painful experience, Teruo probably did not look for work in another flower shop.

15. _____

D. Word Attack. Each of the following sentences contains a blank space. From the words in parentheses, choose the correct homophone to complete each sentence, and write it in the space at the right. *(5 points each)*

16. Teruo wanted to do the _____ (write, right) thing both by his employer and his customers.

16. _____

17. He had _____ (knot, not) worked with a florist before and scarcely knew one flower from another.

17. _____

18. As the days past, he quickly learned _____ (their, there, they're) names and prices.

18. _____

19. _____ (Know, No) person tried harder than Teruo to get everything right.

19. _____

20. What _____ (wood, would) happen to Teruo if he continued to tell the truth?

20. _____

A Running Brook of Horror   *Daniel Mannix*   (Text page 106)

A. Reading Comprehension. In the space at the right, fill in the letter of the best answer to each question. *(5 points each)*

1. The narrator and Grace Wiley had a number of things in common. Which of the following is NOT one of them?
   a. Both loved snakes.   **c.** Both lived in California.
   b. Both sold snakes.   **d.** Both knew a lot about snakes.   1. _____

2. The one snake that Grace Wiley allowed to strike her open palm was a
   a. rattler   **b.** krait   **c.** cobra   **d.** asp   2. _____

3. The article contains a great deal of information about snakes. Which of the following is false?
   a. Cobras are more dangerous than rattlesnakes.
   b. It is impossible to judge the distance of a cobra's strike.
   c. Unlike the rattler, a cobra has to "chew a hole" in its victim.
   d. The king cobra is larger than a boa constrictor.   3. _____

4. Grace Wiley's main source of income was
   a. the sale of her books   **c.** sales of snakes
   b. fees from tourists   **d.** sales of snake serum   4. _____

5. Grace Wiley was fatally bitten because she
   a. was fixing her hair   **c.** had removed her glasses
   b. was blinded by sunlight   **d.** didn't keep her palm open   5. _____

B. Vocabulary. Write the letter of the word or group of words closest in meaning to each of the following numbered words taken from the selection. *(5 points each)*

6. curious   **a.** sure   **b.** strange   **c.** weak   **d.** mean   6. _____

7. reluctant   **a.** angry   **b.** strong   **c.** unwilling   **d.** old   7. _____

8. mishap   **a.** joy   **b.** plan   **c.** grief   **d.** accident   8. _____

9. frustrated **a.** poor   **b.** wary   **c.** discouraged **d.** brave   9. _____

10. trail   **a.** support   **b.** wait   **c.** track   **d.** expect   10. _____

C. Relationships (*Reading Skill*). Each of the following passages makes a comparison or contrast. Answer the question that follows each passage. *(5 points each)*

11. ". . . A picture of a tiny woman with a gigantic king cobra draped over her shoulders like a garden hose." This comparison shows that the cobra was
    a. green   **c.** limp and relaxed
    b. tightly coiled about her neck **d.** angry   11. _____

12. "'Grace lives in a little house full of poisonous snakes imported from all over the world. She lets them wander around like cats.'" This comparison tells us that the snakes
    a. sleep most of the time   **c.** are playful
    b. roam like house pets   **d.** are very curious   **12.** _____

13. "Although Grace was sixty-four years old, she was as active as a boy and worked with smooth dexterity." This comparison tells us that Grace was as
    a. restless as a boy   **c.** strong as a boy
    b. energetic as a boy   **d.** playful as a boy   **13.** _____

14. "Hunters have been mauled by wounded elephants and lived to tell about it, but no one survives a body bite from a big cobra." This contrast tells us that elephants
    a. never kill hunters   **c.** are not willing to attack people
    b. are not as deadly as cobras   **d.** attack only when wounded   **14.** _____

15. "[The cobra's] fangs are short and do not fold back. Instead of stabbing like the rattler, he must actually bite." Compared to the rattler, the cobra
    a. is less aggressive   **c.** has different fangs
    b. is less dangerous   **d.** is more primitive   **15.** _____

D. Word Attack. Each of the following passages contains an *italicized* word. Using the context to help you find the meaning, pick the correct definition for each italicized word, and write its letter in the space provided. *(5 points each)*

16. "She was a surprisingly little lady, *scarcely* over five feet, and probably weighed less than a hundred pounds."
    a. actually   **b.** barely   **c.** greatly   **d.** obviously   **16.** _____

17. "Grace stopped at each cage, casually lifting the *occupant* and pointing out his fine points while she stroked and examined him."
    a. cover   **b.** weight   **c.** dweller   **d.** door   **17.** _____

18. "I have seen children laugh with excitement at the roar of a lion, but I have never seen anyone who did not *cringe* at that cold, uncanny sound [of a cobra]."
    a. joke   **c.** look closely
    b. talk indifferently   **d.** shrink in fear   **18.** _____

19. "Suddenly the snake went *limp* and his hood began to close. Grace slipped her other hand under the snake's body and lifted him out of the cage."
    a. slack   **b.** threatening   **c.** stiff   **d.** alert   **19.** _____

20. "Also, the blow of a cobra is comparatively slow. A man with steady nerves can *jerk* away in time to avoid being bitten."
    a. push   **b.** move quickly   **c.** run   **d.** walk   **20.** _____ .

The Dying Detective   *Michael and Mollie Hardwick*   (Text page 122)

A. Reading Comprehension. In the space at the right, fill in the letter of the best answer to each question. *(5 points each)*

1. During this play Sherlock Holmes never leaves his bed, because he
   a. is lazy   **c.** is actually very ill
   b. is playing an elaborate trick   **d.** has been injured   1. _____

2. The small box on Holmes's bedside table is
   a. one that Holmes bought on the London docks
   b. Holmes's favorite cigarette box
   c. Culverton Smith's deadly "murder weapon"
   d. Dr. Watson's pill box   2. _____

3. Mrs. Hudson and Dr. Watson react to Holmes's illness in the same way, in that they both
   a. urge him to get out of   **c.** urge him to seek treatment
      bed and move around   **d.** send for an ambulance
   b. think that his illness is   3. _____
      minor

4. All of the following statements about Culverton Smith are true EXCEPT one. Which one is false?
   a. Culverton Smith is an expert on Tapanuli Fever.
   b. He runs a plantation.
   c. He has murdered someone named Victor Savage.
   d. Holmes once sent him to prison.   4. _____

5. The play reveals a number of Holmes's habits and character traits. Which of the following is NOT one of them?
   a. He is very shrewd and clever.
   b. He is a tireless investigator.
   c. He is eccentric and unconventional.
   d. He is gullible, and easily fooled.   5. _____

B. Vocabulary. Write the letter of the word or group of words closest in meaning to each *italicized* word. *(5 points each)*

6. "Quite fair—if he hadn't put such *sarcasm* into saying it."
   a. joy   **b.** mocking tone   **c.** deep anger   **d.** friendliness   6. _____

7. ". . . he'll pretend I've said anything he cares to invent that will *corroborate* his insane suspicions."
   a. confirm   **b.** ignore   **c.** contradict   **d.** disguise   7. _____

8. "You saved an *invalid* trouble by giving my signal . . ."
   a. friend   **c.** clever person
   b. enemy   **d.** sick person   8. _____

9. "Your face! You really do look *ghastly*."
   a. silly   **b.** horrible   **c.** hopeless   **d.** fearful   9. _____

10. ". . . just be nice time for something *nutritious* at our little place in the Strand."
   a. well-cooked   **c.** rich and expensive
   b. nourishing   **d.** simple and plain   **10.** _____

C. Relationships (*Reading Skill*). Each of the following sentences contains a word or phrase that signals a contrast relationship. Find the word or phrase and write it in the space at the right. *(5 points each)*

11. Sherlock Holmes looked very ill, but he was actually only pretending.   **11.** _____

12. Although Dr. Watson was an experienced medical man, he had never heard of Tapanuli Fever.   **12.** _____

13. Holmes looked pale and sickly; by contrast, Dr. Watson looked exceedingly well-nourished.   **13.** _____

14. Culverton Smith gloated over the dying Holmes, but his moment of triumph was much shorter than Holmes's.   **14.** _____

15. In spite of Holmes's thorough precautions, Dr. Watson would have seen through them had he been allowed to examine the dying man.   **15.** _____

D. Word Attack. Each of the following sentences contains an *italicized* word. Choose the definition of the italicized word that best fits the context of each sentence, and write its letter in the space at the right. *(5 points each)*

16. "What? This is *monstrous*! I, his oldest friend, and . . ."
   a. shocking, or outrageous   **c.** malformed
   b. like a monster   **d.** very large   **16.** _____

17. "Good heavens, do you suppose such a *consideration* weighs with me? Even if I weren't a doctor . . ."
   a. careful thought; deliberation   **c.** fee, or compensation
   b. idea contributing to a decision   **d.** sympathetic regard for others   **17.** _____

18. "As a medical man, you're a mere general practitioner, of limited *experience* . . ."
   a. everything that has happened in one's life   **c.** an individual reaction to events
   b. a specific event in one's life   **d.** knowledge and skill   **18.** _____

19. "Now, is there any further service I can *render* you?"
   a. yield   **c.** give
   b. melt   **d.** translate   **19.** _____

20. "Really? Watson, have you any *change* in your pocket?"
   a. variety   **b.** alteration   **c.** fickleness   **d.** coins   **20.** _____

Big Red   *Jim Kjelgaard*   *(Text page 143)*

A. Reading Comprehension. In the space at the right, fill in the letter of the best answer to each question. *(5 points each)*

1. Danny has a number of reasons for tracking down and killing Old Majesty. Which of the following is NOT one of them?
   a. The bear injured his father and killed some of their dogs.
   b. The bear must not be allowed to rule the wilderness.
   c. Danny knows his father expects him to hunt down the bear.
   d. Danny wishes to train his bird dog to be a bear hunter.   1. _____

2. Red is
   a. a brave, intelligent animal   **c.** a dog trained to track animals
   b. a beautiful show dog   **d.** an experienced bear hunter   2. _____

3. While Danny and Red track him, Old Majesty is
   a. waiting in ambush   **c.** letting his wounds heal
   b. stealing farmers' stock   **d.** eating grubs   3. _____

4. An unusual aspect of the encounter with the bear is that
   a. Danny's rifle jams at a crucial moment
   b. the bear has circled around and is tracking Danny and Red
   c. Red proves to be cowardly
   d. Danny is caught out in the open   4. _____

5. Danny and Red
   a. save each other's life
   b. fail to kill the bear
   c. show the bear to be a coward
   d. catch the bear completely by surprise   5. _____

B. Vocabulary. Write the letter of the word or group of words closest in meaning to each of the following numbered words taken from the selection. *(5 points each)*

6. crest	**a.** sign	**b.** worry	**c.** hunt	**d.** top	6. _____
7. strode	**a.** fell	**b.** flew	**c.** walked	**d.** hit	7. _____
8. alight	**a.** run	**b.** flee	**c.** observe	**d.** land	8. _____
9. stray	**a.** wander	**b.** come	**c.** play	**d.** shoot	9. _____
10. quailed	**a.** fled	**b.** chased	**c.** faced	**d.** trembled	10. _____

C. Relationships (*Reading Skill*). Read each of the following excerpts carefully; then answer the question that follows. *(5 points each)*

11. "Red padded behind him as he toiled up one mountain, down its other side, and up the mountain beyond. He paused on the summit to stare down the slope. Red edged around him, pricked up his ears, and raised his hackles. He growled, looked up and wagged his tail." When Red looks up, he looks

a. up the mountainside at   c. down the steep slope
   its summit   d. back the way they had come   11. _____
b. at Danny

12. "Twilight came, and erratic bats swooped up and down the little stream before him. But pitch darkness had descended on the wilderness . . ." Where is the stream in relation to Danny?

a. behind him   c. circling around him
b. in front of him   d. to his side   12. _____

13. "The wind still blew steadily from the west. A whippoorwill shrieked, and Red halted to peer toward the sound. Danny waited for the big dog to catch up with him. He was still a hundred feet below the mountain's crest when he stooped to crawl." Red is

a. ranging ahead of Danny
b. walking at Danny's side
c. downslope from Danny
d. waiting at the mountain's crest for Danny   13. _____

14. "Now the bear was just a little way down the hill, looking them over, reading them with his nose, and listening for their next move." Where are Danny and Red in relation to the bear?

a. above him   c. below him
b. to his side   d. behind him   14. _____

15. "Danny snapped the light on. Its white beam travelled into the night to fall like a silver cage about something huge and black, something that stood scarcely twenty yards up the spine of the ridge. The wind blowing out of the valley eddied around it, curling the long hair that hung from its belly." Where is the bear in relation to Danny and Red?

a. just above them on the ridge
b. high above them on the mountain's summit
c. just down the slope from them
d. right next to them   15. _____

D. Word Attack. Each of the following words contains a root. Underline the root; then write the meaning of the new word in the space provided. Use a dictionary if you need help. *(5 points each)*

16. entitled   16. _____

17. winning   17. _____

18. suppress   18. _____

19. undisturbed   19. _____

20. imperceptible   20. _____

The Wall   *Noël Murchie*   (Text page 154)

A. Reading Comprehension. In the space at the right, fill in the letter of the best answer to each question. *(5 points each)*

1. The ascent of the Wall is
   a. Jo's initiation into the world of climbing
   b. Jo's first and last climbing experience
   c. Gunner's last climb
   d. simple and easy   1. _____

2. Carefully planned and safe climbing requires many things. Which of the following is NOT one of them?
   a. proper equipment   **c.** a complete absence of fear
   b. proper technique   **d.** brains and agility   2. _____

3. Someone nearly gets killed during the group's ascent of the Wall. Who saves whom?
   a. Gunner Benner saves Jo.   **c.** Tom saves Jo's mother.
   b. Jo saves Gunner.   **d.** Jo's mother saves Gunner.   3. _____

4. When Jo begins to climb the Wall, her father yells up at her to correct a mistake she makes. What is the mistake?
   a. climbing too fast   **c.** using her knees to climb
   b. looking down   **d.** using her hands alone   4. _____

5. By successfully completing the climb, Jo
   a. decides to become a writer
   b. finds confidence in herself
   c. stops feeling sorry for her brother
   d. decides to become a professional climber   5. _____

B. Vocabulary. Write the letter of the word or group of words closest in meaning to each *italicized* word. *(5 points each)*

6. "... I finally knew the *exhilaration* of propelling myself through free space."
   a. fear   **c.** great
   b. great excitement   **d.** real danger   6. _____

7. "... we made trips to the closet to *assemble* our gear."
   a. clean   **b.** check   **c.** collect in one place   **d.** look over   7. _____

8. "Women are *agile* and clever."
   a. strong   **b.** alert   **c.** brave   **d.** nimble   8. _____

9. "It was *humiliating* to be caught using my knees."
   a. very embarrassing   **c.** sobering
   b. surprising   **d.** frustrating   9. _____

10. "... the belay rope became *taut* and I rested."
    a. slack   **b.** tight   **c.** damp   **d.** even   10. _____

C. Relationships (*Reading Skill*). Each of the following short lists consists of objects, character traits, or experiences—one list for each of the five characters in the story. One item in each list does NOT belong. Identify it and write its letter in the space provided. *(5 points each)*

11. Jo: **a.** lack of experience   **b.** new climbing boots   **c.** youth
    d. portable typewriter   11. _____

12. Will: **a.** chronic illness   **b.** literary ambitions   **c.** an attic room
    d. a dislike of climbing   12. _____

13. Jo's father: **a.** portable typewriter   **b.** much climbing experience
    c. two children   **d.** rescue work in Austria   13. _____

14. Jo's mother: **a.** a love of climbing   **b.** dressing table   **c.** portable
    typewriter   **d.** avalanche rescue work   14. _____

15. Gunner: **a.** lecturing activities   **b.** musical talent   **c.** worldwide
    fame   **d.** a green hat with an enamel pin   15. _____

D. Word Attack. The following jargon words are used in mountaineering. Look up each one in a dictionary. Then choose the word that best completes each of the following sentences, and write its letter in the space at the right. *(5 points each)*

a. lug boots   **d.** overhang
b. rappel   **e.** traverse
c. chimney

16. We gradually worked our way up the narrow _____.   16. _____

17. The ledge we rested on was under a broad _____.   17. _____

18. Before climbing, we made sure that our _____ were tied tightly.   18. _____

19. The first time I had to _____ down a sheer cliff I was frightened.   19. _____

20. We had to _____ across the steep slope in order to reach a good
    resting place.   20. _____

24

PERSPECTIVES

Alone on the Hilltop   *Lame Deer and Richard Erdoes*   *(Text page 186)*

A. Reading Comprehension. In the space at the right, fill in the letter of the best answer to each question. *(5 points each)*

1. While Lame Deer is in the vision pit, he feels the presence of a number of visitors. Which of the following is NOT one of them?
   a. his great-grandfather   **c.** the fowl people
   b. a large bird   **d.** his grandmother   1. _____

2. Lame Deer's main ambition is
   a. to become a warrior   **c.** to become a medicine man
   b. to become a chief   **d.** to prove his courage   2. _____

3. What Lame Deer most hopes to receive from his experience is
   a. a vision   **c.** clues about his people's future
   b. rest   **d.** his grandmother's blessing   3. _____

4. During the four days and nights, Lame Deer
   a. eats very little   **c.** smokes but eats nothing
   b. drinks only water   **d.** eats special food   4. _____

5. Before old man Chest reappears, Lame Deer knows that he will be
   a. a great leader   **c.** a famous warrior
   b. a medicine man   **d.** an upside-down man   5. _____

B. Vocabulary. Write the letter of the word or group of words closest in meaning to each *italicized* word. *(5 points each)*

6. "Imagine, performing such an ancient *ceremony* with a razor blade instead of a flint knife!"
   a. game   **b.** play   **c.** role   **d.** ritual   6. _____

7. ". . . here I was, *crouched* in my vision pit . . ."
   a. hidden   **b.** invisible   **c.** huddled; squatting   **d.** lying down   7. _____

8. "I *treasure* it; someday I shall be buried in it."
   a. fear   **c.** keep hidden
   b. value very highly   **d.** use   8. _____

9. "There are so many things to *distract* you."
   a. make angry   **c.** soothe
   b. divert attention   **d.** gladden   9. _____

10. ". . . to help me pray and make me *stronghearted*."
    a. brave   **b.** healthy   **c.** religious   **d.** calm   10. _____

C. Judgments (*Reading Skill*). Read each of the following passages written by Lame Deer. Then indicate whether he is acting as a primary or a secondary source of information in each passage, using the following code. *(5 points each)*

    a. *primary* source of information
    b. *secondary* source of information

11. "I was all alone on the hilltop. I sat there in the vision pit, a hole dug into the hill, my arms hugging my knees as I watched old man Chest, the medicine man who had brought me there, disappear far down in the valley."

11. _____

12. "Now I was all by myself, left on the hilltop for four days and nights . . . You know, we Indians are not like some white folks—a man and a wife, two children, and one baby sitter who watches the TV set while the parents are out visiting somewhere."

12. _____

13. "Some people need a church house, a preacher, and a pipe organ to get into a praying mood."

13. _____

14. "An old holy man can teach you about herbs and the right ways to perform a ceremony where everything must be in its proper place . . ."

14. _____

15. "As Chest poured water over the rocks, hissing white steam enveloped me and filled my lungs. I thought the heat would kill me, burn the eyelids off my face!"

15. _____

D. Word Attack. Read each of the following passages and decide whether direct context clues help to define each *italicized* word or not. Using the code below, write your answer in the space at the right. *(5 points each)*

    a. context clues DO help to define the word
    b. context clues DO NOT help to define the word

16. "I sat there in the *vision pit,* a hole dug into the hill, my arms hugging my knees as I watched old man Chest . . ."

16. _____

17. "If *Wakan Tanka,* the Great Spirit, would give me the vision and the power, I would become a medicine man . . ."

17. _____

18. "Sometimes it speaks from the *Badlands,* a stone, or even from the water."

18. _____

19. "'*Tunkashila,* grandfather spirit, help me.'"

19. _____

20. "What if I failed, if I had no vision? Or if I dreamed of the *Thunder Beings,* or lightning struck the hill?"

20. _____

The Contest   *Paul Darcy Boles*   (Text page 197)

A. Reading Comprehension. In the space at the right, fill in the letter of the best answer to each question. (*5 points each*)

1. Joey's stepfather disapproves of his trumpet playing for a number of reasons. Which of the following is NOT one of those reasons?
   a. He thinks playing the trumpet hurts Joey's grades.
   b. He thinks that music is just a frivolous hobby.
   c. He wants Joey to devote more time to athletics.
   d. He thinks that hard work and a profession are more important than music.   1. _____

2. The relationship between Joey and his stepfather at the beginning of the story is
   a. warm and loving   **c.** friendly but with a tension
   b. openly hostile   underneath
                                 d. indifferent   2. _____

3. The attitude of Joey's real father toward his trumpet playing was
   a. encouraging and supportive   **c.** hostile and discouraging
   b. indifferent   **d.** one of amusement   3. _____

4. Why does Joey's stepfather attend the contest?
   a. He wants to find out how serious and how good a musician Joey really is.
   b. He had to be in town on business and decides to stop by.
   c. Joey's mother insisted that he go.
   d. He wants to prove to Joey that trumpet playing is really a waste of time.   4. _____

5. What does Joey do with the prize medal that he wins?
   a. He gives it to his stepfather.
   b. He hangs it in his trophy chest at home.
   c. He gives it to his girl friend.
   d. He hangs it on the picture of his landlady's son.   5. _____

B. Vocabulary. Write the letter of the word or group of words closest in meaning to each *italicized* word. (*5 points each*)

6. "So I couldn't keep from being a little *sardonic*."
   a. friendly   **c.** confused and uncertain
   b. sarcastic, or scornful   **d.** fearful   6. _____

7. "It was snowing, fresh and full of *enchantment*, by the time I got to the trumpet-registration building."
   a. magic   **c.** anger
   b. tension   **d.** busy movement   7. _____

8. "They lined us up in the *wings* and told us to be quiet while the other people were playing."
   a. aisles   **c.** offstage area
   b. balcony   **d.** middle of the stage   8. _____

9. "When he came off, he was red-faced and his hair style was slightly *mussed*."
   a. neat   **c.** unusual
   b. old-fashioned   **d.** disordered

9. _____

10. ". . . hard work, a profession, that was the thing to *cultivate*."
   a. ignore   **c.** do without
   b. develop   **d.** discuss

10. _____

C. Judgments (*Reading Skill*). Read each of the statements below and decide whether it is a statement of fact or of opinion. Then write either *fact* or *opinion* in the space at the right. *(5 points each)*

11. ". . . I knew he was thinking I'd get a lot better grades if I'd forget about playing the trumpet."

11. _____

12. "He seemed to think music was something I did the way other people collect stamps or work out on the parallel bars."

12. _____

13. "After I'd bought my ticket for downstate I looked out again, but the car was gone."

13. _____

14. "I mean, I thought that in some secret way, from now on, nothing was going to be lost in the world or the nation . . ."

14. _____

15. "I was third on the program."

15. _____

D. Word Attack. Each of the following sentences contains an *italicized* figurative expression that refers to an animal. Write the meaning of each italicized figurative expression in the space provided. Use a dictionary if you need help. *(5 points each)*

16. After school, we *horse around* in the playground.

16. _____

17. I was in a hurry and *wolfed* my dinner.

17. _____

18. The winner got *the lion's share* of the prize money.

18. _____

19. The burglar entered the room with *catlike* steps.

19. _____

20. When I practice dancing, my little sister likes to *ape* my movements.

20. _____

Night Rider   *Steven Otfinoski*   (Text page 208)

A. Reading Comprehension. In the space at the right, fill in the letter of the best answer to each question. *(5 points each)*

1. Jake can be described by all of the following EXCEPT one. Which one?
   a. a reasonable, compassionate person
   b. an experienced, ordinarily careful driver
   c. someone who likes people and makes friends easily
   d. a man with a prison record who hates the police

   1. _____

2. Where and when does Jake pick up the hitchhiker?
   a. at dusk in Bakerville   **c.** at dawn in the mountains
   b. at night on a lonely highway **d.** at night in the Mohave Desert

   2. _____

3. The hitchhiker is unusual in several ways. Which of the following is NOT one of them?
   a. He knows little English.   **c.** He has excellent vision.
   b. He has no name of his own.   **d.** He is friendly and harmless.

   3. _____

4. Jake performs several acts of kindness and assistance. Which of the following is NOT one of them?
   a. He gives a stranger a lift.
   b. He offers to buy food and coffee.
   c. He helps to repair the space ship.
   d. He shows XT-115 how to avoid the police.

   4. _____

5. At the end of the story, Jake
   a. believes he has had a dream
   b. knows he has helped an alien from outer space
   c. tells the state troopers all that he knows
   d. thinks he is losing his mind

   5. _____

B. Vocabulary. Write the letter of the word or group of words closest in meaning to each of the following numbered words taken from the selection. *(5 points each)*

6. reaction	**a.** fear	**b.** wish	**c.** question	**d.** response	6. _____
7. weird	**a.** pretty	**b.** tame	**c.** strange	**d.** very big	7. _____
8. area	**a.** valley	**b.** route	**c.** game	**d.** region	8. _____
9. annoyed	**a.** happy	**b.** weak	**c.** irritated	**d.** poor	9. _____
10. halt	**a.** see	**b.** stop	**c.** expect	**d.** worry	10. _____

C. Judgments (*Reading Skill*). Read each of the following sentences, and decide whether it contains only statements of fact, only statements of opinion, or a mixture of fact and opinion. Using the key below, write your answer in the space at the right. *(5 points each)*

    a. The sentence contains only statements of fact.
    b. The sentence contains only statements of opinion.
    c. The sentence contains both statements of fact and statements of opinion.

11. It seemed odd to Jake that anyone would be trying to hitch a ride at this hour, but he stopped anyway.

11. _____

12. The hitchhiker was seventeen.

12. _____

13. It was pleasant to drive through the clear, cool night with the windows open.

13. _____

14. Jake answered a call on his CB radio, and his passenger asked questions about the CB slang.

14. _____

15. Jake had a feeling that XT-115 wasn't being completely truthful; still, he had agreed to drive him to his destination.

15. _____

D. Word Attack. Each of the following passages contains an *italicized* word or phrase. Choose the best definition of each italicized word or phrase and write its letter in the space at the right. *(5 points each)*

16. "And yet there was something different about him. I couldn't *put my finger on it.*"
    a. understand it   **c.** touch it with my hand
    b. identify it clearly   **d.** forget it completely

16. _____

17. "'I just want to be sure that you don't have *the law on your tail.*'"
    a. a police record   **c.** an irrational fear of the police
    b. the legal right on your side   **d.** the police after you

17. _____

18. "They must have thought I was *off my rocker,* but I didn't have time to worry about that."
    a. joking   **b.** crazy   **c.** too hasty   **d.** angry

18. _____

19. "'This is XT-115 heading west toward the Big Dipper. Do you *copy me,* White Lightning?'"
    a. know me   **c.** agree with me
    b. hear me   **d.** imitate me

19. _____

20. "The radio *clicked off.*"
    a. went into static   **c.** switched channels
    b. broke down   **d.** automatically shut off

20. _____

The Sin of Madame Phloi   *Lilian Jackson Braun*   (Text page 219)

A. Reading Comprehension. In the space at the right, fill in the letter of the best answer to each question. *(5 points each)*

1. Madame Phloi allows no one to take advantage of her EXCEPT
   a. the fat man   **b.** her owners   **c.** Thapthim   **d.** Charlie

   1. _____

2. What kind of pet does the fat man have?
   a. a dog   **c.** a cat
   b. a fish   **d.** a bird

   2. _____

3. How does Madame Phloi feel about her son, Thapthim?
   a. She is not particularly fond of him.
   b. She thinks he is very wise.
   c. She loves him but disapproves of his uncatlike behavior.
   d. She is indifferent to him.

   3. _____

4. Which of the following is NOT a reason why the fat man kills Thapthim?
   a. He hates all cats.
   b. He is brutal and cruel.
   c. He thinks Thapthim is after his pet bird.
   d. He thinks Thapthim is going to bite him.

   4. _____

5. How does the fat man die?
   a. He commits suicide.
   b. Madame Phloi lures him to his death.
   c. He has a heart attack.
   d. He falls from the window completely by accident.

   5. _____

B. Vocabulary. Write the letter of the word or group of words closest in meaning to each *italicized* word. *(5 points each)*

6. "... Madame Phloi felt an *instinctive* distaste for the man ..."
   a. very great   **c.** moderate
   b. inborn   **d.** unusual

   6. _____

7. "They met for the first time in the *decrepit* elevator ..."
   a. large   **c.** old and worn out
   b. narrow   **d.** newly built

   7. _____

8. "He was bulky, *uncouth*, and sloppily attired."
   a. attractive   **c.** overweight
   b. ugly   **d.** ill-mannered

   8. _____

9. "She had two companions in her tenth-floor apartment—*genial* creatures ..."
   a. friendly   **c.** very large
   b. unpredictable   **d.** hateful

   9. _____

10. "An *interminable* screech was coming out of that wall . . ."

    a. awful   **c.** unending

    b. loud   **d.** soft   **10.** _____

C. Judgments (*Reading Skill*). Each of the following items contains two statements, one of which is a stereotype. Identify the stereotype, and write its letter in the space at the right. *(5 points each)*

11. a. All violinists are overweight.

    b. All obese people are overweight.   **11.** _____

12. a. Most violinists are wealthy.

    b. All airline pilots have good eyesight.   **12.** _____

13. a. Most musicians are untrustworthy.

    b. Many Siamese cats have crossed eyes.   **13.** _____

14. a. Gymnasts are agile.

    b. Women are bad drivers.   **14.** _____

15. a. Tall men are good basketball players.

    b. Most good professional basketball players are tall.   **15.** _____

D. Word Attack. Each of the following lists of words contains one word that does NOT have a negative prefix. Write the word in the space at the right. *(5 points each)*

16. ignore, invisible, illegal, unwise   **16.** _____

17. unfeeling, displeased, expect, impossible   **17.** _____

18. unpleasant, after, invalidate, disqualify   **18.** _____

19. unplanned, unusual, mispronounce, defend   **19.** _____

20. dislike, immoral, inedible, involved   **20.** _____

How the Leopard Got Its Spots   *Forbes Stuart*   (Text page 233)

A. Reading Comprehension. In the space at the right, fill in the letter of the best answer to each question. *(5 points each)*

1. Why does the hyena put the tortoise in the tree?
   a. to be helpful
   b. as a mean joke
   c. to keep the tortoise safe
   d. to teach the tortoise how to fly

   1. _____

2. The least admirable animal in the story is the
   a. hyena   **c.** leopard
   b. tortoise   **d.** zebra

   2. _____

3. Why does the tortoise paint the leopard's coat?
   a. to repay him for his good   **c.** for revenge
   deed   **d.** so the other animals will fear the
   b. as a mean joke   leopard

   3. _____

4. Why does the tortoise paint the hyena?
   a. to have some innocent fun
   b. to show off his skill
   c. to make the hyena invisible
   d. to get revenge

   4. _____

5. Which of the following statements best sums up the lesson of the story?
   a. A jokester should watch out for retaliation.
   b. Never trust a paint-mad artist.
   c. Beauty is only skin deep.
   d. Spotted animals are the prettiest animals.

   5. _____

B. Vocabulary. Write the letter of the word or group of words closest in meaning to the *italicized* word. *(5 points each)*

6. "... the hyena went *loping* through the jungle."
   a. moping   **c.** slinking
   b. running easily   **d.** running at top speed

   6. _____

7. "... he leaped down again, laughing diabolically at the tortoise's *plight* ..."
   a. appearance   **c.** difficult situation
   b. voice   **d.** pleas for help

   7. _____

8. "The leopard's dull coat was completely *transformed* by the black spots ..."
   a. ruined   **c.** covered
   b. helped   **d.** changed, or altered

   8. _____

9. "... he paused to nibble at a *succulent* bush ..."
   a. sweet and juicy   **c.** small
   b. thorny   **d.** dry

   9. _____

10. "... the animals laughed and jeered *derisively* at him."
a. hopefully   c. scornfully
b. pleasantly   d. loudly

10. _____

C. Judgments (*Reading Skill*). Each of the following lists contains one word which is loaded to create an unfavorable impression. Identify the loaded word and write it in the space provided. *(5 points each)*

11. confident, self-reliant, egotistical, assured

11. _____

12. brave, bold, confident, foolhardy

12. _____

13. easygoing, leisurely, lazy, slow

13. _____

14. cautious, careful, cowardly, prudent

14. _____

15. thrifty, frugal, miserly, economical

15. _____

D. Word Attack. Each of the following passages contains an *italicized* word that can be defined by context clues. Choose the definition closest in meaning to each italicized word and write its letter in the space provided. *(5 points each)*

16. "*Seizing* the tortoise between his strong teeth, he jumped up into the tree ..."
a. grasping   c. playing
b. dropping   d. eating

16. _____

17. "Afraid to move, *clinging* to the branch, the tortoise stayed up there for hours ..."
a. sliding   c. waiting
b. having   d. holding tight

17. _____

18. "The gray zebra was so impressed ... that he *galloped* as fast as he could to the tortoise ..."
a. walked   c. ran
b. crawled   d. strolled

18. _____

19. "'Certainly I'll paint you, hyena,' the tortoise *drawled* in his deep slow voice."
a. blurted out   c. cried
b. spoke slowly   d. spoke rapidly

19. _____

20. "... he shouted to them, *strutting* and prancing in his pride, 'Look at this coat!'"
a. slinking   c. loping
b. hiding in shame   d. walking proudly

20. _____

Winter Thunder *Mari Sandoz* (Text page 250)

A. Reading Comprehension. In the space at the right, fill in the letter of the best answer to each question. *(5 points each)*

1. Why do the passengers leave their school bus?
   a. It gets stuck in a drift and catches fire.
   b. The driver panics and refuses to drive farther.
   c. The bus runs out of gas.
   d. They think they are close to the schoolhouse.

   1. _____

2. Most of the schoolchildren are
   a. tough and able to take care of themselves
   b. frightened and helpless
   c. indifferent to their own safety
   d. playful and carefree

   2. _____

3. The group finds some shelter in
   a. a haystack
   b. a willow thicket
   c. another stranded bus
   d. a small cabin

   3. _____

4. During the eight days and nights of the storm, the little group
   a. has nothing to eat or drink except willow bark and willow tea
   b. eats only bits of school lunches and fresh meat
   c. eats leftover apples and oranges from a Christmas party
   d. lives on parachuted parcels of food

   4. _____

5. The group courageously faces and overcomes a number of serious dangers. Which one of the following is the LEAST threatening to them?
   a. sickness, including pneumonia
   b. starvation
   c. death by freezing
   d. rebellion by several children

   5. _____

B. Vocabulary. Write the letter of the word or group of words closest in meaning to each *italicized* word. *(5 points each)*

6. ". . . Chuck shouted as he tried to *peer* back under his shielding cap."
   a. look
   b. duck
   c. hide
   d. push

   6. _____

7. "Even when all *discernible* direction or purpose was finally gone, it still moved . . ."
   a. forward
   b. slow
   c. halting
   d. noticeable

   7. _____

8. "But the *bold* talk did not quiet the sobbing . . ."
   a. quiet
   b. loud
   c. brave
   d. foolish

   8. _____

9. "Chuck was at the tail end of the clumsy little *queue* . . ."
   a. huddle   **c.** line of people
   b. small circle   **d.** shelter   **9.** _____

10. ". . . a shaking of thunder, *ominous* winter thunder . . ."
   a. threatening   **b.** noisy   **c.** unexpected   **d.** repeated   **10.** _____

VISTAS

Beware of the Dog   *Roald Dahl*   (Text page 285)

A. Reading Comprehension. In the space at the right, fill in the letter of the best answer to each question. *(5 points each)*

1. At the beginning of the story we learn a number of facts. Which of the following is NOT one of them?
   a. A pilot is returning to England in his Spitfire fighter plane.
   b. He has been badly wounded.
   c. The sky is cloudless, and he can see the English Channel far below.
   d. He thinks of what he will say to his friends when he lands.   1. _____

2. The pilot bails out of his plane because
   a. it has caught fire   c. he thinks he is lost
   b. it is rapidly losing altitude   d. he is about to pass out   2. _____

3. While Peter is in the hospital, he is told a number of things, most of them lies. Which one of the following is NOT a lie?
   a. He is in a hospital in Brighton, England.
   b. He has undergone a successful operation.
   c. The Brighton drinking water is very hard.
   d. A British wing Commander wants to question him.   3. _____

4. Which one of the following does NOT contribute to Peter's suspicions?
   a. the sound of German aircraft
   b. the hardness of the water
   c. a sign written in French
   d. the nurse's accent   4. _____

5. By the end of the story we realize that the "English" hospital and Wing Commander Roberts are
   a. only a dream
   b. exactly what they appear to be
   c. a trap intended to gain military information
   d. Peter's last thoughts just before he crashes and dies   5. _____

B. Vocabulary. Write the letter of the word or group of words closest in meaning to each *italicized* word. *(5 points each)*

6. "He realized that he . . . was sick and *giddy*."
   a. alert   b. amused   c. hypnotized   d. dizzy   6. _____

7. ". . . *frantically* he tried to slide back the hood with his left hand . . ."
   a. in a wildly excited manner   c. with great difficulty
   b. easily   d. slowly   7. _____

8. ". . . his actions became orderly and *precise*."
   a. awkward   c. hasty
   b. correct and exact   d. automatic   8. _____

9. "The idea became an *obsession* with him . . ."
   a. game   **c.** comfort
   b. a thought that comes and   **d.** a persistent or compulsive thought   **9.** _____
      goes

10. "Perhaps I am a little *delirious*."
   a. optimistic   **c.** irrational from fever
   b. foolish   **d.** dried out from a lack of water   **10.** _____

C. Inferences (*Reading Skill*). Read each of the following passages and write the letter of the most reasonable inference in the space at the right. *(5 points each)*

11. "Then he saw the sun shining on the engine cowling of his machine. He saw the rivets in the metal, and he remembered where he was."
We can infer from this that he has been
   a. injured and unconscious
   b. imagining himself somewhere else
   c. aware of his situation all along
   d. wondering if it would rain   **11.** _____

12. "Anyone who has been bombed can tell the noise of a Junkers 88. They can tell most other German bombers for that matter, but especially a Junkers 88."
We can infer from this that
   a. most German bombers are Junkers 88's
   b. it is difficult to tell one plane from another
   c. the Junkers 88 has a particularly recognizable sound
   d. people who have been bombed have very active imaginations   **12.** _____

13. "Then slowly he opened his eyes, looked down at his hand, and saw that he was holding something which was white. It was the edge of a sheet. He knew it was a sheet because he could see the texture of the material and the stitchings on the hem. He screwed up his eyes, and opened them again quickly."
We can infer from this that
   a. he is not used to sheets   **c.** he is not sure where he is
   b. his eyes are weak   **d.** German sheets are uncomfortable   **13.** _____

14. "He remembered that sometimes they were given calcium tablets because the school doctor used to say that soft water was bad for the teeth."
We can infer that the doctor thought the water was
   a. full of teeth-rotting minerals   **c.** polluted
   b. deficient in calcium   **d.** too hard to drink   **14.** _____

15. ". . . once he sat up in bed and said aloud, 'I will prove that I am not crazy. I will make a little speech about something complicated and intellectual. I will talk about what to do with Germany after the war.'"
We can infer that he
   a. feels certain Germany will be defeated
   b. thinks the war is over
   c. believes he shortly will have visitors
   d. is a former political science expert   **15.** _____

D. Word Attack. Each of the following sentences contains an *italicized* word. Decide whether the italicized word is a noun or a verb, and write your answer in the space at the right. *(5 points each)*

16. The insect on the ceiling would *fly* a short distance, then land again.

16. _____

17. Should he *call* the home airfield over his radio, or wait until he was closer before trying to contact them?

17. _____

18. With a final desperate *push* he managed to move back the plane's hood.

18. _____

19. He tried to turn off the *light*.

19. _____

20. He let the tips of his fingers *play* with the cover.

20. _____

Otero's Visitor   *Manuela Williams Crosno*   *(Text page 298)*

A. Reading Comprehension. In the space at the right, fill in the letter of the best answer to each question. *(5 points each)*

1. The beginning of the story establishes several important points. Which of the following is NOT one of them?
   a. Otero is a wealthy and well-liked man.
   b. He builds a hacienda somewhere in the present American Southwest.
   c. His father had come to Mexico from distant Spain.
   d. His wealth comes from a silver mine worked by convicts.   1. _____

2. When a stranger leaves a small box with Don Otero, we learn only that the stranger is
   a. a much-admired robber   **c.** a close friend of Otero's
   b. an anxious, pursued man   **d.** a distant relative   2. _____

3. The little box remains hidden for years, and Otero tells no one about it because he
   a. is a man of honor
   b. is certain the box has been stolen
   c. doesn't want to get involved in a crime
   d. wants to enjoy its contents secretly   3. _____

4. When the stranger returns many years later to claim his box,
   a. Reyes sends him away
   b. the ghost of Don Otero gives it to him
   c. Don Otero's wife gives it to him
   d. the box turns out to be empty   4. _____

5. The story does not tell us a number of facts. Which of the following details IS told us?
   a. the identity of the stranger
   b. the contents of the little box
   c. the exact way the box is gotten from its hiding place
   d. the source of Don Otero's wealth   5. _____

B. Vocabulary. Write the letter of the word or group of words closest in meaning to each *italicized* word. *(5 points each)*

6. "...always there was about it the feeling of warm *hospitality*."
   a. cooking   **c.** argument
   b. tropical climate   **d.** a friendly welcome to strangers   6. _____

7. "...the wind did not *abate*."
   a. vary   **b.** increase   **c.** freshen   **d.** decrease   7. _____

8. "He seemed in great *agitation*."
   a. peace   **b.** nervous excitement   **c.** anger   **d.** uncertainty   8. _____

9. ". . . all of his *obligations* known to them were dutifully discharged."
   a. fears
   b. possessions
   c. duties and responsibilities
   d. expectations

9. _____

10. :. . . there was a *reassurance* in the walk that quieted their fears."
   a. boring monotony
   b. secret message
   c. irregular movement
   d. a confidence-restoring quality

10. _____

C. Inferences (*Reading Skill*). Read each of the following passages and write the letter of the most reasonable inference in the space at the right. *(5 points each)*

11. "Adolfo [Otero] built for himself a beautiful hacienda, and furnished it with possessions the family had brought with them from Spain."
   We can infer that Adolfo Otero
   a. is a vain man
   b. enjoys a comfortable, gracious way of life
   c. is a greedy man
   d. does not like the New World

11. _____

12. "There were many sons and daughters born in the hacienda of Adolfo Otero, and it became a place of laughter and song and music."
   We can infer that the sons and daughters
   a. cared only for singing and dancing
   b. were always giving dances and parties
   c. grew up happy and contented
   d. quarreled a good deal

12. _____

13. ". . . now Don Adolfo lived alone except for his wife and two servants. But still there came to the house many who were friends and some who were strangers . . ."
   We can infer that Don Adolfo
   a. does not trust strangers
   b. is open-hearted in his hospitality
   c. likes old friends best
   d. has ordered his children to live elsewhere

13. _____

14. ". . . the great carved door swung open to admit a stranger. He seemed in great agitation and would not remove his hat; nor would he partake of the warmth before the fire, or wait for some of the wine Otero offered to bring for him."
   We can infer that the stranger
   a. is Otero's secret enemy
   b. is the son of an old friend of the family
   c. does not like wine
   d. feels too upset and hurried to be polite

14. _____

15. "The eldest son, Reyes, moved into the hacienda with his wife, in order to be with his mother, who was also grown quite old."
   We may infer that Reyes is
   a. his mother's favorite son
   b. eager to acquire the valuable hacienda
   c. a loyal, loving son
   d. poor and needs a place to live

15. _____

D. Word Attack. Each of the following sentences can be completed by using one of the Spanish words below. Choose the word that best fits the context in each sentence, and write its letter in the space at the right. Use a dictionary if you need help. *(5 points each)*

a. adobe   d. senoritas
b. caballero   e. fiesta
c. hacienda

16. Because Don Otero was a real gentleman, a _____, he never asked what was in the box.

16. _____

17. Don Otero lived in a large _____ that he had built himself.

17. _____

18. The walls of the house were made of _____.

18. _____

19. Sometimes Don Otero would have a large _____, lasting for several days, to which he would invite all of his old friends.

19. _____

20. Don Otero's daughters were lovely _____.

20. _____

Back There *Rod Serling* (Text page 310)

A. Reading Comprehension. In the space at the right, fill in the letter of the best answer to each question. *(5 points each)*

1. At the beginning of the play, the time and place are
   a. Washington, D.C., 1920 **c.** New York City, 1980
   b. Washington, D.C., 1965 **d.** New York City, 2006   1. _____

2. The play does NOT tell us
   a. the time and place of Lincoln's assassination
   b. how Corrigan is shifted back in time
   c. who Lincoln's assassin was
   d. why Corrigan loses his skepticism   2. _____

3. The principal character in the play is
   a. President Lincoln **c.** Corrigan
   b. Millard **d.** Wellington   3. _____

4. The villain of the play is first identified as
   a. Wellington **c.** a Police Captain
   b. Millard **d.** William   4. _____

5. By the end of the play Corrigan has had a number of painful accidents. Which of the following is NOT one of them?
   a. He has been knocked to the ground.
   b. He has been drugged.
   c. He has been locked up in jail.
   d. He has undergone a brain operation.   5. _____

B. Vocabulary. Write the letter of the word or group of words closest in meaning to each *italicized* word. *(5 points each)*

6. "Either keep him out of there or put a *cordon* of men around him."
   a. small group of soldiers **c.** line, or ring
   b. cavalry regiment **d.** wooden barricade   6. _____

7. "That man you just had *incarcerated*."
   a. freed **c.** executed
   b. burned up **d.** put in jail   7. _____

8. "On the word of some *demented* fool who probably left his mind someplace in Gettysburg."
   a. mad, or crazy **c.** troublemaking
   b. determined **d.** heartless   8. _____

9. "It has to do with the best ways of *amassing* a fortune."
   a. losing **c.** spending
   b. investing **d.** accumulating   9. _____

10. "Then come on over and listen to a lot of *palaver* from self-made swindlers. William here has the best method."
   a. anecdotes
   b. insider's advice
   c. sly comments
   d. idle talk

10. _____

C. **Inferences (*Reading Skill*).** Read each of the following passages and write the letter of the most reasonable inference in the space at the right. *(5 points each)*

11. "CORRIGAN: Gentlemen, I'm afraid I'll have to leave this time travel to H.G. Wells. I'm much too tired to get into any more metaphysics this evening. And since nobody has ever gone back in time, the whole blamed thing is much too theoretical. I'll probably see you over the weekend."
   We can infer that Corrigan feels
   a. worried and uncertain
   b. very happy
   c. somewhat bored and weary
   d. angry and upset

11. _____

12. "CORRIGAN: I tried to tell you. I tried to warn you. Why didn't anybody listen? Why? Why didn't anyone listen to me? (*His fist beats a steady staccato on the window frame.*)"
   We can infer that Corrigan feels
   a. frustrated and defeated
   b. happy and contented
   c. bored
   d. calm and indifferent

12. _____

13. "MRS. LANDERS: Well now really, young man. I can't spend the whole evening standing here talking about silly things like which is the oldest building in the section. Now if there's nothing else . . ."
   We can infer that Mrs. Landers feels
   a. happy
   b. impatient
   c. frightened
   d. worried

13. _____

14. "CAPTAIN: Now what's this one done? (*He peers up over his glasses and eyes Corrigan up and down.*) Fancy Dan with too much money in his pockets, huh?"
   We can infer that the Captain feels
   a. suspicious
   b. frightened
   c. threatened
   d. insulted and defensive

14. _____

15. "CORRIGAN: William? (*He sees the attendant from Act One but now meticulously dressed, a middle-aged millionaire obviously, with a totally different manner, who puts a cigarette in a holder with manicured hands in the manner of a man totally accustomed to wealth. William looks up and smiles.*)"
   We can infer that William feels
   a. proud and superior
   b. confused; exasperated
   c. suspicious
   d. angry and resentful

15. _____

D. Word Attack. Complete each of the following sentences using the adverb form of the adjective in parentheses. Write your answer in the space at the right. Use a dictionary if you need help. *(5 points each)*

16. The police captain looked up (angry).

16. _____

17. With a dignified air, Wellington walked (slow) to the captain's table.

17. _____

18. The police captain answered Wellington (prompt).

18. _____

19. The uneasy attendant examined the stranger's face (careful).

19. _____

20. Williams was (contented) smoking a cigarette.

20. _____

Crime on Mars   *Arthur C. Clarke*   *(Text page 330)*

A. Reading Comprehension. In the space at the right, fill in the letter of the best answer to each question. *(5 points each)*

1. Mars has little crime because
   a. there is almost nothing to steal
   b. law enforcement is very strict
   c. all Martians are naturally honest
   d. criminals have no place to hide   1. _____

2. Which one of the following descriptions of the Siren Goddess is NOT accurate?
   a. diamond-studded statue   **c.** mystery to historians
   b. statue of a woman's head   **d.** inspiration for religious sects   2. _____

3. Apparently, Danny planned to steal the Siren Goddess in order to
   a. keep it as a souvenir
   b. add it to his collection of art
   c. sell it to an unethical art collector
   d. blackmail the Martian government   3. _____

4. Danny is caught because he forgot to
   a. finish the job before daylight
   b. plan his escape route
   c. take the International Date Line into account
   d. bribe the night watchman   4. _____

5. Which one of the following does NOT happen at the end of the story?
   a. Danny is not thrown into a jail, because there is none.
   b. Danny is forced to work as the museum night watchman.
   c. Mr. Maccar suddenly looks suspiciously ill.
   d. The Siren Goddess is lost forever.   5. _____

B. Vocabulary. Write the letter of the word or group of words closest in meaning to each *italicized* word. *(5 points each)*

6. "The Inspector grinned, rather *mirthlessly*."
   a. quietly   **b.** slyly   **c.** secretly   **d.** joylessly   6. _____

7. "Maybe the *motive* was the same."
   a. greed   **b.** punishment   **c.** reason   **d.** payment   7. _____

8. ". . . guaranteeing that 'this *full-scale* reproduction is an exact copy of the so-called Siren Goddess . . .'"
   a. detailed but smaller   **c.** the same size as the original
   b. mechanically made   **d.** poorly imitated   8. _____

9. "It's quite a tiny thing to have caused so much *controversy*."
   a. disagreement, or dispute   **c.** study
   b. joy   **d.** awe, or astonishment   9. _____

10. "He'd have Saturday for *reconnoitering* the museum . . ."
a. locating   c. examining, or surveying
b. escaping from   d. breaking into

10. _____

C. Inferences (*Reading Skill*). Read each of the following passages and decide whether it contains *fantastic* details or *realistic* details or both. Write your answer in the space provided, using the following key. *(5 points each)*

    a. contains realistic details only
    b. contains fantastic details only
    c. contains both fantastic and realistic details.

11. "But [the Siren Goddess] is an enigma so baffling that it has inspired a hundred religious sects. . ."

11. _____

12. "Beyond those electronic shields is the utterly hostile emptiness of the Martian Outback."

12. _____

13. "Danny has to work for a living."

13. _____

14. "[The International Date Line] is something that doesn't bother us on Earth, where we've been able to dump the problem in the Pacific Ocean."

14. _____

15. "Danny's plan was beautifully simple. . . . You know how absolutely dead a Martian city gets. . ."

15. _____

D. Word Attack. Each of the following passages contains an *italicized* word or term. Choose the definition of each that best fits the context, and write its letter in the space provided. *(5 points each)*

16. ". . . every city on Mars is a closed little world of its own beneath the *force field* that protects it from the freezing near-vacuum. Beyond those electronic shields is the utterly hostile emptiness of the Martian Outback . . ."
a. athletic stadium   c. space ship
b. protective electronic shield   d. atmosphere

16. _____

17. "The Spaceport P.A. system apologized for a further slight delay owing to final fuel checks, and asked a number of passengers to report to Information. While we were waiting for the *announcement* to finish, I recalled what little I knew about the Siren Goddess."
a. fueling   c. delay
b. signal   d. public notice

17. _____

18. "For a perfectly human head has no right whatsoever to be found on Mars, whose only *intelligent* inhabitants were crustaceans—'educated lobsters,' as the newspapers are fond of calling them."
a. talented   c. native to an area
b. human   d. rational, or smart

18. _____

50

19. "... there's a big stone slab in the park with the *Prime Meridian* engraved on it, so that visitors can get themselves photographed standing in two hemispheres at once."

a. line dividing two hemispheres
c. official proclamation
b. famous quotation
d. directions for tourists

19. _____

20. "'It must have been a *weird* business, working in that darkened gallery with all those million-year-old carvings and unexplainable artifacts around him.'"

a. exciting   b. strange   c. quiet   d. challenging

20. _____

Avalanche   *Robb White*   *(Text page 341)*

A. Reading Comprehension. In the space at the right, fill in the letter of the best answer to each question. *(5 points each)*

1. The opening sentence tells us that this story will involve
   a. love   **c.** fun
   b. danger   **d.** amusing characters   1. _____

2. The story describes a number of struggles and conflicts. Which of the following is NOT one of them?
   a. a conflict between Scotty and Marick over Marick's plans
   b. a struggle for life between man and nature
   c. Scotty's struggle between reason and despair when he is buried
   d. a conflict between Scotty and the TV crew at the story's end   2. _____

3. The only person who does not fear an avalanche is
   a. Marick   **c.** the TV cameraman
   b. Scotty   **d.** the village doctor   3. _____

4. When Scotty begins to dig himself out of the avalanche, he realizes that
   a. his situation is hopeless
   b. he can't breathe
   c. the avalanche was unexplainable
   d. he doesn't know which way is up   4. _____

5. When Scotty returns to the town with Marick, he discovers that
   a. the townspeople are anxiously waiting for them
   b. the cameraman has a perfect record of Marick's ski run
   c. the town has been buried by the avalanche
   d. the cameraman forgot to put film in his camera   5. _____

B. Vocabulary. Write the letter of the word or group of words closest in meaning to each *italicized* word. *(5 points each)*

6. "For a moment Scotty was *overwhelmed* by the sheer pressure of the sound."
   a. made happy   **c.** completely overcome, or upset
   b. saddened   **d.** slightly irritated, or angered   6. _____

7. "The smooth, curving *contour* of the snowcap had been broken."
   a. outline   **b.** weight   **c.** bulk   **d.** movement   7. _____

8. "...as the *constant* and increasing thunder of the avalanche poured around him."
   a. distant   **b.** continuous   **c.** alarming   **d.** advancing   8. _____

9. "...a great avalanche started as the tons of snow *catapulted* down the slope..."
   a. spread out   **c.** moved quickly
   b. rumbled loudly   **d.** melted   9. _____

10. "Other men, walking like *zombies*, came slowly to the window . . ."
    a. fugitives   **c.** walking dead men
    b. scarecrows   **d.** children   10. _____

C. Inferences (*Reading Skill*). Read each of the following passages and write the letter of the most reasonable inference in the space at the right. *(5 points each)*

11. "Marick stopped and looked with those cold, brilliant eyes at Scotty. 'I've spent years preparing for this, studying this mountain; I've spent a small fortune. Now the time has come and I'm going to do it. Understand?'"
We can infer that
a. nothing Scotty will say will change Marick's mind
b. Marick will seek other mountains to conquer
c. Marick will spend the rest of his life in poverty
d. Scotty will wish to set records too   11. _____

12. "'You've got the tension on the releases set up pretty high, Mr. Marick. You may need to get out of these bindings a lot faster than these will let you.'
    "'I said knock off with the advice,' Marick told Scotty."
We can infer from this that
a. Marick's tight bindings will later cause him trouble
b. Scotty is being too cautious
c. Marick will later succeed only because of his tight bindings
d. Marick will welcome any further comments Scotty might make   12. _____

13. "And then the avalanche was upon Scotty and he had no more time to think of Marick. Afraid the ice axes would stab him, he threw them away, then ripped Marick's boots from around his neck and dropped them."
We can infer from this that Scotty will
a. be killed
b. continue to act reasonably to try to save his own life
c. panic
d. have to pay for the abandoned equipment   13. _____

14. "But now in the silent stillness, he slowly began to feel his body again. With one hand, he touched his face. His helmet and snow goggles had been ripped off and were gone, and his face was encased in snow."
We can infer that Scotty will
a. check the rest of his body
b. search for his helmet
c. become paralyzed with fear
d. look for his goggles   14. _____

15. "He could not afford this fear; it was using up the small amount of air he had. Almost saying it out loud, Scotty talked to himself. 'Cut it *out*! *Stop* this!'"
We can infer that the buried Scotty will next
    a. shout out loud   **c.** attempt to control himself
    b. be unable to control his emotions   **d.** give up   15. _____

D. Word Attack. One word in each of the following lists is a compound word made up of two smaller words. Write this compound word in the space at the right. *(5 points each)*

16. beautiful, threatening, summit, overrun   16. _____

17. anywhere, serious, releases, accomplish   17. _____

18. tranquility, downhill, canisters, protection   18. _____

19. protruding, particles, something, compressed   19. _____

20. darkness, jubilation, insanity, oncoming   20. _____

Crow Call   *Lois Lowry*   *(Text page 358)*

A. Reading Comprehension. In the space at the right, fill in the letter of the best answer to each question. *(5 points each)*

1. This is a story about
   a. a successful crow hunt
   b. a father and daughter getting to know each other again
   c. two people behaving badly
   d. a girl's initiation into hunting   1. _____

2. What is the mood of the girl at the beginning of the story?
   a. angry   **c.** very frightened
   b. eager but a little unsure **d.** very sure of herself   2. _____

3. The episode in the diner suggests all of the following, with one exception. Which is the exception?
   a. Both father and daughter have a good sense of humor.
   b. The two will get along very well in the future.
   c. The girl will be able to trust her father.
   d. The father will disappoint the girl.   3. _____

4. The father shoots no crows because
   a. there are too few of them
   b. they won't come within range of his shotgun
   c. his daughter scares them away
   d. he knows it would upset his daughter   4. _____

5. At the end of the story both characters are
   a. very happy   **c.** uncomfortable about each other
   b. very unhappy   **d.** ready to shoot crows   5. _____

B. Vocabulary. Write the letter of the word or group of words closest in meaning to each *italicized* word. *(5 points each)*

6. "'Daddy,' I said, the title coming *uncertainly* . . ."
   a. happily   **b.** unsurely   **c.** cheerfully   **d.** casually   6. _____

7. ". . . ruddy *mannequins* holding guns and duck decoys . . ."
   a. servants   **b.** salespeople   **c.** display dummies   **d.** hangers   7. _____

8. "My sister had rolled her eyes in *disdain*!"
   a. scorn, or disapproval   **c.** mischieviously
   b. happiness   **d.** enviously   8. _____

9. ". . . from the *bulky* thickness of rolled-back cuffs my hands were exposed."
   a. hot   **b.** annoying   **c.** surprising   **d.** heavy   9. _____

10. "'Hey, boy,' my father said to me in an imitation of the *groggy* waitress' voice . . ."
    a. heavy   **c.** loud
    b. sleepy   **d.** harsh   **10.** _____

C. Inferences (*Reading Skill*). Read each of the following passages and write the letter of the most reasonable inference in the space at the right. *(5 points each)*

11. "It was morning, early, barely light, cold for November. I was nine and the war was over. At home, in the bed next to mine, my older sister still slept, adolescent, her blond hair streaming over the edge of the sheet."
We can infer that the older sister
    a. is disappointed   **c.** is happy to remain in bed
    b. was not asked to go hunting **d.** has overslept   **11.** _____

12. "I had lingered in front of Kornenberg's window every chance I had since the hunting shirts had appeared."
We can infer that
    a. the narrator wanted to   **c.** Kronenberg's is on a busy corner
        become a hunter   **d.** Kronenberg's sells girls' clothing **12.** _____
    b. the narrator wanted a
        hunting shirt

13. "I wanted to scamper ahead of him like a puppy, kicking the dead leaves and reaching the unknown places first, but there was an uneasy feeling along the edge of my back at the thought of walking in front of someone carrying a gun. Carefully I stayed at his side."
We can infer that the narrator
    a. doesn't want to leave her father behind
    b. doesn't completely trust her father
    c. is being prudent and cautious
    d. doesn't want to appear childish   **13.** _____

14. "But most leaves were already gone from the trees; those that remained seemed caught there by accident, waiting for the wind that would free them. Our breath was steam."
We can infer that the morning is
    a. windy   **c.** dark and cloudy
    b. warm   **d.** quite cold   **14.** _____

15. "The waitress, middle-aged and dawn-sleepy, asked, 'What about your boy? What does he want?'
    "My father winked at me, and I hoped that my pigtails would stay hidden inside the plaid wool collar."
We can infer that
    a. the girl would really rather be a boy
    b. father and daughter are sharing a harmless trick
    c. the waitress is incompetent
    d. the father is sorry he doesn't have a son   **15.** _____

D. Word Attack. Find each of the following words in a dictionary and divide it into syllables. *(5 points each)*

16. surrounded

17. occasional

18. acknowledged

19. afterthought

20. speculatively

16. _____

17. _____

18. _____

19. _____

20. _____

One Alaska Night   *Barrett Willoughby*   (Text page 371)

A. Reading Comprehension. In the space at the right, fill in the letter of the best answer to each question. *(5 points each)*

1. Early in the story, the narrator describes herself in a number of ways. Which one of the following is NOT one of them?
   a. superstitious   **b.** alone   **c.** a greenhorn   **d.** weary   1. _____

2. The narrator is first frightened by
   a. the approach of dusk   **c.** bear fur and bear tracks
   b. the strange landscape   **d.** strange noises   2. _____

3. The cabin frightens the narrator for a number of reasons. Which of the following is NOT one of them?
   a. She thinks that it is probably a murderer's cabin.
   b. She finds parts of his "victims" nearby.
   c. The door will not lock or even shut properly.
   d. There are strange, terrifying noises.   3. _____

4. Even after Dad's explanation, the narrator remains half convinced that the strange noises had been made by
   a. flying squirrels   **c.** a ghost
   b. huge brown bears   **d.** the wind   4. _____

5. What primary feeling does the narrator admit to having during much of her ordeal?
   a. anger   **c.** impatience
   b. fear   **d.** boredom   5. _____

B. Vocabulary. Write the letter of the word or group of words closest in meaning to each *italicized* word. *(5 points each)*

6. "I found myself stepping *furtively*, trying not to make any noise, and straining to hear the slightest sound."
   a. cautiously, or secretively   **c.** awkwardly
   b. hastily   **d.** reluctantly, or hesitantly   6. _____

7. "There was something distinctly *sinister* in the very quality of the silence . . ."
   a. novel   **c.** challenging
   b. evil   **d.** defiant   7. _____

8. "The . . . faint *rancid* odor that clings to a cabin in which raw furs have been stored."
   a. woodsy   **c.** painful
   b. unfamiliar   **d.** rotten   8. _____

9. "I assumed a *nonchalant* manner and strolled out to meet them."
   a. terrified   **c.** dejected
   b. casual   **d.** hurt   9. _____

10. "I must have looked uncommonly foolish for he patted my shoulder *consolingly*."

   a. comfortingly   **c.** idly

   b. impatiently   **d.** repeatedly   **10.** _____

C. Inferences (*Reading Skill*). Read each of the following passages and write the letter of the most reasonable inference in the space at the right. *(5 points each)*

11. "For a moment I was too tired to stir. I lay there, face on my arms, feeling that I'd been foolhardy to start out alone on a ten-mile hike . . ."

   We can infer that the narrator

   a. had slept badly the previous night

   b. had already walked a long distance

   c. had earlier taken a brief nap

   d. had decided to retrace her steps   **11.** _____

12. "But I got hold of myself, decided on a course, and with forced calmness went forward, watching tensely for that breaking away of the timber which foretells an approach to the sea."

   We can infer that the narrator

   a. had never been in the woods before

   b. had a general idea of what to do when lost in the woods

   c. never gets upset

   d. enjoys a good walk in the woods even if she is lost   **12.** _____

13. "The sensible thing to do now was build a fire and then eat a sandwich. Luckily I had a couple remaining from lunch."

   We can infer that she

   a. had been hiking much of the day

   b. had been too frightened to eat lunch

   c. had forgotten to stop for lunch

   d. had eaten lunch at home   **13.** _____

14. "And in the dense bear weed I saw twelve skeleton hands, all cut off at the wrist. There wasn't a skull or bone of any other kind. Somehow I got back inside the candlelit cabin with an armload of wood."

   We can infer that she

   a. has seen skeletons before

   b. is very frightened

   c. was cold

   d. forgot to blow out the candle   **14.** _____

15. "After a dozen seconds, I had a sudden, desperate impulse to end the suspense. I . . . flung open the door, and looked out."

   We can infer that earlier she had

   a. looked out the door

   b. felt safe and cheerful

   c. tried to lock the door

   d. been badly frightened   **15.** _____

D. Word Attack. Each of the following lists of phrases contains one phrase that is a simile. Write its letter in the space at the right. *(5 points each)*

16. **a.** face on my arms
    b. coarse brown hair
    c. big as a truck horse
    d. walking quickly

    16. _____

17. **a.** not a good hunter
    b. a foolish idea
    c. the rank odor of bear
    d. as bright as day

    17. _____

18. **a.** set of bony fingers
    b. a frightening experience
    c. as cold as the hand of death
    d. my legs moved slowly

    18. _____

19. **a.** food tasting like sawdust
    b. an eerie sound
    c. larger than a rabbit
    d. a cold evening

    19. _____

20. **a.** a meadow full of flowers
    b. a noise like distant thunder
    c. an old fellow
    d. tough luck, all right

    20. _____

The Night the Ghost Got In   *James Thurber*   (Text page 384)

A. Reading Comprehension. In the space at the right, fill in the letter of the best answer to each question. *(5 points each)*

1. When Jamie first hears footsteps in the family dining room, he
   a. thinks they are his grandfather's
   b. thinks his father or brother is downstairs
   c. is certain they belong to a burglar
   d. thinks his brother is downstairs   1. _____

2. Jamie's family can best be described as
   a. dull   **c.** odd, or eccentric
   b. happy and ordinary   **d.** rich and arrogant   2. _____

3. How does Jamie's mother call the police?
   a. She uses an upstairs telephone in her bedroom.
   b. She shouts loudly, "Help! Fire!"
   c. She throws a shoe through a neighbor's window.
   d. She fires a gun.   3. _____

4. Grandfather shoots
   a. a burglar   **c.** a policeman
   b. Jamie   **d.** a would-be murderer   4. _____

5. At breakfast on the following morning, Grandfather
   a. apologizes for his actions
   b. has forgotten everything that happened
   c. is happy and full of life
   d. says that he has decided to buy a pistol   5. _____

B. Vocabulary. Write the letter of the word or group of words closest in meaning to each *italicized* word. *(5 points each)*

6. "'Awp,' he said in the low, hopeless tone of a *despondent* beagle . . ."
   a. eager   **b.** frightened   **c.** very sad   **d.** ferocious   6. _____

7. "We listened together. There was no sound. The steps had *ceased.*"
   a. gotten quicker   **b.** stopped   **c.** resumed   **d.** gotten louder   7. _____

8. "The police were on hand in a *commendably* short time . . ."
   a. praiseworthily   **c.** endless
   b. lengthening   **d.** absurdly   8. _____

9. "They began to *ransack* the floor: pulled beds away from walls, tore clothes off hooks in closets, pulled suitcases and boxes off shelves."
   a. examine   **b.** clean   **c.** cross-examine   **d.** search violently   9. _____

10. "The cops were *reluctant* to leave without getting their hands on somebody . . ."
    a. eager   **c.** unwilling
    b. determined   **d.** unable   10. _____

C. Inferences (*Reading Skill*). Read each of the following items and decide whether it sets an amused tone or not. Write your answer in the space at the right, using the following key. *(5 points each)*

    a. sets an amused tone
    b. does not set an amused tone

11. "I had just stepped out of the bathtub and was busily rubbing myself with a towel when I heard the steps.

11. _____

12. "Bodwell was at the window in a minute, shouting, frothing a little, shaking his fist. 'We'll sell the house and go back to Peoria,' we could hear Mrs. Bodwell saying."

12. _____

13. "They caught me standing in my towel at the top [of the stairs]. A heavy policeman bounded up the steps. 'Who are you?' he demanded. 'I live here,' I said. "Well, whattsa matta, ya hot?'"

13. _____

14. "A half-dozen policemen emerged out of the darkness of the front hallway upstairs."

14. _____

15. "'The lady seems historical.'"

15. _____

D. Word Attack. Read each of the following items and decide whether it contains a figurative expression or not. Write your answer in the space at the right, using the following key. *(5 points each)*

    a. contains a figurative expression
    b. does not contain a figurative expression

16. "They began about a quarter past one o'clock in the morning, a rhythmic, quick-cadenced walking around the dining-room table."

16. _____

17. "We listened together. There was no sound. The steps had ceased."

17. _____

18. "One of them found an old zither that Roy had won in a pool tournament. 'Looky here, Joe,' he said, strumming it with a big paw."

18. _____

19. "... the night had been distinctly a defeat for them. Furthermore, they obviously didn't like the 'layout'; something looked—and I can see their viewpoint—phony."

19. _____

20. "'I'm gonna get my gun back from that old bird,' said the zither-cop. 'Yeh,' said Joe. 'You—and who else?' I told them I would bring it to the station house the next day."

20. _____

MOSAIC

On the Edge   *Robert Russell*   (Text page 404)

A. Reading Comprehension. In the space at the right, fill in the letter of the best answer to each question. *(5 points each)*

1. Frank Summers has broken one of the basic rules of mountain climbing by
   a. climbing a strange mountain   **c.** forgetting key equipment
   b. climbing alone   **d.** climbing at night   1. _____

2. Frank falls to the ledge because he
   a. stumbles on a rock   **c.** gets drowsy and dizzy
   b. slips on the smooth, steep   **d.** doesn't watch where he puts his
   granite   feet   2. _____

3. We learn a number of facts about Frank Summers in the story. Which of the following is NOT one of them?
   a. He is sixteen years old.
   b. He is a beginner at mountain climbing.
   c. He is strong and courageous.
   d. He is too poor to own proper climbing gear.   3. _____

4. The makeshift rope that Frank uses to save himself is made of
   a. his belt   **c.** strips of blue jeans
   b. strips of shoe leather   **d.** his shirt   4. _____

5. Frank experiences a variety of emotions during his ordeal. Which of the following is NOT one of them?
   a. fright   **b.** frustration   **c.** anger   **d.** amusement   5. _____

B. Vocabulary. Write the letter of the word or group of words closest in meaning to each *italicized* word. *(5 points each)*

6. "The silver thread *glinted* far below, spreading out into a shadowy blur . . ."
   a. curved   **b.** flashed   **c.** appeared   **d.** blinked   6. _____

7. ". . . if he could hang on somehow, *shuffle* sideways . . ."
   a. slide his feet   **c.** ease his shoulders
   b. step carefully   **d.** crawl slowly   7. _____

8. "Picking up his right shoe, he *flexed* the heavy leather."
   a. pulled   **b.** cut   **c.** tore   **d.** bent   8. _____

9. "With his *makeshift* rope, he made two tight loops . . ."
   a. temporary substitute   **c.** for a desperate purpose
   b. strong and secure   **d.** short and risky   9. _____

10. "The shoe *scuffed* on the rock, then stuck."
    a. slipped   **b.** bounced   **c.** scraped   **d.** rolled   10. _____

C. Main Idea (*Reading Skill*). Find the topic sentence of each of the following paragraphs and write its letter in the space at the right. *(5 points each)*

11. (a) "'Nobody'—Mr. Johnson's voice echoed in Frank's mind. (b) 'That means nobody goes into the mountains alone.' (c) Frank understood now. (d) If he had had a partner up there with a rope—but nobody was there."   11. _____

12. (a) "He studied the cliff. (b) He had fallen only about twelve feet. (c) But even twelve feet *down* means twelve feet up. (d) It might as well be miles."   12. _____

13. (a) "He sighed. (b) If he had only left his rope buckled to his belt! (c) But what good would a rope do? (d) He couldn't just toss the end up into the air and then climb up. (e) It would have to be tied to something at the top, and that meant there'd have to be someone up there to tie it."   13. _____

14. (a) "'All right,' he said, 'that's what I'll do.' (b) He laid his knife on the ledge and unlaced and removed his shoes. (c) He took off his jeans, and cut them into long, even strips, tying them carefully together, testing each knot."   14. _____

15. (a) "Frank studied the face of rock. (b) He could see nothing promising. (c) *That must be ten or eleven feet to the crack, and from there I could reach the top.* (d) It looked like twelve miles. (e) The crack ran diagonally down, but it looked only about an inch wide."   15. _____

D. Word Attack. Each of the following sentences contains two *italicized* words, one used as a noun and one used as a verb. In the spaces provided, identify each word as a verb or a noun. *(5 points each)*

	First Word	**Second Word**
16. "I'll *paint* the garage, but house *paint* isn't my favorite artistic medium."	16. _____	_____
17. The sky's color was a pink *rose*; he *rose* to see better.	17. _____	_____
18. He *slit* the material, then eyed the narrow *slit* in the cliff overhead.	18. _____	_____
19. *Stop* feeling uncertain, he told himself; any *stop* now would be foolish.	19. _____	_____
20. He must *throw* it properly, or it might be his last *throw*.	20. _____	_____

My First Life Line   *Maya Angelou*   (Text page 413)

A. Reading Comprehension. In the space at the right, fill in the letter of the best answer to each question. *(5 points each)*

1. Before Mrs. Flowers came into her life, Marguerite was
   a. unintelligent and lazy
   b. intelligent, but unwilling to talk to people
   c. happy and carefree
   d. conceited and snobbish

   1. _____

2. We learn a number of facts about Mrs. Flowers. Which of the following is NOT one of them?
   a. She has a large family and a noisy household.
   b. She is cultured and educated.
   c. She values people for their real worth.
   d. She likes to help worthy young people.

   2. _____

3. Mrs. Flowers gives Marguerite all of the following. Which is the LEAST important?
   a. someone to use as a model
   b. standards of taste and culture
   c. praise and encouragement
   d. food and lemonade

   3. _____

4. Which one of the following descriptions of Momma is NOT accurate?
   a. a black storeowner in Stamps
   b. a good, dear friend of Mrs. Flowers
   c. a bad, incompetent seamstress
   d. a poorly educated but respected individual

   4. _____

5. After her first afternoon with Mrs. Flowers, Marguerite
   a. walks home sadly
   b. promises never to return
   c. runs home happily
   d. decides that she would rather play with her friends

   5. _____

B. Vocabulary. Write the letter of the word or group of words closest in meaning to each *italicized* word. *(5 points each)*

6. "When she chose to smile on me, I always wanted to thank her. The action was so graceful and inclusively *benign*."
   a. pointed   **b.** personal   **c.** frightening   **d.** gracious and kind

   6. _____

7. "... neither of the women was in the least shaken by what I thought an *unceremonious* greeting."
   a. violent
   b. friendly
   c. too informal, or inappropriate
   d. happy

   7. _____

8. "... drinking tea *incessantly* from silver trays full of scones and crumpets."
   a. slowly   **b.** constantly   **c.** elegantly   **d.** now and then

   8. _____

9. "I knew I shouldn't put on a Sunday dress. It might be *sacrilegious*."
  a. irreverent, or disrespectful
  b. humiliating
  c. appropriate, or fitting
  d. elegant

9. _____

10. "Words mean more than what is set down on paper. It takes the human voice to *infuse* them with the shades of deeper meaning."
  a. confuse **b.** underline **c.** focus **d.** instill, or fill

10. _____

C. Main Idea (*Reading Skill*). Read each of the following paragraphs, then answer the questions that follow. *(5 points each)*

"Momma had a strange relationship with [Mrs. Flowers]. Most often when she passed on the road in front of the Store, she spoke to Momma in that soft yet carrying voice, 'Good day, Mrs. Henderson.' Momma responded with "How you, Sister Flowers?'"

11. The topic of this paragraph is
  a. the Store
  b. the road
  c. Momma and Mrs. Flowers
  d. Mrs. Flowers' voice

11. _____

12. The main idea of this paragraph is
  a. Mrs. Flowers walked by the store regularly.
  b. Momma and Mrs. Flowers had an unusual relationship.
  c. Momma usually sat in front of the Store.
  d. Mrs. Flowers spoke in a soft voice.

12. _____

"[Mrs. Flowers] appealed to me because she was like people I never met personally. Like women in English novels who walked the moors (whatever they were) with their loyal dogs racing at a respectful distance. Like the women who sat in front of roaring fireplaces, drinking tea incessantly from silver trays full of scones and crumpets. Women who walked over the 'heath' and read morocco-bound books and had two last names divided by a hyphen. It would be safe to say that she made me proud to be black, just by being herself."

13. The topic of this paragraph is
  a. Mrs. Flowers
  b. English women
  c. Marguerite
  d. tea and crumpets

13. _____

14. The main idea of this paragraph is
  a. Marguerite wanted to go to a tea party.
  b. Women with hyphens in their names are sophisticated.
  c. Marguerite was ashamed of being American.
  d. Mrs. Flowers made Marguerite proud to be black.

14. _____

"Momma was enjoying the seldom-received compliments. Since everyone we knew (except Mrs. Flowers, of course) could sew competently, praise was rarely handed out for the commonly practiced craft."

70

15. The main idea of this paragraph is
   a. Everyone knew how to sew.   **c.** Momma was pleased.
   b. Momma was embarrassed.   **d.** Mrs. Flowers didn't know how to sew.

15. _____

D. Word Attack. Use a dictionary to find the meaning of each of the following compound words. Write the definition of each in the space provided. *(5 points each)*

16. cloud-capped

16. _____

17. dead-end

17. _____

18. gun-shy

18. _____

19. half-mast

19. _____

20. part-time

20. _____

The Little Lizard's Sorrow   *Mai Vo-Dinh*   (Text page 428)

A. Reading Comprehension. In the space at the right, fill in the letter of the best answer to each question. *(5 points each)*

1. The human motive at the heart of this story is
   a. fear   **b.** envy   **c.** vanity, or pride   **d.** hatred, or anger

   1. _____

2. The rich man's game consists of
   a. comparing possessions   **c.** several physical tests
   b. comparing knowledge   **d.** answering riddles

   2. _____

3. The stranger who shows up at the rich man's door appears to be
   a. a fugitive   **c.** very poor
   b. very wealthy   **d.** a thief

   3. _____

4. The rich man loses the game with the stranger when he cannot come up with
   a. an old hat   **c.** a chipped coconut cup
   b. fifty buffalos   **d.** a child

   4. _____

5. After the stranger wins the game, he
   a. gives the rich man's possessions to the poor
   b. becomes just as vain as the rich man had been
   c. becomes greedy and corrupt
   d. sells the man's possessions and disappears

   5. _____

B. Vocabulary. Write the letter of the word or group of words closest in meaning to each *italicized* word. *(5 points each)*

6. "His land was so *extensive* that, as the Viet-Namese say, 'Cranes fly over it with outstretched wings . . .'"
   a. fertile   **b.** vast   **c.** desirable   **d.** famous

   6. _____

7. "It was then his turn to announce, 'I sleep in an all-teak bed *encrusted* with mother-of-pearl.'"
   a. covered   **c.** bought
   b. comparable in value   **d.** supported

   7. _____

8. "Moreover, his face was *gaunt* and pale as if he had not had a good meal in days."
   a. flushed   **b.** thin   **c.** wrinkled   **d.** serene

   8. _____

9. "*Intrigued,* the man ordered that the pauper be ushered in."
   a. angered   **c.** bored
   b. very impatient   **d.** very interested

   9. _____

10. "The visitor was apparently unimpressed by the rich surroundings, giving them only a passing, *casual* look."
    a. appraising, or judging   **c.** nonchalant, or indifferent
    b. envious   **d.** thoughtful

    10. _____

C. Main Idea (*Reading Skill*). Three main ideas from the story are listed below, followed by a number of supporting details. Match each of the supporting details to a main idea, and write the letter of the main idea in the space provided. *(5 points each)*

    a. The gatekeeper thought that the stranger was a madman.
    b. The rich man was surprised when the stranger produced a chipped coconut cup.
    c. The rich man tried to conceal his curiosity in the stranger.

11. The rich man looked at the cup as if he had never seen one before.   **11.** _____

12. The stranger was dressed in clothes that had been mended over and over.   **12.** _____

13. The rich man offered the stranger hot tea.   **13.** _____

14. The stranger was gaunt and pale.   **14.** _____

15. The rich man offered the stranger his best chair.   **15.** _____

D. Word Attack. Choose the word that has the same, or almost the same, meaning as each of the following words and write its letter in the space at the right. *(5 points each)*

16. counter
    a. suggest   **b.** oppose   **c.** disturb   **d.** ignore   **16.** _____

17. beating
    a. losing   **b.** scolding   **c.** defeating   **d.** joking   **17.** _____

18. master
    a. friend   **b.** boss   **c.** companion   **d.** instructor   **18.** _____

19. mended
    a. useless   **b.** clean   **c.** old   **d.** repaired   **19.** _____

20. conceal
    a. show   **b.** question   **c.** admire   **d.** hide   **20.** _____

The Baroque Marble   *E. A. Proulx*   (Text page 437)

A. Reading Comprehension. In the space at the right, fill in the letter of the best answer to each question. (*5 points each*)

1. Which one of the following best describes Sister Opal's character?
   a. happy-go-lucky
   b. lazy and idle
   c. proud and determined
   d. sophisticated and knowledgeable

   1. _____

2. Sister Opal wants to buy a baroque pearl because she wants to collect valuable
   a. jewels
   b. marbles
   c. works of art
   d. antiques

   2. _____

3. Which one of the following best describes Mr. Sonnier?
   a. greedy and bad-tempered
   b. reasonable and businesslike
   c. sly and untrustworthy
   d. mean and malicious

   3. _____

4. When Sister Opal learns that her baroque marble has been sold, she feels
   a. very sad and disappointed
   b. relieved
   c. rather happy
   d. indifferent

   4. _____

5. At the end of the story, Sister Opal's father advises her to
   a. forget about jewels
   b. give her money to charity
   c. buy another baroque pearl
   d. save her money for college

   5. _____

B. Vocabulary. Write the letter of the word or group of words closest in meaning to each *italicized* word. (*5 points each*)

6. "... children's voices slid under the window *muffled* and changed ..."
   a. warmed
   b. deadened, or made indistinct
   c. amplified, or made louder
   d. distant

   6. _____

7. "... some queer, *garbled* language."
   a. obscure   b. unknown   c. mixed-up   d. foreign

   7. _____

8. "... the unfamiliar angle gave it a *sinister* look."
   a. funny   b. beautiful   c. correct   d. evil

   8. _____

9. "... it took on a silver, *translucent* glow."
   a. clear
   b. many-colored
   c. very lopsided
   d. partly transparent

   9. _____

10. "Immediately they became *hostile* ..."
    a. frightened   b. unfriendly   c. critical   d. helpful

    10. _____

C. Main Idea (*Reading Skill*). Read each of the following paragraphs. Then choose the answer that best expresses the main idea of each paragraph, and write its letter in the space provided. (*5 points each*)

11. "There was no escape. Sister Opal took a deep breath and began telling about the art class and Essex Street and the baroque pearl in R. Sonnier's shop. Her father's face was first incredulous, then angry, then sad. He said nothing for a long time. Opal sat miserably waiting for the lecture."

a. Opal didn't want to escape.
b. Opal was very unhappy as she waited for her father's response.
c. Opal wanted the baroque pearl a great deal.
d. Opal's father refused to speak to her.

11. _____

12. "'I am old enough and able enough to get a job after school in the evenings and earn enough money to *buy* that baroque pearl myself, and I am going to do it!' Opal spoke slowly."

a. Opal was old enough to take care of herself.
b. Opal spoke slowly.
c. Opal was determined to take a part-time job and buy the pearl.
d. Opal was eager to get a job and get out into the world.

12. _____

13. "'Yeah,' said Andrew to Roy, 'at least he doesn't go in for harpsichords and statues.' This joke about harpsichords and statues was one that Roy had never quite fathomed, and he eventually grew so confused on the matter that he was convinced that he really did take an extraordinary interest in keyboard music and sculpture."

a. Opal's interest in art began to spread to the rest of the family.
b. Roy was actually a baseball fan.
c. Roy resented Andrew's jokes.
d. Roy was so confused at the joke that he began to think he actually was interested in music and art.

13. _____

14. "Sister Opal's weeks turned into months, and the long drugstore nights dragged through winter into spring. She had two bank accounts, one for college money and one for the baroque pearl. In March on a Friday night, she had four hundred dollars in the school account, and four hundred fifty in the pearl account. It was enough. She got permission from Mr. Esdall to take the next day off to go to R. Sonnier's to buy the pearl."

a. After months of saving, Opal finally had enough money to buy the pearl.
b. Opal had two bank accounts—one for the pearl, one for college.
c. Opal got permission from her boss to go buy the pearl.
d. Opal was a very hard worker.

14. _____

15. "Patiently Sister Opal explained about the baroque pearl she had asked him to save for her last fall, and then she expectantly waited for the shock of recognition, the rummaging in a desk drawer, and the uncovering of the baroque pearl. She hadn't even yet seen it up close or held it. R. Sonnier looked annoyed."

a. Sister Opal didn't really know what the pearl looked like up close.
b. Sister Opal waited for R. Sonnier to produce the pearl.
c. Sister Opal wondered where the pearl was.
d. R. Sonnier was annoyed.

15. _____

D. Word Attack. Read each of the following comparisons. Then choose the answer that correctly identifies the two things being described, and write its letter in the space at the right. *(5 points each)*

16. "Most of them were mob marbles, as much alike as the faces of the crowd to a dictator on his balcony."
    a. marbles and dictator
    b. marbles and faces
    c. faces and dictator
    d. dictator and crowd

    16. _____

17. "Sister Opal thought the children sounded as if they were speaking Russian or Basque—some queer, garbled language."
    a. Opal and Basque
    b. Opal and children
    c. children's cries and a strange language
    d. thought and language

    17. _____

18. "[Opal] took a miser's satisfaction in pouring them out onto the bed, watching them roll into the valleys, gathering up their heavy, glassy weight . . ."
    a. Opal and miser
    b. marbles and misers
    c. Opal and marbles
    d. marbles and weight

    18. _____

19. "Her warm breath made a milky fog on the window glass and her warm finger wrote, 'All the sailors have died of scurvy, yours truly, Opal Foote.'"
    a. sailors and scurvy
    b. finger and sailors
    c. breath and finger
    d. breath and fog

    19. _____

20. "Sister Opal's mother came in, tired and with a sharp edge to her tongue."
    a. mother and Opal
    b. Opal and tongue
    c. tongue and cutting tool
    d. mother and edge

    20. _____

The Hobbit   *J.R.R. Tolkien*   *Dramatized by Patricia Gray*   (Text page 463)

A. Reading Comprehension. In the space at the right, fill in the letter of the best answer to each question. *(5 points each)*

1. Which one of the following statements about the beginning of the play is NOT true?
   a. The place is Underhill, Middle Earth.
   b. The time is long ago.
   c. The villain is an old troublemaker named Gandalf.
   d. The main character is a small man named Bilbo.   1. _____

2. Bilbo Baggins loves
   a. adventures   **c.** his thriving business
   b. his own home   **d.** crowds   2. _____

3. Which one of the following statements about the band of plotters is NOT true?
   a. Bilbo is tricked into joining the party.
   b. The party is fourteen in number.
   c. Their journey will be dangerous and long.
   d. They plan to kill all of the world's last few dragons.   3. _____

4. Bilbo's job is to
   a. kill a dragon   **c.** act as a lookout
   b. be a burglar   **d.** divide up the treasure   4. _____

5. All of the following items EXCEPT one help to make the plot to slay the dragon a success. Which is the exception?
   a. a magic ring   **c.** the dragon's cowardice
   b. Bilbo's cleverness   **d.** the Elven Queen's sword   5. _____

B. Vocabulary. Choose the best definition for each of the following words and write its letter in the space at the right. *(5 points each)*

6. incredulously
   a. very fearfully   **c.** unwillingly
   b. very skeptically   **d.** angrily   6. _____

7. icily
   a. happily   **c.** angrily
   b. reluctantly   **d.** coldly   7. _____

8. diary
   a. secret directions   **c.** favorite book
   b. hidden map   **d.** personal journal   8. _____

9. panic
   a. patience   **c.** unease
   b. great fear   **d.** destruction   9. _____

10. despondency
    a. great pleasure   **c.** great sadness
    b. anger   **d.** uncertainty   10. _____

COMPOSITION

Sentence Combining   *(Text page 66)*

Combine each group of three sentences into one sentence. Remember to use
the first word as your base. Then remove the repeated words in the second
and third sentences. Finally, use the commas and connecting word that appear
in parentheses.

1. Harry wrapped the package.
    Harry put a label on it.
    Harry placed it under the tree.   (, and)

_____

_____

2. Denise turned on some music.
    Denise sat down in the easy chair.
    Denise closed her eyes.   (, and)

_____

_____

3. Lois hit the ball.
    Lois ran like the wind.
    Lois slid into first base.   (, and)

_____

_____

4. Gus washed the lettuce.
    Gus sliced the tomatoes.
    Gus diced the celery.   (, and)

_____

_____

5. Joyce selected the color.
    Joyce bought the paint.
    Joyce carried the can home.   (, and)

_____

_____

Test Booklet   Cascade   81

COMPOSITION

Sentence Combining   *(Text page 172)*

Combine each pair of sentences below by using the signal word contained in parentheses after the second sentence. (If a punctuation mark appears in parentheses, use this too.)

1. I studied hard.

I didn't want to fail.   (because)

_____

_____

2. Carrie decided to audition for the lead in the play.

She found out her best friend already had a part.   (when)

_____

_____

3. Pat didn't like to go to parties.

He usually had a good time once he got there.   (, even though)

_____

_____

4. Janet wanted to go bowling.

Her parents wanted her to do some chores.   (; however)

_____

_____

5. The workers decided to strike.

Their demands had not been met.   (, since)

_____

_____

COMPOSITION

Narration

(Text page 242)

Choose one of the topics below. Develop ideas about this topic through making lists. Create a rough outline. Then write a narrative paragraph on your topic.

1. the best day in your life.

2. how you met your best friend

3. an embarrassing situation

4. a surprising event

5. preparing for a date

_____

_____

_____

_____

_____

_____

_____

_____

_____

_____

_____

_____

_____

_____

_____

COMPOSITION

Description   *(Text page 394)*

Choose one of the following topics. Use clustering to develop ideas about this topic. Create a rough outline. Then write a descriptive paragraph on your topic.

1. your room

2. a special place

3. your grandmother's home

4. the view from your window

5. your dream house

_____

_____

_____

_____

_____

_____

_____

_____

_____

_____

_____

_____

_____

_____

_____

_____

COMPOSITION

Exposition

(Text page 454)

Choose one of the topics below. Use questions and answers to develop ideas about this topic. Narrow the topic. Create a rough outline. Then write an expository paragraph about this topic.

1. music

2. health

3. school

4. food

5. movies

_____

_____

_____

_____

_____

_____

_____

_____

_____

_____

_____

_____

_____

_____

_____

_____

TEACHER'S NOTES

TEACHER'S NOTES

TEACHER'S NOTES

TEACHER'S NOTES

TEACHER'S NOTES

TEACHER'S NOTES